DOMINICAN COLLEGE
LIBRARY
SAN RAFAEL

LETTERS OF
FRANCIS PARKMAN

FRANCIS PARKMAN, *c.* 1855

From a daguerreotype.
Courtesy of Mrs. John Forbes Perkins

LETTERS OF
Francis Parkman

Edited and with an Introduction by
WILBUR R. JACOBS

VOLUME I

Published in co-operation with
The Massachusetts Historical Society

NORMAN: UNIVERSITY OF OKLAHOMA PRESS

DOMINICAN COLLEGE
LIBRARY
SAN RAFAEL

B
P231le
v.1

By Wilbur R. Jacobs

Diplomacy and Indian Gifts: Anglo-French Rivalry along the Ohio and Northwest Frontiers, 1748–1763 (Stanford, 1950)

Indians of the Southern Colonial Frontier: The Edmond Atkin Report and Plan of 1755 (Editor) (Columbia, 1954)

Letters of Francis Parkman (Editor) (Norman, 1960)

57327

Library of Congress Catalog Card Number: 60–8754

COPYRIGHT 1960 BY THE UNIVERSITY OF OKLAHOMA PRESS,
PUBLISHING DIVISION OF THE UNIVERSITY.
COMPOSED AND PRINTED AT NORMAN, OKLAHOMA, U.S.A.,
BY THE UNIVERSITY OF OKLAHOMA PRESS.
FIRST EDITION.

TO BETH

PREFACE

FRANCIS PARKMAN'S MULTI-VOLUMED SAGA of *France and England in North America* has often been acclaimed as the greatest history written by an American. William H. Prescott's books on Spain in the New World and the Old, John Lothrop Motley's history of the rise of the Dutch Republic, and George Bancroft's history of the United States proved that America of the nineteenth century had its eminent historians; but among them Parkman's stature remains the highest.

Boston-born of a leading New England family, Parkman made his literary debut with *The Oregon Trail* of 1849, a vivid account of his tour of the prairies that has become, in the century since it appeared, one of the widest-read personal narratives in the English-speaking world. Although partial infirmity prevented his concentration on historical writing in subsequent years, he was nevertheless able to complete his elaborate set of volumes describing the epic struggle between France and England for mastery of an empire in North America.

Parkman's narrative told a romantic story of the Old West. His main characters, explorers and soldiers in plumed helmets, black-robed priests, and painted Indian warriors, acted against a magnificent backdrop of living nature, the stately forests and waterways of the interior wilderness frontier. Through a kind of alchemy that bridged the gulf of centuries, Parkman, with dramatic presentation and vital prose, wrought a history in which men and women are alive. His vibrant representations of the life and spirit of another age were based, as he wrote in his preface to *The Pioneers*, "on authentic documents or on personal observation." The hallmark of Parkman's *History* is its vitality, the eternal youthfulness of a creative work of art. His *History* has withstood the test of time because of his penetrating, accurate research; his skill in the use of literary devices that made his narrative fascinating to the reader; his sensitivity to nature's beauties; and his understanding of the mainsprings that motivate the actions of mankind. While his theme was restricted, Parkman attained his lifelong objective of creating a romantic but authentic image of a complex panorama in North American history.

His own life story is a heroic struggle against illness, projected and reflected in the heroic characters of his *History*—La Salle, Frontenac, Montcalm, and the great Jesuit martyrs. In writing about Catholic New France, Parkman exhibited remarkable sympathy and understanding, despite his Protestant heritage. His letters provide many hitherto unknown details of his adventurous career and his personal battle against illness to finish the task of writing his *History*. Included in this edition are Parkman's unpublished letters written from the Oregon trail in 1846 to his parents, and his letters to Frederic Remington, Lewis H. Morgan, George Bancroft, Lyman C. Draper, Charles Eliot Norton, and many other eminent figures of the nineteenth century.

Additional facts on Parkman's life and correspondence are provided in the Introduction, the Editorial Note, and the prefatory notes at the beginning of each section of Parkman's letters. Material based on parts of the Introduction has appeared in the *Pacific Historical Review*, the *New England Quarterly*, and the *American Quarterly*.

An acknowledgment of my indebtedness to a number of persons and institutions in the preparation of Parkman's letters is found at the end of Volume II.

WILBUR R. JACOBS

Santa Barbara, California
April 19, 1960

CONTENTS

CONTENTS

CONTENTS

CONTENTS

ILLUSTRATIONS

INTRODUCTION

From Conway, New Hampshire, on Thursday evening, July 22, 1841, seventeen-year-old Francis Parkman penned a letter to his anxious father: "I write, as in duty bound," he said, "to relieve your spirit of the overwhelming load of anxiety which doubtless oppresses you, seeing that your son is a wanderer in a strange land—a land of precipices and lakes, bears, wolves, and wildcats."

Perhaps Conway, a quiet New England village and gateway to New Hampshire's magnificent White Mountain country, was not exactly the center of a howling wilderness as Parkman with a bit of light sarcasm pretended; but this first letter of his preserved correspondence does display an imaginative mind, preoccupied with the hidden beauties and dangers of the forest. Thirty-four years later, after an expedition to the mountains of old Acadia, he recaptured in his thoughts, as he wrote a Paris friend, "the time of the *coureurs de bois*. One often comes on bears, foxes, lynx, and other wild animals. It is an immense forest, broken up by rivers, lakes, and mountains."[1] The passion for the solitude of the wilderness was as much a part of the mature historian at fifty-two as of the boy of seventeen.

Parkman's first letter, written in the summer after his freshman term at Harvard College, is the beginning of a series that spans over half a century to the time of his death in 1893. The letters, many of them intimate and autobiographical, are a record of his life story: his ambitions, his frustrations, and his attainments.

[1] FP to Pierre Margry, September 13 [1875]. FP letters cited in the notes are printed herein. A list of abbreviations used in footnotes is on page lxv.

With the exception of several letters in which Parkman recalled incidents from his childhood and youth, the gap between his birth in Boston on September 16, 1823, and his first year in college is filled by family papers, together with memoirs written by those who knew him.[2] The Parkmans, who had come to New England in Puritan times, rose to prominence through commerce and the church. Among the historian's ancestors were prominent clergymen, including Cotton Mather, the Puritan divine. His paternal grandfather, Samuel Parkman, a colorful Boston merchant who acquired wealth in shipping, loved Spanish wine and silver plate. Grandfather Samuel's three-story mansion facing Bowdoin Square, with its garden and fruit trees and stable in the rear, was a comfortable home for his wife and numerous sons and daughters. One of these children, the Reverend Dr. Francis Parkman, was the historian's father.

Although Dr. Parkman was a leading Unitarian minister of Boston, he was known, in later years, as the son of a prominent merchant or the father of a famous American historian. As a boy, Frank was often exposed to his father's wide circle of eminent friends and no doubt read widely in the family library, which contained a wealth of history, literature, and biography in addition to works on theology.[3] After deciding that the law was not a suitable career for his son, Dr. Parkman gave substantial encouragement to Frank's literary ambitions.

Those who knew Parkman as a youth said he resembled his mother more closely than his father in personality and in appearance. A gracious woman with auburn hair, a prominent chin, and clear blue eyes, Caroline Hall Parkman was regarded as a person of charm and intelligence who loved her home and managed it with no little success. Carrie, Mary, and later Lizzie, Frank's affectionate sisters, often practiced penmanship by making copies of their brother's historical documents. A younger brother, John, or "Elly," soon made known his desire to enter the navy despite his promise as painter and writer.

[2] Barrett Wendell, "Francis Parkman," *Proceedings* of the American Academy of Arts and Sciences, XXIX (1894), 435–77, and Edward Wheelwright, "Memoir of Francis Parkman," *Publications* of the Colonial Society of Massachusetts, I (1895), 304–50, are the best short published memoirs. Charles H. Farnham, *A Life of Francis Parkman* (Frontenac edition of FP's writings, Boston, 1904) is an early study of Parkman by his former secretary and copyist. In the PP, MHS, are three "Reminiscences" by FP's sister Eliza, and one by his daughter, Katharine (Mrs. J. T. Coolidge).

[3] "Library Catalogue of [the Reverend Dr.] Francis Parkman," PP, MHS. The notes accompanying Mason Wade's excellent edition of *The Journals of Francis Parkman* (2 vols., New York, 1947) contain information on FP's early reading interests.

On Thanksgiving and on other holidays there were gay family reunions in the old Parkman mansion on Bowdoin Square, the scene of Frank's boyhood experiments in chemistry and playwriting. Today the thronged, noisy streets and unsightly buildings of Bowdoin Square form a marked contrast to the square of Parkman's youth, when handsome white colonial houses in the area were owned by dignified families like the Parkmans, the Shaws, and the Everetts.

The Parkman mansion, former home of Grandfather Samuel, had the stir and activity of a large family in its many rooms. Like the young women of Jane Austen's novels who liked to sketch, Frank's sisters delighted in making pencil drawings of its elegant interiors.[4] Through the columned doorway into the spacious entrance hall with its balustered spiral staircase came many visitors, even whole conclaves of ministers and their wives. There was a constant round of parties and dinners which were a source of pleasure for Dr. Parkman and his children. These affairs, according to family letters, did not always afford such enjoyment for Mrs. Parkman, who seemed to be continually engaged in preparing for the arrival of guests.[5]

There was also a gloomy side to the picture. One would think, from reading family correspondence, that the Boston of the Victorian era was one vast sickroom. One has the impression that not many of the leading families went through the month without having a member confined to bed. The Parkmans had their particular problems. Dr. Parkman, for example, occasionally had periods of dejection which threw a cloud of gloom over his entire household. Frank himself had frequent headaches; Carrie had serious difficulty with her eyes; and John Eliot, or Jack, as he came to be known, increasingly complained about pains in his head which made it difficult for him to study as he grew older. Yet Jack eventually outgrew his illness and had an adventurous career in India and in the United States Navy. Jack's experience as a Southern prisoner during the Civil War is the subject of one of his brother's letters to the press.[6]

Tension in the Parkman family resulting from Dr. Parkman's attacks of depression was relieved by his frequent travels. New York, Montreal, Baltimore, St. Louis, and even London and Dublin were

[4] Several of these drawings are in the PP, MHS.

[5] The social life of the Parkmans is described in a number of letters written by FP's mother in the 1840's. PP, MHS.

[6] See FP's letter to the editors of the *Boston Daily Advertiser*, September 29, 1864.

on his itinerary. After exchanging pulpits with other ministers in distant cities and enjoying a fill of sightseeing, he came home to his family laden with gifts, frequently books for his children. When traveling, Dr. Parkman usually kept a diary, a record of his more entertaining experiences, which Frank, no doubt, read with keen interest.[7]

Mrs. Parkman remained at home during these trips to care for her children, but she did make occasional visits to her parents' farm in near-by Medford, where Frank had spent many happy months as a small boy. When the oven heat descended on Boston in July, the whole family moved to Phillips Beach to occupy a summer house, large enough to be comfortable for the seven Parkmans. Here, as Carrie said, they loafed on the seashore or took pleasant horseback rides over the low-tide sands of Nahant. During the rest of the year Frank was a student at the Chauncy Place School of Boston, where he was drilled in Greek, Latin, and mathematics in preparation for the Harvard entrance examinations. Such was Francis Parkman's world just before he entered Harvard.[8]

Parkman's college letters indicate that he led an active social life as a student. They are filled with lively nonsense about the opposite sex, more particularly with allusions to Pamela Prentiss, a spirited young woman from Keene, New Hampshire. He records the hilarity of Joe Peabody's suppers, polished off with whiskey punch and Indian war cries. But pretty girls and horses, he wrote, were "the 'first-ratest' things in nature."[9]

In these letters a serious theme is also present. During a period of almost six years, from 1840, when he entered Harvard, to 1846, when he was graduated from law school, Parkman formulated his grand scheme for a history of France and England in North America. His initial plan was to write a history of the "Old French War," a subject that he chose with deliberate care. Here was an opportunity, as he said, of combining his love of the forest with the life of a writer. It was a unique theme, one that enabled him to satisfy his youthful obsession of writing about America's romantic wilderness heritage. When he recalled his youthful literary aspirations in an autobiographical letter, Parkman wrote that "his thoughts were always in the forests" and

[7] Dr. Parkman's diaries in the PP, MHS.

[8] Material for the above paragraph is drawn from family letters of the 1830's and 1840's. PP, MHS.

[9] To Charles W. Dabney, Jr., Feb. 10, 1845.

"possessed his waking and sleeping dreams, filling him with vague cravings impossible to satisfy."[10]

Analysis of the records Parkman left behind, especially his early attempts at fiction and his preserved reading lists,[11] discloses that the ideas behind his theme were nourished by Cooper's *Leather Stocking Tales* and Scott's *Waverly Novels*. Parkman's early letters reveal that he was tormented day and night with the urge to show the arrogant English literary world that a Yankee could write a good book on a North American theme. The extremity of the case made it necessary that his creation be a brilliant work of art, not merely a success. From his animated letters to Charles Eliot Norton one has the impression that Parkman had a passionate compulsion to succeed. In pursuing his dream, he was urged on by a proud, sensitive nature and a feeling that he was competing with the artistry of such literary lions as William H. Prescott. Moreover, he had to show his father that he could make his way as a writer.

The background of Parkman's career as a writer is further illuminated by a view of his college studies which emerges not only from his letters, but from his journals, the Harvard Archives records, and the Parkman family papers. Of special interest are the books from Parkman's personal library, decorated with his marginalia.

Frank, along with a large percentage of his class, was placed on academic probation when admitted to Harvard. At this time the Harvard faculty was obliged to use the recitation-drill method of teaching, in which the daily performances of each pupil were recorded on a scale of eight. Although Frank accumulated credits, his class records show that he, like many of his classmates, was sometimes penalized. For instance, he lost credits for tardiness, and on one occasion was even reprimanded by a faculty committee on discipline for excessive absences from compulsory prayers and recitations, conduct that undoubtedly caused his father embarrassment as an Overseer of the college. Yet Parkman's academic work was, according to the term book records, more than satisfactory; and a year and a half after his entrance he was admitted to full standing.[12]

The curriculum, sternly set forth in the old Harvard catalogs, had centered on instruction in the classics. Yet Parkman never com-

[10] Autobiographical letter to George E. Ellis [1864].
[11] Library charge lists, 1840–44, HA.
[12] "Records of the College Faculty," XII, 4, 23, HA.

plained, and his term book records show that he performed well in Latin, Greek, rhetoric, and composition—that is, when he attended classes. Although he had the air of a young man of leisure, available evidence shows that he actually drove himself to exhaustion by a strenuous physical conditioning program and strained his eyes with an ambitious reading schedule in history, literature, and ethnology. During his junior and senior years Parkman was enrolled in four language classes simultaneously, Latin, Greek, French, and Italian.[13] This linguistic background later enabled him to learn Spanish for purposes of research. In addition to English, Parkman thus had five languages at his command. If the necessity arose, he could also read German. Certainly Parkman's talents as a linguist facilitated his research and enriched his vocabulary.

As a young man Parkman read almost as many books in other languages as he did in English. No translations were necessary for him to know the great historians of antiquity or Italian authors like Machiavelli. His library charge lists give sure evidence of his fascination with French literature and history. During this formative period the whole story of the French past inflamed and exalted his imagination. The young Parkman was drawn to the romantic themes of Chateaubriand and Michelet as he had been attracted to Scott. Sismondi and Guizot along with Montesquieu and Voltaire were among his favorites. Nor were the plays of Molière, Racine, and Corneille neglected.[14]

There is little question that Parkman's knowledge of Greek drama, acquired in college, had an effect on the structure of his *History*. *La Salle,* for example, is a biography that exhibits elements of classic Greek tragedy. A heroic figure with an indomitable will battles the forces of nature. His violent death results in part from a "tragic flaw" of character.

Yet it was not only from his formal studies and from the self-education so characteristic of the Yankee of his day that Parkman obtained the training necessary for his future work. Equally significant was his youthful association with Jared Sparks, sometimes called the "Nestor of American historians" in spite of his shortcomings as editor of Washington's writings.

In 1838, when Sparks accepted the appointment of McLean Professor of Ancient and Modern History at Harvard, he demanded and

[13] Term Books, HA.
[14] Library charge lists, HA; "Entry of Books Borrowed," Boston Athenaeum.

received assurance that he would have ample time for archival research. Moreover, he made it clear that he would have no part of the recitation system that seemed designed to rob the instructor of any chance to make his subject stimulating. Although he reported credits for each pupil, he threw out the textbooks, and taught by lectures, by assigned readings, and by requiring his pupils to write essays. When Parkman began his classes with Sparks, in which he made a good academic record, he was exposed to a man who already had had a notable career as minister, editor, and historian. But Sparks was more than a distinguished figure of nineteenth-century Cambridge. Immersing himself in documents and old maps, he became excited by the adventure of exploration; he not only wrote about such figures as La Salle and John Ledyard, but actually planned, at one time, an expedition to Timbuktu. He even considered the feasibility of circumnavigating Africa. In addition, Sparks was probably the first American who had the adventure of probing through archival repositories in Paris and London.[15] One can imagine the impact such a teacher had on Frank Parkman, the impressionable college freshman!

Frank had known Sparks before entering college. In the days when he was a Unitarian minister, Sparks had been an associate of Frank's father, a fellow-cleric, and had been a visitor at the Parkman home on Bowdoin Square.[16] The early correspondence between pupil and teacher, extremely reserved as it was, contains evidence of growing friendship. One suspects that they had long talks on such topics as "the nature of historical evidence," or "the rules of historical composition," titles that Sparks had chosen for two of his lectures. It was Sparks who gave Parkman, the fledgling historian, his first reading list on the "Old French War," and introduced him to copyists who could obtain transcripts of documents from foreign archives. Sparks came to regard his pupil as a protégé and opened many doors for him by cordial letters of introduction. Through such a letter Parkman in 1845 met Lyman C. Draper, who shared his enthusiasm for early Americana.[17]

One of the important histories Parkman was required to read for Sparks' classes was Henry Hallam's scholarly *Constitutional History of England*, noted for its vitriolic attack on political and ecclesiastical

[15] Part of this sketch is from the Sparks Papers, HCL. See also Samuel E. Morison's superb essay on Sparks in the *DAB*.

[16] There are a number of letters from Sparks to the Reverend Dr. Francis Parkman, the historian's father, in the PP, MHS.

[17] FP to Lyman C. Draper, Oct. 8, 1845.

tyranny. Another historian he came to know through Sparks was J. C. L. Sismondi, whose monumental *Histoire des Français* appeared on Parkman's reading lists throughout middle life. It has been said that Sismondi was the avowed enemy of all kings and priests of the past. This view of history was not lost on the young Parkman. It was probably strengthened by his reading Gibbon's *Decline and Fall of the Roman Empire,* a work his father purchased for the family library. That Parkman was fascinated with Gibbon is affirmed by one of his unpublished college notebooks in which he scrawled out choice selections on "Roman tyranny" and other topics.[18] Gibbon's rationalism, his impatience with superstition, his stress on accuracy, design, and authorities must have deeply impressed the youthful Parkman, for these concepts are omnipresent in the *History*. Even Gibbon's idea that decay is inherent in despotic governments is noticeable in Parkman's description of the French colonial system. Gibbon, Hallam, and Sismondi told a European story of conflict between liberty and authority. It remained for the mature Parkman to show how spiritual and political despotism contributed to the decline and fall of New France.

In the college years Parkman's youthful capacity for self-training led him to read Joseph François Lafitau's celebrated *Moeurs des Sauvages*. Lafitau, an early Jesuit, formulated research principles now considered basic for the field ethnologist. Parkman's decision to study the Sioux of the nineteenth century in order to understand the primitive Iroquois was probably stimulated by Lafitau's idea that contemporary Indian cultures throw light on older cultures.

Still another writer who provided inspiration for Parkman was George Bancroft. The early volumes of Bancroft's *History* were in his father's library, and Parkman's penciled notations disclose that he pored over every line that Bancroft wrote on New France.[19] Close analysis of Bancroft's treatment of early Canadian history reveals basic proportions and emphases to be repeated in Parkman's writings. An example is the detailed treatment given the Jesuit missions, and a still more pointed illustration is the dramatic portrayal of La Salle. In short, Bancroft furnished a miniature framework for Parkman's later use.

If Bancroft provided a framework for the *History,* a debt that

[18] Two paper notebooks in the PP, MHS, labeled "F. Parkman History Europe Aug. '44" and "History Europe No. 2."

[19] FP's annotated copy of Bancroft's *History of the United States* is owned by the HCL.

Parkman indirectly acknowledged in correspondence with the older historian, many of the details were provided by yet another author. This was Thomas Mante, an eighteenth-century British officer who had fought under Bradstreet in Pontiac's war. Mante's *History of the Late War . . .* , published in 1772, has an accurate, blow-by-blow narrative of all important military actions between 1755 and 1764. Parkman's copy of this book and a copy he borrowed from the Harvard College Library when he was a student are both dotted with his marginalia. Perhaps Mante's *History* was, as he wrote Lyman C. Draper, "clumsily written," but it still was the most authoritative account of the "Old French War."[20] This important book with its detailed maps and charts was the source for Parkman's chronological table of events when he later wrote *Pontiac* and *Montcalm and Wolfe*.

Such authors as Mante, Bancroft, and Lafitau are representative of the kind of reading that equipped Parkman for the years ahead, for he was not as self-pollenizing as he has usually been portrayed. By an extremely varied scheme of study and other activities he anticipated his future needs to a remarkable degree. In these formative college years he crystallized many of the ideas which he was to retain through life and which were to be incorporated into his writings.

Just as the reading Parkman did for his college classes and on his own initiative was of real consequence for his later work, so his career in law school had an overlapping influence on his future career as a writer. His discreet reserves of judgment and timely skepticism are not unrelated to this part of his education. Although Parkman never practiced law, he had a lawyer's persistence in sifting facts. What lengths he went to is demonstrated by the years he spent collating seventeenth-century journals which finally exposed Father Hennepin as one of the most insolent liars in history.[21] Sometimes, during his mature years, the last particle of conclusive evidence almost curdled the milk of his narrative, yet he did not hesitate to set down the facts as he saw them. Parkman's judicious approach to writing is best summarized in a line he wrote one of his most bitter critics. "I wish," he said, "to preserve an entirely judicial, and not controversial, frame of mind in all that relates to Canadian matters."[22]

Parkman's training in the law was thorough and he had excellent

[20] To Lyman C. Draper, Dec. 23, 1845.

[21] *La Salle and the Discovery of the Great West*, 136. All citations to FP's *History* are from the Frontenac edition, containing his last revisions.

[22] To Abbé Henri-Raymond Casgrain, May 9, 1875.

teachers. One of these, Joseph Story, surpassed even John Marshall in legal scholarship according to a prominent law historian. Simon Greenleaf, another instructor, was an exacting teacher who demanded results from his students. An important book Parkman studied was Greenleaf's famous text on *Evidence,* along with commentaries of Blackstone and Kent. Despite Parkman's lack of enthusiasm for studying law, he was interested in the subject to the extent that he read international law on his own initiative.[23]

While books and teachers helped to shape Parkman's views during his formative period, his method of gathering information, as affirmed by his letters and journals, was personal observation. Fortunately his plans required him to travel, to leave the provincial society of Boston. His journeys broadened an ingrained Federalist view of the world, and, in some respects, broke down his aloofness toward fellow-Americans. Yet, as demonstrated by his later letters to the press, he never came to the point of being able to appreciate all the merits of a bumptious coonskin democracy.[24] Although he tried, it was very difficult for him to throw off a cloak of superiority.

In these early years he exhausted college friends in summer expeditions through the New England woods and Canada. After a breakdown in his health in his senior year at college, he made a grand tour of Europe with the design of observing the Roman Church at close range, and in 1845 he explored historic sites of the Old Northwest. The journey that was to leave its impression on almost all his writings began in March of the following year when he embarked on a tour of the prairies.

Parkman's Oregon Trail letters give ample evidence of his conscious preparation for a lifelong task. They convey the impression that he had at last satisfied his desire for a full taste of life in the raw wilderness. The trip gave him, he wrote his family, "a cartload of practical experience." "One season on the prairies," he said, "will teach a man more than a half a dozen in the settlements. There is no place on earth where he is thrown more completely on his own resources."[25]

[23] The library charge lists of Harvard, HA, shows that in 1842–43 FP was reading Emmerich de Vattel's celebrated *Le droit des gens.*

[24] See, for example, FP's letter to the editors of the *Boston Daily Advertiser,* Jan. 8, 1862.

[25] To his Father, Sept. 26, 1846.

Indeed, one who follows Parkman's tortuous path through the wild, desolate Sybille Canyon to the arid basin of the Medicine Bow, where he lived with the Sioux, becomes acutely aware of his fierce determination to see what he wanted to see and to bear the hardships of the frontiersman.[26]

Parkman's Oregon Trail letters are perhaps the most fascinating in his entire correspondence. Because he was writing to his father and mother, the letters are marked with a personal touch, with vivid glimpses of life on the Great Plains during the surge of the westward movement in 1846. Doubtless the publication of these letters will reopen the question of Parkman's attitude toward fellow-Americans he saw on the trail. Critics of the published account of his journey, his *Oregon Trail*, have marked him as a "Boston Brahmin," who looked down on the westward-moving pioneers with aristocratic disdain. It has been said that Parkman's Federalist background prevented him from understanding the significance of this great nineteenth-century westward expansion, although he perfectly grasped the importance of its colonial counterpart, as indicated in his *History*. The late Bernard DeVoto took this latter position,[27] but Samuel E. Morison has defended Parkman by pointing out that the westward movement "was simply not his dish," because Parkman went west to hunt and study the Plains Indians.[28] Evidence in the letters will lend support to both opinions, and the reader will have to reach his own conclusions.

There are seven letters in this series of 1846, beginning with one from Cincinnati and ending with one from St. Louis. That Parkman sent additional communications to his parents is certain, but these have yet to be discovered. Actually the last two extant summarize part of the story, the details of which may well be contained in missing letters; but unfortunately we have nothing at all from Bent's Fort or from the Santa Fe Trail.

Perhaps the most significant aspect of the letters is that they provide new information concerning the beginning and ending of his journey. His journals, for example, have an entry of April 9, but nothing is said of Parkman's visit in Cincinnati. His letter from St. Louis, written six days after the final entry in his journal, contains a reaction

[26] The editor has had the pleasure of following FP's route of 1846 and has traced his college expeditions through the beautiful "Parkman country" of New York and New England.

[27] *The Year of Decision, 1846* (Boston, 1943), 140 ff.

[28] Samuel E. Morison (ed.), *The Parkman Reader* (Boston, 1955), 16.

to his experiences ("I feel about ten years older than I did five months ago") and a description of the unusual assortment of clothing he wore on the plains.

Parkman's classic in American literature, his *Oregon Trail,* was one of the first popular books that called attention to the romance and adventure of the prairies across the Missouri River. The excellent edition of Parkman's journals by Mason Wade provided many of the previously unknown details of his expedition, and now Parkman's unpublished letters throw still more light on the journey that took him from St. Louis to Independence, northward to Fort Leavenworth, and thence westward across the grasslands to the Platte River, which he followed to Fort Laramie. After his side trip into the country of the Medicine Bow, he turned south to Bent's Fort to pick up the northern branch of the Santa Fe Trail which took him back to Independence.

What remains of the primitive West that Parkman saw in 1846? For a twentieth-century generation it is of interest to know that many of the landmarks Parkman observed remain practically unchanged for one who retraces his route as nearly as it can be followed by automobile and on foot. Madame Jarrot's mansion in Cahokia, the scene of Pontiac's demise, is almost exactly as Parkman saw it, a sturdy brick building with graceful white columns and shutters. Fort Leavenworth surrounds a few ruins of white-walled fortifications mentioned in Parkman's journals, but the area is dominated by brick barracks of the Civil War era. Turning westward toward the Platte, one crosses the Big Blue River, which is in mid-summer a chocolate rivulet that hardly justifies its name. However, the panorama of the gradual northwestern slope of the land at the California Crossing of the Platte with its wagon-wheel scars on virgin soil meets all expectations. Farther along the trail, Ash Hollow, famed as a wooded sanctuary, is an oasis on the plains. Deep wheel ruts mark an adjacent hill where wagons made their perilous descent down to the cool bottom lands. The timeless landmark of Chimney Rock thrusts its lonely pinnacle skyward as conspicuously as when the emigrants in wagons counted the days it was still in sight. Always near by, the blue-green waters of the North Platte wind through a broad bed interrupted at times by chalk cliffs marked by carved initials and names dating back to the 1840's. Several combinations of initials have the appearance of "F.P.," and might well be Parkman's, for decorating dormitory woodwork with initials was an old student custom at Harvard. Finally, Scott's Bluff looms ahead, where the wind howls through cool ravines and where the wagon trail winds below pine- and cedar-covered escarpments.

The Fort Laramie Parkman described so vividly has completely disappeared. Only on a knoll near a bend on Laramie Creek, belted by willows and cottonwoods, may one discover remains of the proud fur company post by picking up old pieces of glass and crockery from the gravel soil. The picturesque ruins and reconstructed buildings near by, part of the Fort Laramie National Monument, belong to the period after 1849 when the post was owned by the U. S. Army.

The extreme hazardousness of Parkman's side expedition from Fort Laramie to join a roving band of Oglala Sioux is revealed by tracing his route through the rocky Sybille Canyon to the basin of the Medicine Bow. Although accessible by narrow paved road, the desolate canyon conveys the impression of isolation, relieved only by a narrow meadow where bison graze peacefully under government protection. Many of the piercing rock formations must have recalled, for Parkman, his beloved Dixville Notch of the White Mountains, although the Sybille has no resemblance to the gushing rivers of New Hampshire.

After returning to Fort Laramie, he passed over the future site of Denver. He later wrote a friend that when he saw the place in 1846 it was "an absolute solitude, inhabited solely by rattlesnakes of which we killed one four feet in length."[29] One may still attempt to trace Parkman's southward path down to Bent's Fort and follow the Santa Fe Trail back to Independence, but disappointingly enough, nothing remains of Bent's Fort except excavated foundations in an open field along the Arkansas.

Parkman's bold enterprise on the prairies almost cost him his life. Suffering from eye irritation caused by the hot glare of the plains and attacks of dysentery resulting from a meat diet and the peculiar concoctions served up by the Sioux, he staggered when he walked and could hardly keep himself in the saddle. That he was fortunate to survive the dangers he faced, there can be little doubt. Yet it was these very dangers and hardships of the summer of 1846 that gave tremendous vitality to his historical writings. He knew from personal experience the kind of heroic courage that scorned weakness, such courage as that found in the characters of explorers like La Salle. Moreover, he had had the unique experience of observing western

[29] To Pierre Margry, Oct. 17, 1882.

tribesmen, who in many respects resembled the Iroquois of colonial times.

His real period of literary productivity began after this sojourn in the West, for he now belonged to the soil of the frontier as well as to the provincial ground of Boston. He became, in truth, an American historian, rather than a writer confined to New England tastes and ideas. His amateurish tales of blood-and-thunder printed in *The Knickerbocker* in college days make a pale comparison to *The Oregon Trail,* written out of the authenticity of his own experience. This was followed by his first historical work, *The Conspiracy of Pontiac.* In his letters, he modestly refers to the first as "a simple narrative of the incidents of a journey to the Rocky Mountains, with descriptions of scenery, Indian life, etc."[30] In reality it is a superb adventure story. *Pontiac,* which followed soon thereafter, was in large part the product of his ethnological observations on the plains, a remarkable history of the Anglo-French conflict leading up to the Indian uprising under a great Ottawa chief. Indeed, the value of this work is still not fully appreciated by modern scholars.

At the time these books were being written, Parkman's letters reveal that he was approaching one of the worst crises in his health—a combination of partial blindness and severe head pains which he thought might be a prelude to loss of mind. Largely as a result of the excessive strain of his western expedition, he was reduced to semi-invalidism, an embarrassing and even mortifying state of affairs for one who admired manliness in others.

He found, as he told Mary Dwight Parkman, his cousin-in-law, a haven of refuge in marriage. Among Parkman's papers is a carefully written note in his hand, "Kate during engagement 1849," identifying a lock of blond hair tied with a blue ribbon. Kate, or Catherine Scollay Bigelow, the daughter of Jacob Bigelow, a distinguished Boston physician and member of Harvard's medical faculty, exhibited no small amount of courage in pledging herself to a man who seemed at the time doomed to a mysterious infirmity.

The news of the engagement, announced by Kate on March 29, 1849, was exciting news for the Parkman household. Caroline Hall Parkman, the historian's mother, had been deeply concerned about her son's illness, but now, with maternal solicitude and delight at her

[30] To Charles Scribner, May 8, 1854.

twenty-six-year-old son's impending marriage, immediately wrote to her daughter, Caroline. "My dear, dear Carrie," she said,

> . . . I write this morning particularly to tell you that Frank is really engaged to Kate Bigelow, & this day it comes out. Aren't you surprised? How much I wanted to talk to you about it, when he first told me of it, which was ten days ago, but *she* wished it should not be generally known just then, so of course I could not speak of it even in my letters to you, for I thought it would only fidget you to know it & have to keep it entirely to yourself—but we are all much pleased, as we have good reason to be, it certainly is as good a connection as we could desire, & everyone says she is one of the finest girls; father is quite satisfied too, which is a great thing, he likes it very much, it makes Frank so happy & gives him something to do & think about; we see little of him, comparatively, no reading in evenings or writing at present. She said she would like to see me, so father & I went down there to call. She received us very prettily indeed, though she blushed a little at first. There was no embarrassment to "make it awkward"—she was perfectly at her ease, she says she wants to see you & hopes we shall like her. I admired her mother's manner too, she is very ladylike, & the Dr. called here the other day, & seemed well pleased.[31]

Parkman's marriage took place in the spring of the next year, and, at his home in Milton, "small snug & comfortable," work continued on *Pontiac* while Kate acted as his amanuensis. In September, 1851, just after the book made its appearance, he announced in a letter to a friend that "a young heiress is yawling in the next room. Mrs. P. quite well."[32] Grace, his eldest daughter, was one of three children. Francis, a son, was born in 1854, but died three years later from scarlet fever.[33] The little boy's death caused much sorrow, especially for Kate, who followed her son to the grave after the birth of Katharine in 1858.

The loss of Parkman's wife brings the reader to what becomes a familiar cycle in the historian's life, a period of depression and semi-infirmity. It is difficult to read his letters without being sensibly depressed by his poor health, a reappearing theme of his correspondence

[31] PP, MHS.
[32] To Ephraim George Squier, Sept. 12, 1851.
[33] To Louis-Joseph Papineau, Feb. 15, 1857.

throughout adult life. Analysis of his letters discloses that he had recurring "attacks," but even when his health is moderately good, one has the impression that acute suffering is in the offing. His correspondence with Lyman C. Draper reveals a congenial understanding between two fellow-sufferers who enlivened their letters with occasional remedies, regimens, and mention of the "water cure."[34]

In 1849, Parkman's sympathetic fiancée, Kate, chaperoned by his mother, had accompanied him to Brattleboro,[35] where one could find, as the town's *Hydropathic Messenger* promised,[36] "cold water and warm hearts." Robert Wesselhoeft's Brattleboro Water Cure Establishment was a popular center for nineteenth-century Bostonians who suffered from all kinds of ailments. Wesselhoeft, an authority on European water cure techniques, could supply his eager convalescents water to suit individual requirements: "Tubbaths, sitzbaths, shower-baths and sprays . . . which could be turned on any part of the body in the strength required, all regulated by faucets and nozzled according to the needs of the patients."[37] That Parkman obtained relief from his suffering by taking the water cure seems probable, for he repeated it several times. He recommended it to Draper, who became so dependent upon it that he was able to predict when he would need treatment.

Parkman's other correspondents had their individual health problems. Abbé Henri-Raymond Casgrain, Parkman's Canadian critic and friend, had a delicate constitution and poor eyesight. Brantz Mayer of Baltimore and even the energetic Ephraim George Squier complained about their eyes. Pierre Margry, the Paris archivist, wrote about his nervous disorder, presumably caused by overwork. George Bancroft was an exception. He had an air of arrogant indestructibility in his "great old age,"[38] but was the victim of curious accidents which kept him bedridden for weeks at a time.[39]

It has been noted that Parkman's immediate family suffered from such disorders as despondency, severe headaches, and poor eyesight.

[34] To Lyman C. Draper, July 13, 1851.

[35] There are several letters written by FP's mother in the PP, MHS, which deal with this trip.

[36] Brattleboro *Hydropathic Messenger*, Vol. I, No. 3 (June 1, 1858), a publication of the Lawrence Water Cure.

[37] Willard Star Cutting, "Robert Wesselhoeft . . . Founder and Director of the First Brattleboro Water Cure Establishment," pp. 301–302, typescript manuscript, Brattleboro Free Library, Brattleboro, Vermont.

[38] Bancroft used this phrase in a letter to his son, George Bancroft, Jr., July 15, 1878, BP, MHS.

[39] See, for instance, FP's letters to Bancroft of Oct. 27 and Nov. 19, 1878.

As a boy, his father tells us, Frank, like his brother Jack, complained of head pains.[40] Yet in mature life Parkman's maladies seem to have been far more numerous than those of his family. His complaints of heart trouble, despondency, terrible headaches, and semi-blindness, insomnia, water on the knee, and finally rheumatism and arthritis, in order of occurrence, are subject matter for a considerable part of his correspondence.

Dr. S. Weir Mitchell, the famed Philadelphia physician, was one of many doctors who aided Parkman, but as Mitchell said, "I fear that the counsel I gave you could have been of little value to a man who had so thoroughly studied his own case."[41] Although Parkman was the most assiduous student of his own bad health, he seems never to have perceived that hypochondria was a contributing cause. Seven modern physicians who have examined his life story, especially the relevant data in his letters, agree that his symptoms are indicative of an underlying neurosis.[42] Unconsciously he created for himself what is called a "struggle situation." He forced himself to play the part of an exceedingly vigorous and aggressive man of action at the cost of tremendous physical and mental tension. Struggle became the keynote of his life, and through adherence to it he maintained his self-respect. He saw himself as forever battling a relentless foe, the illness which he personified as the "Enemy." Parkman's struggle to master his "Enemy" appears to be in part responsible for the drive and creative force behind his accomplishments as a writer. It throws light on his tendency toward perfectionism and impatience with anything less than excellence. Parkman's penchant for the masculine and active life is omnipresent in his autobiographical novel, *Vassall Morton*,[43] and is often projected into his *History*, especially in heroic figures like Wolfe and La Salle, who also battled against formidable odds.

This analysis of Parkman's illness agrees in substance with that made by the late Bernard DeVoto in notes accompanying Chapter 11

[40] In the PP, MHS, there are several letters of the 1830's written by the Reverend Francis Parkman in which he mentions FP's boyhood headaches.

[41] S. Wier Mitchell to FP, June 9, 1878, PP, MHS.

[42] Consulting physicians of the Mental Hygiene Clinic of Santa Barbara, California. The editor is also indebted to Dr. Henry A. Murray of Harvard University and to Professor William D. Altus of the University of California, Santa Barbara, for assistance in describing FP's illness.

[43] FP's novel (Boston, 1856), is not generally regarded as a work of great literary merit. He refused to have it published with his historical writings, probably for the reason that it is transparent that the hero is FP himself.

of *The Year of Decision.* Some years ago the editor discussed Parkman's illness with DeVoto, and there was agreement that Parkman's exposure on the trail in 1846 probably caused eyestrain and dysentery. DeVoto also pointed out that Parkman's later symptoms were in part evident before he went west. This point is borne out in Parkman's early letters, particularly his letter from Rome in 1844 in which he refers to his mysterious "difficulty."[44] George M. Gould, in his *Biographic Clinics,* shows that competent specialists were unsuccessful in giving Parkman relief from eye trouble by correcting lenses in his spectacles. That Parkman's difficulties with his sight stemmed from complex and severe eye strain is an interpretation given by DeVoto after consultation with the Dartmouth Eye Clinic and also a conclusion reached by ophthalmologists who have conferred with the editor. Yet the possibility of a neurotic element in Parkman's anxiety about his eyes cannot be overlooked, and it is within the realm of probability that there was a neurotic element in his heart trouble and in his arthritis. This latter view is expressed by Dr. Louis Casamajor in an article on Parkman's illness.[45]

Parkman's anxiety about his sight appears to be linked with his struggle to achieve success as a writer. His compulsive approach to his work was motivated by the desire for family approval, and on a broader basis, the approval of the society he knew. In an early letter to Charles Eliot Norton he spoke of the incentive he received from "spectators" who admired his spirit in carrying on in the face of illness. His youthful letters give the impression that his nervous anxiety was, in some degree, rooted in his fear of failure. When he surmounted the handicap of partial blindness, he compared himself with William H. Prescott, who at least had reasonably good sight in one eye. "Prescott," he wrote, "could see a little—confound him he could even look over his proofs, but I am no better off than an owl in the sunlight."[46] This comparison is carried farther in Parkman's use of a "gridiron," a writing device fashioned of wood and wire that could guide his pencil when he wrote

[44] To his Mother, April 5, 1844.

[45] "The Illness of Francis Parkman," *American Journal of Psychiatry,* Vol. CVII (April, 1951), 749–52. Dr. Casamajor points out that many of FP's anxiety symptoms were common ones, such as a tight band around his head and palpitation of the heart, and concludes that if Parkman had real eye symptoms, they were a peg on which was hung a mixed neurosis. Dr. Casamajor questions that Parkman's eye trouble could be traced to compound astigmatism or to aniseikonia, as suggested by George M. Gould, *Biographic Clinics* (Philadelphia, 1904), 131–93, and DeVoto, *Year of Decision,* 496.

[46] See FP's letters to Norton of July 13, 1848 and Sept. 22, 1850.

in semidarkness. It will be recalled that Prescott had a similar device, called the noctograph, a grid crossed with brass wires. Like Prescott, Parkman hired copyists to make transcripts of documents in foreign archives, and later attempted to follow Prescott's system of having his books published. There seems to be little question that the young Parkman lived in the shadow of the older historian and, like Prescott, felt a strong compulsion to overcome the formidable obstacle of illness and make his mark in the world. Parkman would battle his "Enemy" to the last. The advancement of his "highest interest" was an early ambition, "irrespective of happiness or suffering," he wrote in an intimate letter to Mary Dwight Parkman.

Mary, his cousin-in-law, an unusual woman of keen intelligence and understanding sympathy, was the recipient of a series of remarkable letters from Parkman. Reticence caused him to conceal his deepest emotions from even his wife, Catherine, whom he shielded from the black despair which his illness provoked. To spare his wife's feelings, he took his troubles to Mary Dwight Parkman, concealing little, for Mary was able to console him when he thought infirmity doomed him to "a weary death in life." She was undoubtedly the original Mrs. Ashland, whose tender responsiveness caused the hero to break into tears, in Parkman's autobiographical novel, *Vassall Morton.* In his widower years she almost became the voice of his conscience as he contemplated the merits and demerits of a second marriage. "You and I," Parkman wrote, "have certain vital aims and feelings in common, and I feel that a friendship founded on such sympathies must be enduring."[47]

It was Mary Dwight Parkman who helped Parkman carry the burden of his despondency and despair in the "dark years" following the loss of his wife. As an active nurseryman, developing much skill in the cultivation of flowers, he gradually improved his health. Although his "Enemy" arose to deliver new attacks, Parkman's rearguard action enabled him to resist any prolonged engagements. When the Civil War reached its climax, he had triumphed over his foe of illness to the extent that he was able to publish his *Pioneers of France in the New World*, a romantic but authoritative account of French exploration and settlement that set the stage for subsequent volumes of his *History*.

[47] To Mary Dwight Parkman [1852].

In the twenty-seven years after the Civil War, Parkman managed, by conserving his energy, to complete his elaborate series with six more historical works in addition to *The Pioneers*. His *Jesuits in North America* (1867) is an eloquent portrayal of the sufferings and courage of the Canadian Jesuits whose missions were almost exterminated by the fierce attacks of the Six Nations Iroquois. Parkman's *La Salle*, first published in 1869, but later revised, is, in many respects, one of the greatest one-volume biographies in the English language. It is great because so much of Parkman is within its pages; the heroic, tragic figure of La Salle, a man who displayed almost superhuman strength and gallantry in fighting overwhelming odds, was a perfect subject for Parkman's pen. Each of Parkman's characters was gradually molded from an inert mass of clay into a recognizable individual; and *Count Frontenac* (1877), the story of New France under its most able governor, portrays a man of vanity, energy, and courage. Parkman was convinced that Frontenac's vanity would have led him to have his portrait painted.[48] Parkman never did find the portrait, but at Versailles he discovered a painting of the Governor's wife and used it to describe her physical appearance as she made a grand entrance into his narrative. In *Montcalm and Wolfe*, published in 1884, Parkman reached a high point in his portrayal of character when he depicted the affectionate, domestic side of Montcalm and the poetic sentiment of Wolfe. After reading Montcalm's autobiography, he was somewhat disturbed to note that a martial figure should have such a tender concern for his family. "The autobiography of Montcalm spends too much time over his wife's child bearing," he wrote Pierre Margry. "Still his nervous choppy style gives more the feel of a soldier than of a family man."[49] Domestic considerations were important in appraising a man's motives and aspirations. For this reason Parkman had questioned John G. Shea about Champlain's strange child bride who wanted to leave her husband to become a nun. The story of Champlain's twelve-year-old bride became one of the more interesting sidelights in *The Pioneers* and provided more than a little insight into the explorer's character.

Parkman's *Old Régime in Canada*, published in 1874, is by contrast a brilliant combination of narrative and social history, an intriguing description of the society of New France in the seventeenth century. While this book is a pioneer work in the difficult field of writing

[48] To Abbé Henri-Raymond Casgrain, June 25, 1871.
[49] May 6, 1878.

social history, it is nevertheless, like Parkman's other volumes, dramatic and interesting enough to appeal to anyone who likes a good story. It is no easy task to pick out and label economic, political, or institutional history in his works, because they are woven into the dramatic fabric by the hand of a master craftsman. The reader who seeks these subheadings of the professional historian which Parkman disdained to use must stop to unravel the threads. Such elements of literary artistry are particularly evident in *A Half-Century of Conflict* (1892), a complex but carefully designed narrative of Anglo-French rivalries leading to the outbreak of the French and Indian War.

Parkman's social ideas are among the many threads woven into the fabric of his *History*. As he discarded the myth of the noble Indian and shocked contemporaries such as Theodore Parker and Herman Melville by an unbrotherly depiction of the warrior as a barbarian of the Stone Age,[50] so Parkman also perceived the weaknesses of the nineteenth-century legend of the "noble Democrat." He wished to have the leadership of society under the control of a vigorous, educated aristocracy with a heritage of self-reliance, a "palladium of democracy."[51] For Parkman, George Washington and William Pitt symbolized this kind of leadership in the eighteenth century;[52] but there were no men of their caliber in post–Civil War politics. Parkman was much concerned about the problem of leadership in his day and hammered on the point with increasing blows of emphasis in letters to the press. Parkman's sympathies were with the old "cultivated class" that had been squeezed out of the Boston State House by the professional politicians of his day. The virtues of the proud New England culture he admired are best described in two of his letters to the press: "Aristocrats and Democrats" and "Our Best Class in National Politics."[53]

In Parkman's *History* there are many projections of his concept of the cultured leader. La Salle, he wrote, "was no rude son of toil, but a man of thought, trained amid arts and letters."[54] La Salle, La Mothe Cadillac, and Bienville represented a class of gentlemen, Park-

[50] See Parker to FP, Dec. 22, 1851, PP, MHS, and Melville's review of *The Oregon Trail* in the *Literary World*, Vol. IV, No. 113 (March 31, 1849), 291–93.

[51] "The Tale of the 'Ripe Scholar,'" *Nation*, Vol. IX (December 23, 1869), 558–60.

[52] Wendell, "Francis Parkman," *Proceedings* of the American Academy of Arts and Sciences, XXIX, 447; *Montcalm and Wolfe*, II, 247–49.

[53] See FP's letters to the editors of the *Boston Daily Advertiser* of July 14 and July 21, 1863.

[54] *La Salle*, 198 & n.

man wrote in *The Old Régime*, "who discovered the Ohio, explored the Mississippi to its mouth, discovered the Rocky Mountains, and founded Detroit, St. Louis, and New Orleans."[55] The Canadian *noblesse* demonstrated, for Parkman, the historic accuracy of his concept of leadership. Although he was attracted to these men as individuals, it is possible that, without acknowledging it, he felt they represented a finer and more aristocratic culture than England's in the seventeenth century.

Yet it must be said that Parkman did esteem the masculine virtues when he found them, regardless of a man's education and social position. Henry Chatillon is a good example. This illiterate guide of the plains, whose daguerreotype exhibits a powerful frame and manly countenance, won Parkman's sincere admiration. Nor did Parkman neglect the ordinary man in his *History* if this man was a representative figure of his day; such a man was Seth Pomeroy, a typical soldier, whose journal became a valuable source for two of Parkman's works.[56]

In the same way Parkman's heroes were representative men in that they portrayed the character of their society. It is true that he had his heroes whose faces until only recently adorned the walls of his preserved study;[57] nevertheless, Parkman did not promulgate a "Great Man" interpretation of history. Rather he seized upon a biography that seemed to him a mirror of the times and masterfully employed the life of the great individual to describe the period.

Parkman, the historian, revealed his greatness by rising above any one historical interpretation. Not only institutions shape the character of nations and communities, he said, but climate, geographical position, and many other factors play a part in molding the national and communal character. These influences, he wrote, exert their power through successive generations.[58]

Parkman's *History* is a narrative of intercolonial wars that were a part of a struggle for survival between two rival civilizations. He be-

[55] *The Old Régime,* II, 59.

[56] FP's dog-eared copy of Pomeroy's journal is still preserved in Vols. 107–10, "Notes on Pontiac," PP, MHS. Pomeroy's journal was especially useful for writing *A Half-Century of Conflict* and *Montcalm and Wolfe.*

[57] The editor assisted in the classification and identification of materials in FP's study at 50 Chestnut Street, Boston, when the study was dismantled in the winter of 1955–56. Under the able direction of Walter Muir Whitehill, the study has been faithfully reconstructed at the Mount Vernon Street headquarters of the Colonial Society of Massachusetts.

[58] See FP's chapter on "Canadian Absolutism," Chap. XXIV, *The Old Régime,* II, 197 ff.

lieved that the rustic British colonial population, with a heritage of self-reliance, exemplified the vitality of the representative system. To his mind, the struggle was between "barren absolutism" and "a liberty, crude, incoherent, and chaotic, yet full of prolific vitality."[59] William Dean Howells caught the spirit of Parkman's works when he wrote: "One moral is traced from beginning to end,—that spiritual and political despotism is so bad for men that no zeal, or self-devotion, or heroism can overcome its evil effects."[60] Because Parkman showed us that authoritarianism falls like mildew on a land under its care, it does not follow that he had an "Anglo-Saxon" bias similar to that of the later followers of Social Darwinism.[61] It is true that John Fiske, an ardent disciple of Herbert Spencer, was enthusiastic about Parkman's writings, and saw in the victory of England over France a demonstration of the virility of Anglo-Saxon civilization.[62] Yet Parkman's *History* does not criticize early Canadian civilization because it was Latin rather than Anglo-Saxon; rather, the *History* shows that the growth of French despotism in Canada held back the natural development of the colony.

Parkman's ideas on other subjects, such as national characteristics, religion, and women in politics are mirrored not only in the *History* and in his journals, but in his letters as well. These ideas and interpretations—ideas which often reveal impolite truths that other historians have prudently ignored—are, in many respects, a projection of Parkman's views about the American society of his own day, particularly his reaction to the sordid era of the Grant administration. Although Parkman was a champion of the representative system, he wanted leadership in the hands of the intelligent, public-spirited segment of the population. A vigorous masculine society free from paternalism and liberated from the tyranny of demagoguery and corruption was for him an ideal. A "Mugwump" in his politics, Parkman supported civil service reform and a complete overhaul of the popular educational system. The public schools, he said, give the average citizen little more than a crude, imperfect body of knowledge. The common man learned just enough to savor the sweetened oratory of political charlatans and throw

59 *Montcalm and Wolfe*, I, 38.

60 "Mr. Parkman's Histories," *Atlantic Monthly*, Vol. XXXIV (November, 1874), 602–10.

61 FP has often been accused of "Anglo-Saxonism." As an example, see Harvey Wish, *Society and Thought in Modern America* (New York, 1952), 328.

62 John Fiske, "Introductory Essay" on FP, *Pioneers*, I, x–lxxxvi.

men of ability out of office. We must teach the teachers, Parkman wrote, and also give money to "wisely-established" and "wisely-conducted" universities that could provide the class of thinkers needed for leadership.[63]

Parkman's keen interest in educational and governmental reform led him to form friendships with those who shared his views. One of these was Edwin L. Godkin, well-known New York journalist. "I made Parkman's acquaintance in 1863 at the house of Mr. Charles Eliot Norton in Cambridge," Godkin wrote, "and my later intercourse with him was, if not frequent, continuous. I never went to Boston without spending some hours in his company."[64] At his sister's home on Chestnut Street on Beacon Hill, Parkman had many visitors, who sat on the rosewood parlor sofa before a warm fire and enjoyed his vigorous conversation. Godkin was one of these, and Parkman respected his penetrating intellect and the zeal with which he fought for clean government. The impact of Parkman's alert mind left a vivid impression on Godkin. "There are few subjects of the day on which I did not become intimately acquainted with his views," Godkin wrote, "and I can safely say that he impressed me, of all the men I ever have known, as the most American."[65] Indeed, one suspects that many of Parkman's ideas found their way into Godkin's crusading editorials, for there was an old saying that the *Nation* was the best New York newspaper edited in Massachusetts.

If Godkin valued Parkman's company, many others found him congenial and amiable. At fifty-seven he was one of the leaders in the formation of the St. Botolph Club, a social organization of men interested in letters and art. He became its first president and as late as 1892, the year before his death, served as vice president.[66]

Parkman's enjoyment of social life is illustrated by his membership in other organizations like the Union Club of Boston. "The Club"[67] was still another group that Parkman joined which had informal meetings at members' homes to talk about literature and poli-

[63] "The Tale of the 'Ripe Scholar,'" *Nation*, Vol. IX (December, 23, 1869), 558–60. See also "The Failure of Universal Suffrage," *North American Review*, Vol. CXXVII (July–August, 1878), 1–20.

[64] Godkin is quoted in Charles Wells Moulten (ed.), *The Library of Literary Criticism of English and American Authors*, VIII (Buffalo, N. Y., 1905), 219–20.

[65] *Ibid.*

[66] "Records of the St. Botolph Club," The St. Botolph Club, Boston.

[67] There is a printed schedule of the meetings of "The Club" in the PP, MHS. "The Club" is mentioned in FP's letter to William C. Endicott, Feb. 4, 1886.

tics. He also belonged to the celebrated Saturday Club, closely associated with the early growth of the *Atlantic Monthly*. A seating chart from one of the Parker House meetings of 1873 has Parkman sitting near Longfellow at one end of a wide table, while Emerson, who was with Parkman a member of Harvard's governing body, the Board of Overseers, is opposite. Seated near by is Richard Henry Dana, famous for his dinner stories. Charles W. Eliot, Henry James, Sr., and Louis Agassiz are among the company completing the brilliant assemblage.[68]

Ever since his college days Parkman had exhibited genuine pleasure in social life. He has often been pictured as a solitary recluse, but such a portrait is out of focus. Not only was Parkman acquainted with many leading figures in nineteenth-century America, but he also carried on a wide correspondence with eminent Americans who distinguished themselves in varied fields of specialization. His letters to William Dean Howells give an inkling of Parkman's fascination with novels,[69] and Parkman's reading lists reveal that he read dozens of fictional works, including the imaginative stories of Jules Verne. Throughout Parkman's correspondence there is evidence of his interest in ethnology and archaeology. Lewis H. Morgan, famous student of the Iroquois, and his protégé, Adolph F. A. Bandelier exchanged a number of letters with him. In his correspondence with Morgan, Parkman gave evidence of concurrence with Morgan's theories and showed disdain for writers who concealed their ignorance of Indian culture by "high-flown phrases."[70] Parkman used influence, even money from his own pocket, to assist Bandelier's archaeological investigations in the American Southwest. "Got a letter from Mr. Parkman with $100," reads an entry in Bandelier's journals. "Thank God!"[71] Although there are many letters from Bandelier in Parkman's papers, it is indeed regrettable that diligent search has not revealed the location of Parkman's replies. Parkman, no doubt, derived much pleasure from reading Bandelier's accounts of wild adventures among the Indians of the Southwest.

[68] "Diagram of a Saturday Club Dinner," M. A. DeWolfe Howe, *Boston, the Place and the People* (New York, 1903), 245.

[69] Howells, in his *Literary Friends and Acquaintance* . . . (New York, 1900), 141 ff., gives an interesting account of his associations with FP and describes a curious quarrel with him over the moral in the story of *The Rise of Silas Lapham*.

[70] To Lewis H. Morgan, April 2, 1877.

[71] Entry of Feb. 9, 1886. Bandelier's journals are now at the Museum of New Mexico, Santa Fe. Mr. J. O. Anderson, the museum's director, sent excerpts from the journals to the editor.

Despite his other interests, Parkman's first love was his family. After his wife died, his two small daughters were reared in the home of their Aunt Mary Bigelow (Aunt Mora) and their grandparents, Dr. and Mrs. Jacob Bigelow. The spacious Bigelow mansion, a red brick Bulfinch house with firm stone pillars, is still one of the most attractive buildings on Mount Vernon Street above Louisburg Square. The girls were near enough so that their father saw them frequently. When Aunt Mora took them to the seashore in the summer, usually to Mount Desert or Nahant, Parkman was on hand to see that his daughters were comfortably settled in their hotel.[72]

During the spring and fall they visited him at his large frame house at Jamaica Plain. Roses surrounded his home, for Parkman was a rosarian of considerable reputation and had many varieties in his gardens. In addition to the roses the girls saw colorful beds of irises, asters, and other flowers, bordered by ferns and ornamental grasses. Later his daughters missed seeing his *Lilium Parkmanii,* a spectacular hybrid crimson auratum which he sold to an English nurseryman.[73] His nine species of rhododendron burst into a symphony of red and white in late spring, somewhat compensating for the loss of the "Parkman Lily." His own "Parkman Apple,"[74] a variation of a Japanese tree, was one of his favorites. But the historian also took pride in his large trees, his huge elms and sugar maples, and one magnolia said to be over sixty feet high with a trunk two feet in diameter.[75]

During the winters in Boston, the girls, as they grew older, could skip around the corner to see their father, who lived with Mary and Eliza, his two sisters, and his mother. His mother's home at 8 Walnut Street near the top of Beacon Hill was only a few steps from the Bigelow house; and when he later moved down the hill to 50 Chestnut Street, he was still within close walking distance.

One of Parkman's more interesting letters concerned his daughter Grace, who intended to wed Charles P. Coffin, a young man not very well known to her father. Parkman took the trouble to query John Greenleaf Whittier on Coffin's character as an extra precaution for

[72] FP's granddaughters recall that their mothers spoke of these visits.

[73] See FP's letter to Anthony Waterer, Jan. 15, 1876.

[74] FP's grandson, J. T. Coolidge, has a specimen of this tree on his estate in Milton, Mass. It is a small tree, notable for its delicious fruit and colorful blossoms.

[75] After FP's death in 1893, a descriptive list of all plants and trees on his Jamaica Plain estate was made. A copy of this list is in the PP, MHS. See also *Boston Transcript,* July 25, 1891.

Grace's future happiness.[76] Both girls were married in 1879, somewhat to the surprise of their father. "A curious thing," he wrote Pierre Margry, "the beginning of last year I shouldn't have foretold it for either one."[77] Kate's husband, John Templeman Coolidge, studied painting in France, where their first three children were born. It was Coolidge, "a well brought up young man, small, intelligent, and upstanding,"[78] who later purchased the Wentworth mansion for his family.

The Wentworth mansion, part of which was built by a colonial governor, has a narrow, winding staircase. On summer visits Parkman slept and worked in the "blue room" on the upper floor, where his only furniture was a small table, a chair, and a bed. On the wall he hung his fringed leather shirt and powder horn from his summer of 1846 on the plains. On a wooden brace was his saddle, which had been mounted on "Pontiac" and "Pauline," prairie horses he had made famous in his *Oregon Trail*. When Grandfather Parkman came down the stairs in the mornings, his granddaughters recall that he supported himself on the bannister, or, on occasion, lowered himself in a sitting position from one stair to another. It was here, at the old Wentworth house, that Parkman in 1890 finished the last pages of his *Half-Century of Conflict*. The historic house is described in its pages and several times in his letters.

During the last years it was Lizzie, as Parkman fondly called his youngest sister, a handsome woman with an agreeable disposition, who looked after his every need. She was, as Parkman said, "the beau ideal of sisterhood."[79] If America has Parkman to thank for a great *History*, this country must also be grateful to Lizzie, who gave a lifetime of devotion to her brother. In the winter they were at home on Chestnut Street; and the spring, fall, and large part of the summer found them on the shore of Jamaica Pond.

After a Sunday afternoon's row around the pond Parkman finally yielded to his old "Enemy." Feeling ill, he took to bed, and about noon on Wednesday, November 8, 1893, died peacefully. His funeral, held at historic King's Chapel, was thronged with Boston's elite who had come to pay homage to one of its most eminent literary figures.

[76] To John Greenleaf Whittier, July 29, 1878.

[77] Aug. 3, 1879.

[78] *Ibid.*

[79] To Eliza Parkman, July 10 [1891].

Today on Indian Ridge at Mount Auburn Cemetery a white headstone, overlooking flowers, trees, and a quiet pool, marks his grave.

The editorial pages of the day were flooded with Parkman eulogies, recalling his genius, his love of nature, his simple tastes, and his kindnesses to fellow-writers. For a later generation, however, these traits are brought to life in his correspondence.

In the clubhouse of the St. Botolph Club on Commonwealth Avenue in Boston hangs the only known portrait of Parkman in oils, painted by Frederick R. Vinton, one of the charter members of the club. It is a challenging study, not easily forgotten by the observer. An erect figure with wide shoulders, muscular hands, and square-tipped fingers conveys the idea of strength and purpose. The hair is iron gray, parted on the side and brushed over the ears; the smooth-shaven cheeks have a full color, the eyes are deep blue, and there is a slight smile on the lips. The first president of the St. Botolph Club appears as anything but a chronic invalid. Indeed, the whole portrait has the spirit of vigor and health, a tall, but muscular and big-boned Yankee.

In the background of Parkman's letters is always his enchantment with the American forest. As a youth nothing gave him greater pleasure than tramping and hunting in the unspoiled woods. The reader of his early letters is sometimes surprised at his zeal in maiming or destroying birds and animals that came within range of his beloved rifle, "Satan."[80] But Parkman appears to have outgrown his passion for hunting, and in his *History* protested against the senseless slaughter of beaver.

Parkman's enthusiasm for life in the wilderness is, of course, reflected on many pages of his *History*. In addition to the panoramic scenes of nature's grandeur, Parkman also described the wilderness as a powerful modifying influence on Europeans. Like Frederick Jackson Turner, he took cognizance of the frontier environment as a source of freedom from governmental authority. In recounting the defects of the government of New France, he made this observation: "Canada was at the very portal of the great interior wilderness. The St. Lawrence and the Lakes were the highway to that domain of savage free-

[80] See, for instance, FP's letter to Henry O. White, Feb. 5, 1843.

dom."[81] Indeed, Parkman's letters show that he himself had experienced that kind of freedom on more than one occasion.

His letters help to clarify his literary aspirations, his pride in America, and his desire to enhance her prestige by making a contribution to her literature. They also help to explain the mystery of his illness and its connection with his compulsion to write and project his own struggle with the "Enemy" into his *History*. Of equal importance are the letters that demonstrate that he had periods of reasonably good health which enabled him to accomplish as much as he did.

His correspondence additionally reveals the intense research behind the sensory images in his writings, for his letters are punctuated with requests for maps,[82] charts, plans of fortifications and drawings. When his study at 50 Chestnut Street was recently dismantled, a number of drawings, together with volumes of photographs of Indians and of the historic wilderness, were found.

It must always be remembered that Parkman painstakingly assembled a mass of evidence from a wide variety of sources: not only from maps, photographs, and original manuscripts, but also from personal observation of historic sites and Indians and pioneers in a primitive environment; from the study of nature and human character; from knowledge of French civilization and culture. Parkman's reading lists show that he became an ardent student of French civilization long before he became a historian of New France.

What may be the true significance of Parkman's *History* was perceived by Frederic Remington, illustrator of *The Oregon Trail*. "I believe," wrote Remington, "that you have 'blazed a trail,' which will produce a romantic literature and art in America—"[83] Remington was right, in a sense, because Parkman did "blaze a trail." He did it so well that a generation of historians hesitated to write about a subject he had covered so thoroughly. Although other writers borrowed the structure of his narrative, it was a number of years before anyone attempted to reinterpret the epic of France and England in North America. None have done it so well as Parkman, however. Of *Montcalm and*

[81] *The Old Régime*, II, 198.

[82] FP's map collection included rare, original early American maps as well as copies from European document repositories. The collection is now in the Harvard College Library.

[83] Remington to FP, Jan. 9, 1892. This letter is printed in the notes following FP's letter to Remington of Jan. 7, 1892.

Wolfe, Henry James wrote to Parkman, ". . . it has fascinated me from the first page to the last. . . . It is truly a noble book. . . ."[84]

The broadest trail Parkman blazed was stimulating interest in American history as literature. There were "literary historians" who were guilty of using tricks in writing to conceal sketchy knowledge of their subject. But Parkman was not one of these. His realism, as his letters disclose, was rooted in deep, penetrating research as well as expertness with the pen. He demonstrated that a skilled writer who approaches his subject as a work of art can produce a narrative which is both captivating to the reader and historically accurate. He was so successful that his main figures—Frontenac, Wolfe, Montcalm, Pontiac, and La Salle—are not remembered primarily because of their accomplishments but because Parkman wrote about them. Through Parkman the world came to appreciate the heroic martyrdom of the Canadian missionaries.

In recreating or re-experiencing the past there is always the danger that the end product will merely be the result of the author's imagination. That Parkman was aware of this danger is shown by his letter to John G. Shea in which he revealed the choices he faced. The Isaac Jogues saga in the *Jesuits* was "of such dramatic interest" that he was "tempted," as he said, "to give it more space than is consistent with just historic proportion."[85] But Parkman's integrity as a scholar caused him to keep his dramatic organization within the bounds of "just historic proportion." He had a genius for recognizing interesting and dramatic potentialities in the raw materials of history; but, as he wrote, he wanted "to tell things as they really happened."[86] Parkman wished, he said, "to get at the truth."[87] Truthful, interesting narrative, double-barreled and difficult to write, is also an ideal for the historian of today.

Parkman's letters give an insight on how the ideal may be attained, for he belonged to an aristocracy of excellence among the literary historians. His writings have been an inspiration to novelists like Willa Cather[88] and to historians like Samuel E. Morison and Theodore Roosevelt, who dedicated his *Winning of the West* to Parkman.

[84] August 24, 1885. PP, MHS. Letter is printed in notes following FP's letter to James of Sept. 15, 1885.

[85] Sept. 25, 1857.

[86] To Abbé Henri-Raymond Casgrain, April 13, 1889.

[87] To John G. Shea, Dec. 14, 1869.

[88] E. D. Brown, *Willa Cather, A Critical Biography* (completed by Leon Edel) (New York, 1953), 39, 270, 271.

Another historian, Herbert Eugene Bolton, adopted Parkman's research techniques and followed old trails of the Southwest with pack mules to prepare for writing books on America's Spanish borderlands. It was the eminent Frederick Jackson Turner, an admirer of Parkman and Bolton's teacher, who gave his pupil some good advice on style. "You must water your rum," Turner wrote, "and offer it in a small glass to a man who is brought up on the Parkman light wines."[89] Indeed, the freshness and sparkle of Parkman's *History* will always stimulate the aspiring historian who wants to write a readable book.[90]

[89] Turner to Bolton, January 20, 1916, Bolton Papers, Bancroft Library, University of California. In this letter Turner writes further: "Sometime you are going to complete your Parkman-like work by putting your material in a form of interpretation and generalization suited to the general reader."

[90] For appraisals of Parkman as a writer, see Wilbur R. Jacobs, "Some of Parkman's Literary Devices," *New England Quarterly*, Vol. XXXI (June, 1958), 244–52, and the penetrating analyses by Otis A. Pease, *Parkman's History: The Historian as Literary Artist* (New Haven, 1953), and David Levin, *History as Romantic Art: Bancroft, Prescott, Motley, and Parkman* (Stanford, 1959).

EDITORIAL NOTE

SLIGHTLY MORE THAN four hundred Parkman letters are printed in this edition. While the term "letters" is used here to include letters to the press and occasional drafts and copies, the large majority are actually originals sent by Parkman to his correspondents.

The editor has collected microfilm and photostatic copies of some seven hundred Parkman manuscripts which will be deposited with the Massachusetts Historical Society after the completion of a biographical study of Parkman which is now in progress. The copies of Parkman manuscripts include notes and memoranda as well as drafts of letters. Many of the letters themselves are repetitious, such as those dealing with Pierre Margry's documentary collection. There is additional repetition in the correspondence relating to books and documents. When Parkman was engrossed in a particular volume in his series, he often sent out almost identical epistles requesting information about a rare book or manuscript. Much of his correspondence with John G. Shea is of just such a nature, for the Roman Catholic historian had knowledge of rare works owned by ecclesiastical libraries. Such Parkman correspondence that duplicates letters printed in this edition is mentioned, when necessary, in explanatory notes.

The intent of the editor has been to make easily available all of the preserved letters of Parkman that have literary merit or reveal, so far as letters can, significant information about his life, his work, or his times. With this intent the letters have been selected and printed in chronological order, an order which does in fact allow us to follow the various currents of Parkman's life. In a few instances the justification for printing an entire letter lies in a single line or paragraph of importance. As a result this edition may be considered an autobiography in the form of letters.

Collecting copies of the letters has been a fascinating task, one that involved thousands of miles of travel and an extensive correspondence with letter sleuths in Europe, Canada, and many parts of the United States. A few Parkman originals were discovered in bookstore autograph collections. In most cases, however, they were in private hands or in collections owned by institutions. By far the largest number of Parkman manuscripts is in the collections of the Massachusetts Historical Society.

Probably the best suggestions for locating additional Parkman letters came in response to an inquiry published in the Sunday *New York Times Book Review*. While some of the replies merely expressed an interest in Parkman, others offered specific information about his letters. Finding an original was always a source of real pleasure. Sometimes a suggestion was worth hundreds of miles of travel to trace down clues; indeed, in a few instances, the editor interviewed private owners and librarians who did not know that they possessed Parkman letters. Perhaps the greatest thrill in some eight years of collecting was opening a drawer of an old secretary in Parkman's Chestnut Street study to discover the Oregon Trail letters tightly bound in a faded red string which had cut into the margins of the manuscripts. These letters have since been given to the Massachusetts Historical Society, owner of Parkman's journals, which were found earlier in the same room.

Approximately one-third of the letters chosen for this edition have been previously printed with substantial variations from the original texts, yet without editorial comment. A case in point is the selection of Casgrain letters printed in volumes XXIX–XXXI of *Le Canada Français*. Deletions which altered Parkman's meaning were made in a number of these by the Abbé himself, who prepared the letters for publication. Moreover, a large portion of the letters Parkman wrote in French to Pierre Margry were carelessly copied, with omissions of whole paragraphs, and published with a short introduction by John Spencer Bassett in 1923 in volume eight of the *Smith College Studies in History*. Another selection, Don C. Seitz's *Letters From Francis Parkman to E. G. Squier* (Cedar Rapids, Iowa, 1911), was also hastily edited, as demonstrated by examination of the originals at the Huntington Library which reveal at least one important omission.

Besides these publications, fragments of correspondence have appeared in Parkman biographical studies and in scholarly journals. Of special merit is Howard Doughty's penetrating analysis of seven Parkman letters written to Mary Dwight Parkman (*Harvard Library Bulletin,* Winter, 1950).

In the present edition much effort has been devoted to maintaining an accurate text, although nothing less than a facsimile reproduction could be faithful to the original manuscripts. Many of the originals, especially those written in haste or in times of illness, are scratched in an almost illegible hand, with crossed-out words and phrases. Parkman's deletions which are legible are retained if they exhibit a trend of thought or illustrate his command of alternative modes of expression. A number of these deletions are in Parkman's letters to Thomas W. Higginson on December 19, 1879, and to Abbé Casgrain on September 17, 1888. While Parkman's orthography is not always conventional, his spelling, grammar, and punctuation are preserved with only minor additions and changes. For instance, periods are placed at the ends of sentences when they are necessary for intelligent reading of the text, and contractions have been furnished with apostrophes. In all letters copied from originals, the place, the date-line, and the salutation are as Parkman wrote them. The date-line, however, has been placed at the beginning of the letter, regardless of where it occurs in the manuscript. Postscripts are relegated to the end of the letter despite Parkman's propensity to scrawl them across the top of the first page. Another minor change is that foreign words and titles of publications are italicized when necessary for clarity, although Parkman usually enclosed them with quotation marks. Generally speaking, the editorial policy has been to preserve as much of the original document as possible.

The same general policy has been followed in translating the letters Parkman wrote in French. In the preliminary translations made from film or photostatic copies of the originals, accuracy was stressed. Then the translations were revised and compared again with the originals in an effort to capture the flavor of Parkman's French. When he wrote in French, Parkman at times exhibited an unusual warmth and absence of inhibitions, and, indeed, even in letters written in English to French Canadians, especially to Abbé Casgrain, this same freedom is apparent.

An attempt has been made to provide complete annotation for

each published letter. The first footnote usually furnishes pertinent data about the letter which is not included in the credit line: for example, an explanation for the date assigned to an undated letter. Whenever it is possible to identify persons mentioned by Parkman, a biographical note is provided, with special attention to individuals who were important in Parkman's life and work. The footnotes also contain information on incoming letters acknowledged by Parkman, and occasionally excerpts of these are quoted to explain or clarify points of interest. Books and publications named in the texts are identified when it is possible to do so. In addition, a number of cross references are provided, each reference being to the addressee and the date of the letter, not to the page number. Unless otherwise noted, references to Parkman's historical writings are from the Frontenac edition, which has his final revisions.

In the footnotes the sources of information are furnished, but readily available reference works such as the *Dictionary of American Biography* and the *Dictionary of Canadian Biography* are not usually named. The first time a source is mentioned a complete title is provided, and if a work is frequently cited, a short title is used. A key to the editorial apparatus and a list of abbreviations used in footnotes follow.

Key to Editorial Apparatus

[. . .] [. . . .]: MS illegible or mutilated. Subjoined footnote estimates number of missing words if there are more than two.

[roman]: Editorial insertion. Subjoined footnote indicates conjectural reading of missing or illegible words.

[*italic*]: Words deleted in the MS, but restored in the present printed text.

MS: In the credit line following each letter, MS signifies a signed recipient's copy unless qualified by terms such as "Draft," "Duplicate," "Dictated," or "Translated." A number of Parkman's letters were dictated, but they usually have his signature. A footnote marks the signature that is not in his hand. Parkman's drafts are sometimes rough compositions that differ from the texts of recipient's copies. Drafts have been printed when the recipient's copy cannot be found. The same practice has been followed in the printing of duplicates. A selection of the letters Parkman wrote to Pierre Margry in French has been translated into English for the present printed text. Endorsements on all letters have been disregarded unless they provide pertinent information.

PRINTED: This word in the credit line indicates that the text given is from the printed source named, not from a MS. Printed texts have been used when the original MS has not been found.

Abbreviations Used in Footnotes

BP, MHS	George Bancroft Papers, Massachusetts Historical Society
DAB	Allen Johnson and Dumas Malone, eds., *Dictionary of American Biography* (22 vols., New York, 1928–44)
FP	Francis Parkman
HA	Harvard Archives
HCL	Harvard College Library
PP, MHS	Francis Parkman Papers, Massachusetts Historical Society

I

1841-1851

I

1841-1851

WOODLAND EXPEDITIONS AND COLLEGE YEARS, THE OREGON TRAIL, ILLNESS, AND *THE CONSPIRACY OF PONTIAC*

THE FIRST LETTER of Parkman's preserved correspondence, an account of a wilderness field trip in the scenic White Mountain country of New Hampshire, is a prelude to other travel letters, each of which has its own individual charm, retaining much of the vitality and vigor characteristic of Parkman's historical writings. As the radius of Parkman's movements lengthens in this formative period, his letters are postmarked at increasing distances from his Boston home.

Throughout these early letters there is evidence that young Parkman's thoughts seldom strayed far from the subject of his future historical work. He was fascinated with what he found at historic sites and talked, whenever he could, with those who knew something about the subject matter of the Old West, and the history of New France. He was equally interested, as his letters show, in Passionist monks of Rome and descendants of pioneers from the American frontier. His method was original, and those who have tried to adopt his techniques have not had a similar success, for Parkman imbued himself with the life and spirit of another age. The people he talked with, the places he saw, and the historic sites he examined are noted in his letters as well as his journals and became later the reference pegs from which he hung descriptive sections of his *History*.

Parkman's Oregon Trail letters, as has been noted, relate his unique experiences on the Great Plains in 1846. Still preserved in these letters is the stimulating freshness of the virgin prairies during the heyday of the westward-moving wagon trains. The careful reader will also note Parkman's increasing complaints of illness and occasional references to possibilities of entering the bar or beginning a literary career. As a young Bostonian of a prominent family, Parkman was obliged, as an old saying went, "to make an effort" to establish himself in a worthwhile occupation. Certainly Parkman's intense desire to achieve success as a writer, an ambition partly concealed from his parents at this time, left little room for the idle life of a gentleman of leisure.

Although his college letters tell some of the details of Frank Parkman's share of student frivolity and idle mischief, they also reveal his perseverance in ferreting out books and documents pertaining to the "Old French War." When Parkman began his research, there were few, if any, multi-volumed sets of published documents on the early history of France and England in America. As a result of his voluminous reading, the youthful Parkman soon discovered that existing books on the subject were incomplete and, for the most part, lacked authority. He readily distinguished between accurate historical accounts and fictional treatments, a faculty which led him to begin his own lifelong search for manuscript material such as letters, diaries, legal records, and reports, the primary sources for writing history. It was no accident that his search led him to Lyman C. Draper, who, in the 1840's, had already amassed a collection of rare books and manuscripts on early American frontier history. Parkman's first letters to Draper are the beginning of a lengthy correspondence in which Parkman described his scheme of writing and the kind of documents he wanted. Fortunately Draper proved generous with his collection, and Parkman in turn tried to help Draper with writing projects and building a library at the state historical society in Wisconsin. Parkman's quest for documentary material was to lead him to other members of the historical fraternity who, like Draper, were able to find rare items of reference that Parkman found invaluable, even indispensable, for his *History*. The diligent reader of Parkman's letters will find that a significant portion of his whole correspondence is linked to this search for source materials.

After returning from the plains at the age of twenty-three, Parkman launched his literary career in the teeth of illness. With notable persistence, by writing and dictating, he managed to finish *The Oregon Trail*, first published in installments in the *Knickerbocker Magazine*. Although his malady gave him little respite, Parkman doggedly continued writing *The Conspiracy of Pontiac;* documentary material was read aloud to him by an assistant, and he was able to produce five or six lines a day.

There is enough evidence in Parkman's letters to indicate that the soothing bonds of matrimony were not unrelated to his partial recovery as the book neared its finish. Scarcely mentioned in his letters is Parkman's marriage to Catherine Scollay Bigelow—"Kate"—who did much to ease the burden of his infirmity. Some of his letters were written in her hand, dictated by Parkman while he awaited public reaction to *Pontiac*, his first book on American history. Parkman's letters show that he had no little apprehension that the book might be lost in the fiery dust of rejection, but fortunately there were friends who did their utmost to see that *Pontiac* was favorably received. In later years, after he had won recognition as a writer, the anxiety for approval disappears from his letters.

To His Father[1]

Conway [N.H.], Thursday Eveng.
July 22nd [1841][2]

Dear Father,

I write, as in duty bound, to relieve your spirit of the overwhelming load of anxiety which doubtless oppresses you, seeing that your son is a wanderer in a strange land—a land of precipices and lakes, bears, wolves, and wildcats. Not only has my good genius borne me in safety through such manifold perils, but he has also infused into my heart such a spirit of contentment with my lot that I should be in no wise reconciled to any manner of change. Barring a grievous roasting from the sun, gotten during a thirty miles walk on one of the hottest days that my limited experience can recall, I am as well in mind and body as when I last saw you. I will take care to subject myself to no further cooking operation. Indeed, I have determined, in consequence of the insufferable heat and dryness of the present Tartarean weather, to walk no more, but to perform the whole journey by stage; and, for the same sufficient reason I have judged expedient to push on for the mountains as fast as possible, the prospect of a little coolness being added to their other attractions. Accordingly, I started this afternoon from Senter [Center] Harbor, and arrived at Conway an hour or two ago, it being now about ten o'clock. At five o'clock this morning, we went to Red Mountain[3] at Senter Harbor, saw the deaf and dumb woman, got a breakfast from her, after a long colloquy by means of signs, ascended, and saw—nothing. A mist, or the smoke of burning woods, rose and covered lakes, mountains, and everything else, and nothing was visible but the dim, ragged outline of the ridge of hills, and the faint glistening of the water through the mist. I saw enough, however, to recall to my memory the scene as we saw it in perfection three years ago,[4] so, having duly cursed the beastly practice of burning the woods, I descended and went home.

The first day, Monday, carried us to Alton—more than a hundred miles—the last ten of which we walked. From Alton we proceeded on foot, along the lake, to Meredith, and thence, next day, to Senter Harbor. Tomorrow, at noon, we shall be among the mountains, and if, as is probable, a thunder storm comes up tonight, everything will be favorable to us. There has been no rain here for weeks; the air is sultry and dim—a storm will make all bright again. Slade,[5] my companion, has long legs but is somewhat silly and grievously given to grumbling. The quality, however, which gives me the greatest uneasiness, is an unconquerable aversion to a separation and an oft expressed desire to stick by me wherever I go. I trust in good time, when I have secured another companion, to overcome this foolish prejudice —meantime, Slade is a good deal better than nobody at all.

Give my love to mother and the family in general. If they are apprehensive, tell them that my health is excellent, spirits the same, and my gun in a state of quiescence. I am respectfully and affectionately yours,

F. PARKMAN.

ADDRESSED: Rev. F. Parkman, DD. Boston Mass.
MS: Parkman Papers, Massachusetts Historical Society.

[1] The Reverend Dr. Francis Parkman (1788–1852), D.D., Harvard, 1834, studied theology under William E. Channing, attended the divinity school at the University of Edinburgh, and, after being ordained about 1813, became pastor of the New North Church on Hanover Street in Boston. He was married twice: first to Sarah Cabot (d. 1818) and second to Caroline Hall of Medford (1794–1871), FP's mother. By his first marriage Dr. Parkman had one daughter, Sarah, who was a close member of his family circle during his second marriage. Octavius Brooks Frothingham, *Boston Unitarianism 1820–1850* . . . (New York, 1890), 161–65, has a complimentary appraisal of Dr. Parkman's career as a minister, but Charles Francis Adams, who heard him speak in Washington, complained that he lost Dr. Parkman's text (*Proceedings* of the Massachusetts Historical Society, LXVIII, 270). A number of Dr. Parkman's printed sermons are owned by the

Harvard College Library and the Boston Public Library. He was also editor of a "gift book," *An Offering of Sympathy to the Afflicted* (London, 1842), a work that passed through three printings.

[2] In his journal of 1841, FP notes on July 22 "I occupied myself with writing a letter home." *Journals*, I, 11.

[3] Red Hill, an eminence of some 2,000 feet overlooking Lake Winnepesaukee, is now a popular place for summer hikers.

[4] Unfortunately FP left no known account of this journey of 1838.

[5] Daniel Denison Slade (1823–96) was a member of FP's class of 1844 and a lifetime friend. He studied medicine at Tremont Medical School in Boston and for one year was house surgeon at the Massachusetts General Hospital. Later he was professor of veterinary zoology at Harvard's Bussey Institute, where FP served as professor of horticulture in 1871. Additional information on Slade and FP's other classmates is found in the records of the "Class of 1844," HA. Edward Wheelwright, the class secretary who wrote a memoir of FP, gathered a large mass of materials on class members.

In the summer of 1841, Slade and FP spent a month in the woods of Maine and New Hampshire. Their route took them from Boston to Center Harbor. Thence, they made almost a complete circuit from Conway to Franconia, afterwards moving northward to the then unfrequented country of Dixville Notch and the Magalloway River. Slade became alarmed at the prospect of such a formidable journey, ". . . as if we were bound on an exploring expedition to Hudson's Bay," and ". . . muttered dark hints about his . . . 'not engaging to come so far.'" *Journals*, I, 7–36, 22.

To His Father

Dr. Father, Franconia [N.H.], July 29th, '41

Since the date of my letter from Conway nothing very serious has occurred to disturb my equanimity or abridge my happiness. Indeed, I have seldom enjoyed a week more than the past one. The day after I wrote, I arrived at the mountains, and although I was welcomed to the Notch[1] by a very special and unsparing application of Heaven's shower-bath, whereby I was ducked from head to foot and my progress through Crawford's entry indicated by great puddles of water which streamed down my body like torrents from Mt. Washington—yet, nevertheless, my stay at the mountains was an extremely pleasant one, and my subsequent journey has been of a character in nowise different. As to my ducking, I was not the only sufferer. A young lady[2]—extremely pretty and very witty—received an equal share with myself, but a glass of brandy revived us both. I spent four days at Crawford's.[3] His house was full of pleasant company, and, amongst us, we more than supplied his table with trout. We all—a cavalcade of ten—ascended Mt. Washington, and had a succession of most noble views, though an obstinate cloud was settled on the highest peak and saluted us with a storm of sleet and snow. On our walk to Franconia, I shot some partridges and pigeons. We made a camp on the banks of the

Amonoosuck [Ammonoosuc], cooked and eat our game, and with a good relish too, though the cooking was of a somewhat primitive character. My gun and fishing lines have procured me many a good dinner, though this is the sole instance in which I have attempted an union of the characters of sportsman and cook. I am now at the Notch of Franconia,[4] having visited the Flume[5] and the other curiosities this morning and yesterday, and having spent the afternoon in fishing—an occupation from which my supper received exceeding benefit. Tomorrow I shall go to Lancaster, for I wish to visit the extreme northern parts of the state which I have never travelled before. Thence I intend to return through Vermont and western Massachusetts, as I find going to Lake George out of the question, for that expensive route would completely drain my purse and leave me to beg my way back. I trust to do that, and other things, in another excursion.

Give my love to mother and the family. I have been able, as yet, to secure no wild-cat alive as a companion to our tame grimalkin, but I may still be able to effect that desirable object. In the meantime, let her not be impatient. My exercise today has made me rather sleepy, as is evident, from my hand-writing. I must therefore bid you goodbye at the foot of the second page.

I am, dear Father, respectfully yrs.

F. Parkman

ADDRESSED: Rev. F. Parkman, DD. Boston, Mass.
MS: Parkman Papers, Massachusetts Historical Society.

[1] The Crawford Notch, a three-mile pass following the Saco River and dividing the greater White Mountain area near its center. The Notch was named after pioneer Abel Crawford (1765–1851) and his family, who had a tavern, the "Mount Crawford House," at the southern entrance to the Notch. Frederick W. Kilbourne, *Chronicles of the White Mountains* (Boston, 1916), 158.

[2] Pamela M. Prentiss, born in 1821, was one of eight children of John Prentiss, a Keene, New Hampshire, publisher, and Roxana (Wyman) Prentiss. Pamela was not only "pretty and very witty," but she also won recognition for her skill in cooking at an agricultural fair. She married Judge Henry F. French of Concord, Mass. S. G. Griffin, *A History of the Town of Keene* (Keene, N. H., 1904), 447, 637. Pamela and her father are mentioned in FP's *Journals*, I, 17, 21. They were undoubtedly the inspiration for Vassall Morton's romantic encounter with Colonel Leslie and Edith Leslie at Crawford's. *Vassall Morton*, 10 ff.

[3] Between 1827 and 1829 Abel Crawford and his son Ethan Allen constructed a new "Notch House" on a plateau at the northern gate of the Notch. It became a popular inn for travelers, and Thomas J. Crawford, another son, was proprietor from 1829 to 1852. Later the family made an unsuccessful attempt to build a hotel on the site of the present Crawford House, a sprawling frame hotel. All of Abel's sons were over six feet tall, yet Vassall Morton easily threw Tom Crawford "on

his back" in a wrestling match. *Vassall Morton*, 11. On the Crawfords, see Kilbourne, *Chronicles of the White Mountains*, 85, 162 ff.; Lucy Crawford, *History of the White Mountains* (Portland, Maine, 1886), 113 ff.

[4] A noble pass five or six miles long between the Franconia and Pemigewasset ranges.

[5] The Flume Gorge of Franconia is one of the most interesting spectacles in the White Mountains. Rising on both sides of a narrow chasm are perpendicular walls of granite, sixty to seventy feet high. Spray and mist from the stream at the floor reach the overhead canopy of foliage and forest trees.

To Jared Sparks[1]

Sir, Cambridge, April 29th [1842][2]

I am desirous of studying the history of the Seven Years' War, and find it difficult to discover authorities sufficiently minute to satisfy me. I wish particularly to know the details of the military operations around Lake George—the characters of the officers—the relations of the Indian tribes—the history, the more minute the better, of partisan exploits—in short, all relating to the incidents of the war in that neighborhood. Could you furnish me through the Post Office with the names of such authorities as you can immediately call to mind, you would do me a great kindness.

Yours with great respect,
F. PARKMAN, *Soph. Class.*

ADDRESSED: Professor Sparks, Cambridge.
MS: Sparks Papers, Harvard College Library.

[1] Jared Sparks (1789–1866), a prolific writer and editor, published over one hundred books, although none of them are regarded today as definitive. Born of humble parents, he managed to graduate from Harvard in 1815 after earning money as a tutor. After continuing his education at Harvard's Divinity School, he accepted a pulpit in Baltimore, where he made it his business to carry the message of Unitarianism into the South, even to the extent of preaching in Georgia. During this period Sparks became a close friend of the Reverend Dr. Francis Parkman, the historian's father, who occasionally filled Sparks's pulpit. There are a number of letters from Dr. Parkman to Sparks in the large collection of Sparks Papers, HCL.

Between 1838 and 1849, Sparks taught history at Harvard, during which time, and before Sparks's elevation to the presidency of Harvard, FP was fortunate enough to attend his classes. See Introduction.

Sparks's shortcomings as an editor of Washington's papers are well known to historians. He corrected the first President's spelling and did not hesitate to make omissions and changes in Washington's letters. His system of treating historical documents as if they were articles to be blue-penciled for the *North American Review*, of which he had been an editor, caused a storm of criticism. FP consoled his former teacher in a letter of May 1, 1852, and according to Sparks's daughter, publicly defended him. Lizzie Sparks Pickering to FP, Feb. 17, 1888, PP, MHS.

[2] Dated by Sparks's answer of April 30, 1842, PP, MHS. Sparks's "list of books

relating to the Old French War" is as follows:

Old French War

Mante's *History of the War of 1755* [See Introduction]

Knox's *Campaigns in N. America*

Trumbull's *Hist. of Connecticut* (several Chapters in Vol. II.)

Annual Register (beginning with 1758, chapters relating to America)

Washington's Writings, Vol. II. (for an account of the war in the middle Colonies)

Lake George & Ticonderoga

Mante, Knox, Trumbull.

Major Rogers's *Journal.*

Life of [John] *Stark* (in a small volume)

Life of Putnam

Maps & Plans

Jeffrey's *American Atlas*

A set of Plans & forts in America (See College Cat. of Maps, 189)

To His Father

Stanstead, Canada,
Sunday, July 31 [1842][1]

Dear Father,

All is still well and promising with us. We got here—a border town, just north of Vermont—yesterday; determined to stay here over Sunday, proceed a little further north, and make a leisurely return through New Hampshire. A dozen or more British soldiers are quartered [*here*] at the house, which is kept by Chase, a man from Franconia, who when he heard my name asked me if I was any relation to the gentleman who preached there four years ago. He is greatly troubled by the riotous conduct of his lodgers—young fellows who are ready for any mischief and keep the house continually jarring and shaking with their noise. They got their bugle and kettledrum last night in the entry and kept on beating and blowing every kind of obstreperous tune till about midnight when one of them sat up in bed scraping on a violin till near morning.

We walked most of the way from Burlington, and shall walk more tomorrow. An easterly storm has come up which has changed all the streets to canals. For all that, it is a thousand times better than the suffocating heat we had to endure on the lake, which took all the vigor out of us. I suppose you got the two letters[2] which I dutifully sent home from Lake George and from Burlington. I shall follow them myself in about a fortnight. If, however, any accident, as may possibly be the case—for it is impossible to put any dependence here on the stages or on anything else—should prevent my being at home until a day or two after the time, I beg of you, be not alarmed, for I shall undoubtedly be well and flourishing. The worst thing I have yet encountered in the way of danger was an attack from an old he-goose backed by a little bitch puppy, who assaulted us on the highway but were soon put to flight without loss of life on either side. From all appearances, these are the only perils that will threaten us, and as a venerable old damsel remarked, at the town of Eden, we "go armed enough to beat all Canady"; so there is no great occasion for alarm. We have had good luck at fishing—for other game, the time is not come, though it ought not to be forgotten that White,[3] after firing sixteen shots, actually succeeded in maiming a chip-squirrel for life, and the destructive animal only escaped instant death by means of a hole in a stone wall, into which he crept, thereby escaping the grasp of his eager enemy.

I have been to church today, where I found about twenty people, the storm frightening the rest. There are several churches in this town which is a large one, and, as far as I can see, in all respects like a Yankee town of the same size, except that an occasional soldier stalking about gives rather an unrepublican aspect to the place. There are now, the sargeant at this house told me, more soldiers in Canada than there have been since '12 and '13. But as the noise of those down stairs is rather unfavorable to writing, I will stop here,

Yrs. respectfully,
F. PARKMAN.

P.S. White's money having nearly failed, he has written for a new supply which will reach him at Franconia. I am well off in that respect. With a proper companion I could go over all New England with five dollars, but such a performance would be, as White says, more romantic than pleasant.

Again, Yours, dear Father,
F. P.

ADDRESSED: Rev. F. Parkman, DD. Boston, Mass.
MS: Parkman Papers, Massachusetts Historical Society.

[1] FP mentions writing letters on this date in *Journals*, I, 65.

[2] These letters are not among the Parkman Papers.

[3] Henry Orne White (1824–87) of Salem, Mass., was a member of the class of 1843. After graduating from Harvard, he obtained an M.D. degree at the University of Pennsylvania in 1846 and died at El Cajon, San Diego County, Calif. Quinquennial folder on H. O. White, HA. Additional information on White, other members of the class of 1843, and members of the class of 1844 is found in *Quinquennial Catalogue of Harvard University, 1636–1930* (Cambridge, 1930), 242–43.

Although White and FP were close friends, as indicated by FP's letters of Feb. 5 and April, 1843, White was even more unsatisfactory as a summer companion than Slade. As FP wrote to Abbé Henri-Raymond Casgrain on Sept. 30, 1892, "White did not sympathize with my ideas, and was sometimes rather disgusted at my persistency in searching after localities for which he did not care a pin."

In the summer of 1842, FP and White traveled from Boston to Albany, toured the historic remains of forts in the area of Lake George and Lake Champlain, and then moved north to Stanstead. From here they went eastward to the Magalloway River country and eventually worked their way south to the White Mountains. *Journals*, I, 43–84.

To Henry O. White

My dear Fellow, Boston, Sunday, Feb. 5th '43

I am very sorry not to have had time to reply to your letter before. I have spent most of my days at Medford[1] lately, returning by jerks, and escaping out of town again as soon as possible. The last time I jerked back I found your letter together with three others containing three several invitations to go into the country for a visit. Each writer urgently begged me to "name the day," as otherwise he might be from home. I did so—accepted two invitations—rejected the third—and shall soon set out for New Hampshire. So now, having disposed of business letters, I come to pleasure; my motto being always business first and pleasure afterwards. You called on me the other day, while I was at Medford; as usual in such cases, Fortune seldom favoring me in these affairs. On that day I was enjoying a loaf, on the principle of the Margalloway [River] loafing, but on a smaller scale. I went out to the woods with my cousin,[2] who had stuffed one pocket with a cold chicken and the other with a brandy-bottle. I was provided with cake and fruit. We walked through five or six miles of woods without seeing a man and also, unhappily without seeing any game but a rabbit, which our corpulent pointer followed in such close chase that we were afraid to fire for fear of dropping the wrong beast. The rabbit dodged into a wall, leaving us to vent our wrath in disconsolate oaths. We sat down under a rock, at noon, demolished the chicken and the fruit, finished the brandy—then arose, marvellously refreshed, and got home before night. The game was not quite what we should wish; but we had some good shooting, nevertheless; for we threw stones into the air and shot them before they reached the ground. One great amusement of mine has been to sit in a grove of pine or hemlock, a cigar in my mouth, and rifle across my knee, and take off the heads of the chick-a-dees with the bullet. But I have come to the conclusion that the sport is too barbarous.

I paid a visit to those voluble maidens the Miss Osgoods.[3] They were loud and long in their praises of you; introducing quotations from your letters, and dwelling with particular glee on the philosophic view you take of your exile.[4] The damsels dined at our house the other day—the first time, I believe, within the period of authenticated history—where Miss Lucy repeated to father the passage where you dwell so exultingly on your exemption from the tyranny of tutors and proctors, and the accursed summons of the prayerbell. Father smiled, then seeing me grinning, he looked grave by an effort, shook his head, and remarked that you might pretend to pass it off as a good joke, but he didn't doubt you felt bad enough about it.

I admire your nice appreciation of John Ladde's poetical merits.[5] Indeed, how could any man of taste fail to be enraptured? John is staying at present in the dismal solitude of Cambridge—as disgusting a hole in vacation time as you will find, if you search the whole country. I have been over two or three times lately, and always felt an attack of the blues, which it took several days to get over. I am afraid that, after all, my visit to Salem is likely to prove rather visionary. I shall start soon for N. H. Meantime, I have got three or four scattered engagements which chop my time into such small pieces that it is almost useless. The pickerel of Wenham Pond may appoint a day of general thanksgiving. Those of Spot Pond have been full as fortunate—I have not hurt a fin of them. Next time you write, give me some hint of the spiritual and corporeal condition of Joe Peabody.[6] I have not heard of him this vacation, and have begun to suspect that he must have been suffocated by the fumes of his father's laboratory, or died of a broken heart from the cruelty of some hard hearted fair-one.

Yrs truly
FRANK PARKMAN

ADDRESSED: Mr. Henry O. White Care of Hon D. [I.?] White Salem, Mass.

MS: Professor Gilman M. Ostrander, Department of History, University of Missouri.

1 Medford, Mass. where FP's maternal grandfather, Nathaniel Hall, owned a farm bordering a rocky woodland now known as Middlesex Fells (FP to Martin Brimmer, 1886, PP, MHS) and where the "Miss Osgoods" lived. See note 3 below.

2 Possibly one of FP's cousins from the Hall family. FP also had two cousins at Harvard at this time: Quincy A. Shaw,

class of 1845 and companion on the Oregon trail, and George F. Parkman, a member of FP's class of 1844.

[3] A Miss Lucy Osgood is identified as the daughter of the Reverend Dr. David Osgood, "minister of Medford," in Charles Brooks, *History of the Town of Medford* (Boston, 1886), 242.

[4] White had been dismissed from Harvard College for his part "in assaulting a fellow student," but was readmitted after taking an examination and was allowed to graduate with his class. "Faculty Records," XII, pp. 127, 143, 166, 168, HA.

[5] John Gardner Ladde (d. 1853), a member of White's class of 1843, obtained an M.D. degree at the University of Pennsylvania after graduating from Harvard.

[6] Joseph Peabody (1824–1905) of Salem was a convivial member of FP's class who kept wine in his room and was known for his hospitality in providing abundant food and liquor for his "suppers." (FP to George S. Hale, Nov. 24, 1844.) After graduating from Harvard, Peabody took up the study of chemistry in Boston and later in Europe. Eventually he returned to Salem, where he became a successful manufacturer. "Class of 1844," HA.

To Henry O. White

Cambridge, Sunday
April *the devil knows when*[1] [1843]

My dear fellow,

I rejoice in your spunk and unfailing indignation against your class and the lords of this venerable seat of the muses. I hear that you flourish and grow fat on your wrath; and if you wish to be continued in the same happy circumstances, I counsel you by no means to come near this "blessed dammed hole" as you facetiously denominate. It is astonishing how many of your class bear you out in your unpatriotic opinions and wishes concerning it. This very day, Thaxter[2] dammed his classmates with such energy that I was forced, in my capacity of minister's son, to be shocked at it. Lee[3] curses them with equal virulence; so do most of your good fellows. Webb[4] was out at the Puddings[5] the other night, in a state of absolute misanthropy and desperation. Yes, Moses[6] is president of the supper, and Ladde Lord High Admiral (!!) You should have seen John on parade, issuing forth his mandates to the Navies, with his boots, blacked three weeks ago, pulled over his pantaloons; arrayed in a dingy velvet frock, burst out in the back; his hair straggling over his eyes, and the chapeau bras cocked on one side, and inclined to an angle of forty-five degrees with the ground. He went slouching along at the head of his troop, holding the sword, in a business like manner, with the point close to the ground, and every now and then stopping, turning round, puffing out his breast, throwing back his head, and bellowing forth an authoritative word of command.

I was struck with dumb admiration at your infernally smutty

The Parkman mansion at 5 Bowdoin Square. Built by the merchant, Samuel Parkman, in 1788; the front of the brick building was sheathed with wood in imitation of beveled stone blocks.

Courtesy of Mrs. John Forbes Perkins

Samuel Parkman, paternal grandfather of the historian and leading Boston merchant. Grandfather Samuel "liked Spanish wine and bequeathed the effects to a few of his descendants."

From a painting attributed to Gilbert Stuart.
Courtesy of Mrs. John Forbes Perkins

metaphor about the [. . . .][7] which smacks already of your medical investigations; whereof I give you joy. Should you ever need assistance to accomplish a resurrection, you may count on me to give it. Your profound observations and sage reflections on [. . .] filled me with rapturous delight, and inspired the profoundest reverence for your scientific acumen.

In a true brotherly spirit, you asked me some questions about Birchard[8] and the other "bisces" of your class. The dog himself I believe had no part—if he had got one it would have gone hard for him—that is if your fellows carried out the mighty projects they made. They were to have got conspicuous seats, and sat quiet till Birchard came on the stage—then risen with one accord, and gone out, leaving him to finish his part, and returning when he had done. I know nothing about the rest of the parts except that Very[9] got the oration, which, the story says, he had written in the vacation, having a just confidence that the eminence of his abilities would meet its due notice.

The Fresh are plucking up a spirit, and, having been encouraged by a few town brats, who set the grass of the Delta on fire the other night, they have made sundry goodly bonfires. Last night they went so far as to paint a cross over each of the doors of University, and also to [besmirch][10] the columns on each side. It is to be hoped that we shall have a few rows, all in good time. Meanwhile, let us have your best wishes, in so momentous a matter, and be assured that you have mine in all respects.

Yrs. very truly
FRANK PARKMAN

P.S. I have got a quantity of regards, loves, etc. to give you from various fellows, too numerous to specify. Take them, therefore, in the lot.

ADDRESSED: Mr. Henry O. White Care of Rev. John H. Morison New Bedford.

MS: Professor Gilman M. Ostrander, Department of History, University of Missouri.

[1] MS is marked "ans. May 1, 1843."

[2] Levi Lincoln Thaxter (1824–84), of Boston, class of 1843, later known for his readings of the poetry of Robert Browning. Quinquennial folder on L. L. Thaxter, HA.

[3] Francis L. Lee (1823–86), of Boston, class of 1843, served as a colonel during the Civil War and was widely known for his interest in landscape gardening. Quinquennial folder on F. Lee, HA.

[4] Seth Webb (1823–62) of Scituate,

Mass., class of 1843, later practiced law in Boston and New York. Quinquennial folder on S. Webb, HA.

[5] The Hasty Pudding Club, of which FP was successively vice president and president. "Class of 1844," HA.

[6] Possibly a nickname. FP was known as "The Loquacious" and also as "The Dominie," probably after the grisly character in Scott's *Guy Mannering*. "Class of 1844," HA.

[7] Five illegible words.

[8] The Reverend Eliphalet Birchard (1815–54), of Lebanon, Conn., class of 1843, who was known as a "faithful and acceptable preacher." Quinquennial folder on E. Birchard, HA.

[9] Washington Very (1815–53), class of 1843, a preacher and teacher of Salem, Mass. Quinquennial folder on W. Very, HA.

[10] Conjectural reading of illegible word.

To His Mother

Dear Mother, Rome, April 5th. '44

I have just received a letter from you and father, which was sent to me from Paris by Uncle S.[1]—and glad I was to get it. I have been here nearly two months—that is in Rome and the neighboring country, where I have been travelling a little. The Hunts[2] are here—Mr. and Mrs. Parker[3]—Colonel Winchester, beside a large number of Americans; artists and others. We are in the midst of the fooleries of Holy Week. Tonight the Pope took mass and toasted the high altar, in presence of some ten-thousand people in the Church. The handkerchief on which Christ wiped his face, and which contains the impression of his features, was exhibited in great state from a gallery in St. Peter's, so high that the holy relic could scarce be seen so that the people bowed and crossed themselves on trust. You will perceive from the tenor of my remarks, that the farce of Coolidge Shaw[4] has not been reenacted in my person. It is no fault of the Jesuits, nor of his friend St. Ives[5]—who by the way, is a hypocrite and liar, whom I am surprised Coolidge could tolerate. I have been spending a few days in a convent of the monks called Passionists[6]—the strictest order in Rome,—who thrash themselves daily with iron lashes, wear hair shirts,—get up at midnight to make a procession and prayer—and live on pease and fish. Some of them are, nevertheless, a very good kind of men. They looked with great compassion on my condition of heresy, and seemed very sorry to find they could not rescue me from damnation. Tomorrow the Pope is to bless the people from the gallery above the columns of St. Peter's, and all Rome, together with many thousands from all the neighboring country, will be assembled in the great *piazza* before the Church. When this is over, his Holiness is to wash the feet of some poor pilgrims—then to wait on them at table, and so on.

You may think two months a long time to remain in Rome, but it is not too much to see the place thouroughly—in fact, it is not half enough. I do not think the time could be more profitably spent. I shall not go to Spain, again. I find that, though I am very well indeed, in other respects, there has not been any great change in the difficulty that brought me out here. I am not alone in this—there are several other Americans in the same scrape, and having quite as little success in getting out of it. I have resolved to go to Paris and see Dr. Louis,[7] the head of his profession in the world—and see if he can do anything for me. Uncle S. will be there. I shall see him, at any rate—and see Paris, and acquire consequence in the eyes of George Parkman.[8] And there is some satisfaction in having done the utmost, and left no stone unturned. I have been a perfect anchorite here—have given up wine etc. and live at present on 40 cents a day for provisions—so if I do not thrash the enemy[9] at last it will not be my fault. I shall sail [from Le][10] Havre—make a straight line from here to Paris, where I shall not stay long, but embark about the end of May, or first of June.

Here are four-thousand Englishmen in Rome, importing race-horses, pickles, and straight dickeys—not by any means following the [*proverb*] maxim of doing among the Romans as the Romans do, but trying their utmost to turn Rome into England. They are tolerably hated by the Italians—while we sixty or seventy Americans seem, I am happy to say, liked and esteemed everywhere. My love to all—I shall see them in a month or two. Mr. Parker desires his respects to father.

I am very affectionately yours,
FRANK.

ADDRESSED: Rev. F. Parkman, DD (For Mrs. Parkman) Boston, Mass. *USA*.

MS: Parkman Papers, Massachusetts Historical Society.

[1] Samuel Parkman (1791–1849), brother of FP's father, who was divorced and lived in Paris "and who was truly a jewel to the bewildered traveller." FP to E. G. Squier, Nov. 3, 1851.

[2] William Morris Hunt (1824–79), class of 1844, the painter, with his mother and sister joined FP in a tour of the Apennines. Hunt left college in his senior year and remained in Europe for a number of years to study painting and sculpture. "Class of 1844," HA; *Journals*, I, 182 ff.

[3] Theodore Parker (1810–60), the celebrated Unitarian clergyman, and his

wife. Parker visited the crater of Vesuvius with FP (*Journals*, I, 167–68) and later sent him a penetrating criticism of *Pontiac*. T. Parker to FP, Dec. 22, 1851, PP, MHS.

[4] Joseph Coolidge Shaw (1821–51), class of 1840, was FP's cousin and brother of Quincy A. Shaw. J. C. Shaw became a Catholic convert after graduating from college and studied for the priesthood but died before he was ordained. Quinquennial folder on J. C. Shaw, HA.

[5] "A Virginian, named St. Ives," FP says in his *Journals*, I, 179, "lately converted to Catholicism, has been trying to convert me, along with some of the Jesuits here."

[6] See *ibid.*, I, 191, ff. and FP's article "A Convent at Rome," *Harper's Magazine*, Vol. LXXXI, 448–54, for more detailed accounts of this experience.

[7] Dr. Pierre-Charles-Alexandre Louis (1787–1872) was chief physician at l'Hôtel-Dieu in Paris and is known for his researches and writings on pulmonary tuberculosis. His reputation also rested on "*son beau travail*," *Recherches anatomiques et pathologiques sur plusieurs maladies aiguës et chroniques* (Paris, 1825), which was probably known to FP. See *Larousse du XXe Siècle*, IV (Paris, 1931), 530; Pierre Larousse, *Grand Dictionnaire Universel du XIXe Siècle*, X (Paris, 1873), 722. Dr. Henry Jacob Bigelow of Boston, brother of FP's wife, Catherine, studied under Dr. Louis in the period 1841–44. *DAB*.

[8] George Francis Parkman (1823–1908), FP's cousin and classmate, had been to Paris before he entered the Boston Latin School in 1837. He graduated from Harvard (or Dane) Law School, was admitted to the bar but never practiced. After his father's murder (Dr. George Parkman, physician, member of Harvard's medical faculty, and brother of FP's father), he became a recluse. He is chiefly known for his large bequest for the preservation of the Boston Common. "Class of 1844," HA.

[9] The first indication that FP had personalized his illness by calling it "the enemy."

[10] MS torn, conjectural reading.

To George S. Hale[1]

Cambridge,
Monday Oct. 6 [1844][2]

Dear George,

White tells me that he is about to send to you, and gives me a few moments to write. When shall I hear of you and of your intentions with regard to your profession? Have you decided on the black gown? Believe me, it will turn out the best spec. I am down at Divinity,[3] devoting one hour *per diem* to law,—the rest to my own notions. It is a little dismal here without the *fellers*, and no Cary[4] to laugh at—life [is] a dull unchanging monotony, varied by a constitutional walk, or an evening expedition to see Macready. How is Perry's[5] nigger?—or has that promising scheme evaporated, like the no less magnificent plan of the Rocky Mountains?

We have here in the Law-School a sprinkling of fine fellows from north, south, east, and west—some in the quiet studying line, some in the *all-Hell* style, and some a judicious combination of both. Dr. Walker[6] pronounces a "very good spirit" to prevail among the undergraduates, so that there is no chance of a rebellion or any other recreation to entertain us lookers-on. I hear the Divinities' prayer-bell, which informs me that my time has expired—White is coming, so good bye. Please remember me to your father, mother, and sister.

Yrs. very truly
FRANK PARKMAN

ADDRESSED: Mr. George S. Hale Keene, N. H.
MS: Parkman Papers, Massachusetts Historical Society.

[1] George Silsbee Hale (1825–97), of Keene, N. H., FP's classmate, son of Salma (author of a text, *History of the United States*, *Annals of Keene*, and other works) and Sarah Hale, became a leading attorney of Boston. "Class of 1844," HA; Griffin, *History of the Town of Keene*, 604.

[2] Dated by the contents of the letter.

[3] FP occupied Room 7, Divinity Hall. *Catalogue of . . . Harvard University . . . 1844–45* (Cambridge, 1844), 14.

[4] George Blankern Cary (1824–46), of Boston, FP's classmate and friend, was regarded as one of the most precocious members of the class of 1844. Nicknamed "Mr. Pickwick," he was known for "his sparkling conversation, his sallies of wit and humor." He would have undoubtedly made a literary reputation for himself had he not died in 1846 from an attack of pneumonia after attending a ball at the home of a neighbor. "Class of 1844," HA.

[5] Horatio Justice Perry (1824–91), of Keene, N. H., FP's classmate, attended the Harvard Law School, served in the Mexican War, and for many years held the post of secretary of the legation in Madrid, Spain. He married the Señorita Doña Carolina de Coronado, known for her writings in Spanish lyric poetry. "Class of 1844," HA; Griffin, *History of the Town of Keene*, 635–36.

[6] The Reverend Dr. James Walker (1794–1874), clergyman and president of Harvard (1853–60), was Alford Professor of Natural Religion, Moral Philosophy, and Civil Polity from 1839 to 1853.

To George S. Hale

[Cambridge,
. . . . November 24, 1844][1]

We wanted you the other night. Joe got up one of his old-fashioned suppers, on a scale of double magnificence, inviting thereunto every specimen of the class of '44 that lingered within an accessible distance. There was old S. and Snaggy, N. D.,[2] Ned W.[3] (who, by the way, is off for Chili!), P., etc., etc. The spree was worthy of the entertainment. None got drunk, but all got jolly; and Joe's champagne disappeared first; then his madeira; and his whiskey punch would have followed suit, if its copious supplies had not prevented. At first, all was quiet and dignified, not unworthy of graduates; but at length the steam found vent in three cheers for '44, and after that we did not cease singing and roaring till one o'clock. Even my hideous voice grew musical;[4] I succeeded in actually singing in the chorus to "Yankee Doodle," without perceptibly annoying the rest. At length, all deserted, except a chosen few. Old S. sat on the rocking-chair, with one foot on the table, and the other on his neighbor's shoulder, laughing and making execrable puns. He had the key of the door in his pocket so that nobody could get out. The whole ended with smashing a dozen bottles against the Washington [Elm?],[5] and a war-dance with scalp-yells in the middle of the Common, in the course of which several night-capped heads appeared at the open windows of the astonished neighbors. . . .[6]

PRINTED: Farnham, *Life of Francis Parkman*, 23–24.

[1] Dated by Farnham. *Life of Francis Parkman*, 23–24.

[2] Edmund Dwight (1824–1900), of Boston, class of 1844, was the brother of FP's friend, Mary Dwight Parkman. "Ned" Dwight became a successful New England business leader as treasurer of the Chicopee Manufacturing Company and later treasurer of the Naumkeag Steam Mills. "Class of 1844," HA.

[3] Edward Wheelwright (1824–1900), of Boston, the class secretary who compiled the remarkable series of records for the "Class of 1844," HA.

[4] Katharine Templeman Coolidge, FP's daughter, in her reminiscences (n.d.) PP, MHS, states that her father "did not care for music." FP "is said to have been fond of exclaiming in Harvard Corporation meetings, after reading the annual budget, '*Musica delenda est!*'" Samuel E. Morison, (ed.), *The Development of Harvard University* . . . 1869–1929 (Cambridge, 1930), 111.

[5] Farnham inserts "word illegible."

[6] The complete letter is not printed.

To George B. Cary[1]

Cambridge, Dec. 15, '44.

Dear George,—Here am I, down in Divinity Hall (!) enjoying to my heart's content that *otium cum dignitate* which you so affectionately admire; while you, poor devil, are being jolted in English coaches, or suffering the cramp in both legs on the banquette of a French diligence. Do you not envy me in my literary ease?—a sea-coal fire—a dressing-gown—slippers—a favorite author; all set off by an occasional bottle of champagne, or a bowl of stewed oysters at Washburn's? This is the cream of existence. To lay abed in the morning, till the sun has half melted away the trees and castles on the window-panes, and Nigger Lewis's fire is almost burnt out, listening meanwhile to the steps of the starved Divinities as they rush shivering and panting to their prayers and recitations—then to get up to a fashionable breakfast at eleven—then go to lecture—find it a little too late, and adjourn to Joe Peabody's room, for a novel, conversation, and a morning class of madeira —while you are puckering your lips over bad *vin ordinaire* in a splendid café, and screaming *garçon* in vain hope of relief. If I am not mistaken, George, this is leading a happier life, by your own showing, than to be encountering the hard knocks and vexations of a traveller's existence. After all, man *was* made to be happy; ambition is a humbug —a dream of youth; and exertion another; leave those to Freshmen and divinities. I think the morbid tendency to unnecessary action passes away as manhood comes on; at any rate, I have never been half so quiescent as since I was qualified to vote against Polk and Dallas.[2]

Perhaps you may imagine me under some vinous influence in writing thus. Not at all; yet if I had written this a few nights ago, perhaps it might have smacked more of inspiration. We had a class spree! where, if there was not much wit, there was, as the Vicar of Wakefield says, a great deal of laughing, not to mention singing, roaring, and unseemly noises of a miscellaneous character. There was Gould,[3] and Farnsworth,[4] Wild,[5] Batchelder,[6] and numbers more of the same renown. Joe also gave an entertainment not long ago, where, if there was not so much noise made, there were better jokes cracked and better champagne opened. And now, what are you doing; a cup of coffee at Véry's, perhaps; then a lounge, quizzing glass at eye, in the Louvre, followed by a ditto on the Italian Boulevard, and a fifty-franc dinner at the Trois Frères. What supplement shall I add to this? You will not be sorry, I dare say, to hear a word of some brethren of your *noctes ambrosianae,* though I imagine that those *noctes* do not now appear very ambrosial on the retrospect. Hale vibrates between Law and Gospel. I fear the chances are a little in favor of the Devil. Snow[7] is established in Graduates' Hall, with two pianos, Shelley, and a half-cask of ale. He now and then appears at the one o'clock lecture, rubbing his eyes and gaping. Clarke is here,[8] taking boxing lessons. Ned is in town, a counter-jumper by day, and a literary character by night; on the way to make a very sensible and accomplished man. Perry has been *hunting* deer and *killing* partridges, and would fain persuade a quiet fellow like me to leave Cambridge and join him; but I preferred a pleasant fireside. Old Treadwell is splashing about in the muddy waters of politics and law.[9] Our brothers, whilom of X X,[10] accused me in the beginning of the term of an intention of authorship! probably taking the hint from the circumstance of my never appearing till eleven o'clock, à la Scott; but I believe they no longer suspect me of so ill advised an intention. It would run a little counter to my present principles, though I *do* remember the time when G. B. C.[11] meditated the Baron of B——; and Snow felt sure (in his cups) of being Captain General of Transatlantic literature, while your humble servant's less soaring ambition aspired to the manufacture of blood and thunder chronicles of Indian squabbles and massacres. But I have discovered a new vein of talent, which I think you did not suspect. In fact, *I* did not dream I could play the hypocrite so well as to deceive your discerning eye, on my return from Europe. I think I did, however; and I believe you embarked in the impression that foreign travel had wasted all its charms on my incorrigible idiosyncrasy. You will answer this, will you not? I am very eager to hear from you.

yours truly,
F. PARKMAN.

PRINTED: Farnham, *Life of Francis Parkman*, 19–22.

[1] See note 4, FP to G. S. Hale, Oct. 6 [1844].

[2] James K. Polk of Tennessee and George M. Dallas of Pennsylvania, victors in the presidential election of 1844.

[3] Benjamin Apthorp Gould (1824–96), of Boston, whose father of the same name was principal of the Boston Latin School, was FP's classmate and "chummed" with him as a roommate at 9 Holworthy Hall in FP's freshman year. Gould became an eminent astronomer and remained a lifelong friend. FP's letter to him of Feb. 5, 1868, demonstrates how carefully FP verified the authenticity of his MSS. A great deal of data on Gould's publications and work is in the records of the class of 1844, HA.

[4] Amos Henry Farnsworth (1824–1903), class of 1844, was a graduate of the Harvard Law School and later made his home in Troy, New York. "Class of 1844," HA.

[5] Edward Augustus Wild (1825–91), class of 1844, of Brookline, Mass., obtained an M.D. degree at Jefferson Medical College, Pennsylvania, and reached the rank of brigadier general in the Union forces during the Civil War. "Class of 1844," HA.

[6] Francis Lowell Batchelder (1825–58), class of 1844, graduated from the Harvard Law School and spent a portion of his life in Florida as an attorney. "Class of 1844," HA. He is not to be confused with Eugene Batchelder (see note 3, FP to C. E. Norton, March 3, 1849). Both Batchelders were in law school with FP.

[7] Charles Henry Boylston Snow (1822–75), class of 1844, practiced law in Fitchburg, Mass., after graduating from the Harvard Law School. "Class of 1844," HA.

[8] James Gordon Clarke (1822–1906), class of 1844, of Nashua, N. H., graduated from the Harvard Law School, served in the U. S. diplomatic service, and retired in Nashua. "Class of 1844," HA.

[9] James Parker Treadwell (d. 1884), class of 1844, obtained an M.A. degree from Harvard, and spent most of his life in San Francisco, Calif. "Class of 1844," HA.

[10] Probably a literary club. FP belonged to the "C. C.," the "Chit Chat" or "Lemonade Club"; the P T Δ; and other "secret" organizations largely devoted to the study of literature. "Class of 1844," HA.

[11] George B. Cary.

Unaddressed

Dear Sir: [1845][1]

You may be surprised at my writing to avail myself at this time of a polite offer of yours which I have already once declined. [*At the time when I told*] wrote [*after*] writing you that I was [*daily*] confidently expecting a copy of "Historical and Scientific Sketches of Michigan,"[2] and would not trouble you to send me [*a copy*] the book. I was disappointed in not receiving it; and have not been able to get it to this day, though I have tried every means I could think of, by booksellers, expresses, etc. I suppose it is out of print. I have seen fragments and extracts enough to show me how valuable, or rather indispensable, it would be. May I beg of you, to send me a copy, if now convenient. Should you find it for sale, please pencil in it a note of the price, which I will immediately forward; and let the zeal of an antiquarian (of which title, however, I am a little ashamed) be my excuse for troubling you.

I have devoted what leisure I can get to laboring through an army of musty books, and antiquarian collections, besides getting hold of some valuable MSS, and getting wind of more. I have also read almost all the works on the Indians, from Lafitau[3] and the Jesuits[4] down to the autobiography of Blackhawk;[5] and have arrived at least to one certain result—that their character will always remain more or less of a mystery to one who does not add practical observation to his closest studies. In fact, I am more than half resolved to devote a few months to visiting the distant tribes.—meanwhile I intend visiting Detroit this summer, where I hope to have the pleasure of seeing you and thanking you in person for your politeness.

MS: Draft, Parkman Papers, Massachusetts Historical Society.

[1] Dated by the contents of the next letter, an unaddressed draft of Feb. 1, 1845.

[2] By Lewis Cass, published in Detroit in 1834.

[3] Joseph-François Lafitau (1670–1746), French Jesuit author of the celebrated *Moeurs des Sauvages* . . . (2 vols., Paris, 1724). See Introduction.

[4] Early editions of the *Jesuit Relations.*

[5] *Autobiography of Ma-ka-tai-me-she-kai-kaik- or Black Hawk,* Dictated by Himself (Rock Island, Ill., 1833).

Unaddressed

Boston
Sir, Feb. 1st '45

I have just received your very polite letter, and as you are yourself no stranger to historical investigation, you can readily conceive my satisfaction at the new mine of information which you point out. As for Mr. Richard's M.S. I had never a very high idea of its value. As the original cannot now be come at, I do not care to have the translation copied at present, but prefer to wait until I can myself judge [*of*] whether it would be worth while. I propose to visit Detroit in the course of the summer, and, if I [*can*] am permitted to see the paper, will then determine as to copying it. I [*have*] had already sent, by Saxton and Pierce, for Genl. Cass's[1] pamphlet and will not give you the trouble to send it. Should Gladwin's[2] [*papers*] correspondence and the other papers be published by the legislature, I will procure them in the summer without putting you to the trouble of sending them. I am exceedingly obliged for your kindness, and, permit me to add for the pleasure I have derived from your printed works.

MS: Draft, Parkman Papers, Massachusetts Historical Society.

[1] Lewis Cass, of Michigan, soldier, diplomat, and statesman (secretary of state, 1857–60, during Buchanan's administration), obtained transcripts of French documents relating to the early history of Michigan when he was U. S. minister in France in the 1830's. Cass wrote *Historical and Scientific Sketches of Michigan* (Detroit, 1834) and in 1827 a paper entitled "Early History of Detroit and the Conspiracy of Pontiac," *DAB*. FP appears to have obtained the title for his first historical work from Cass.

[2] Major Henry Gladwin, commander of Fort Detroit during Pontiac's uprising.

To Charles W. Dabney, Jr.[1]

Boston,
Feb. 10th. '45

My Dear Charley,

Returning from the country, I find, to my great gratification, a long letter from you; and the Harbinger is gone on her outward voyage. You must think it very strange that she brought you no answer; and I assure you, I have not felt so uncomfortable since the day I called Joe's sister a little dammed rascal, by mistake. As I may be gone again when the vessel returns, I sit down at once to indite an epistle, which I shall deposit in the hands of Fred. C.[2] to be transmitted on the first opportunity. It was a visit to Keene that lost me the privilege of answering. Joe and I went up together, and shot three four-legged deer, besides desperately wounding in the heart a large number of biped dear. It was a magnanimous exploit, that of the three quadrupeds; and if you audaciously presume to doubt my word, I shall just remark that you are not half so credulous as certain confiding females who devoured the story without wincing. By, the way, speaking of Joe, a story has reached me tonight a little too funny. Joe has been prosecuted for an assault and battery committed a week or two ago in Salem!! The occasion was this. Joe has lately mounted a most gigantic bearskin coat from Russia, which gives him much the appearance of the quadruped to whom the article originally belonged. He attracted the attention, as may well be supposed, of the democratic loafers in Essex Street, who, it seems, made some remarks offensive to Joe's nice sense of dignity, whereupon he valiantly faced about and pulled the nose of the most prominent deviler; and afterward repeated the process upon the olfactories of another one. Joe is spunking up! Tell Lev. of this.—So your expedition to the volcanoes slumped. This is unfortunately the common fate of such plans. I myself cherished a purpose of visiting the White Mts. in the dead of winter; but fell among the girls by the way, who giving me a much warmer reception than I could reasonably expect at the place of my destination, I thought it best to stay where I was. How does your amorous disposition find fuel to support it at Fayal? I tell you for your consolation, my dear Charley, that Boston has been for the last six weeks in a great ebullition of gaiety—enlivened not only by its own quantum suff. of pretty girls, but by large importations from north, south, east, and west. Things are getting a little calmer, now; yet there are whispers of still further commotions to come—*don't you wish you could!*[3] The fact is our merchants feel their pockets growing over corpulent this winter, and are glad to sweat off a little of their extra wealth. —Pray, do you get good horses in Fayal? If so, you can a little better dispense with pretty women, though the two go naturally together, as about the "first-ratest" things in nature. My appetite for horseflesh is probably to you a new trait of my character. The truth is, it is lately developed; and developed so effectually that for the last three weeks I have spent the whole of every morning on horseback. I should like nothing half so well [as] a prairie horse under me, the Rocky Mountains around me, and you by my side;—you remember we once called up this vision before, but I fear it is destined never to be turned to reality.

"Oh ye powers of mind!" I hear the servant in the cellar scraping the dried dirt [*from*], cau[ght][4] during my morning's ride from my boots, and gru[mb]ling to himself during the operation. Cambridge

[went] beyond itself this winter. The mud varies from six inches to two feet and a quarter in depth, and as you ride you are in the midst of a vortex like that that surrounded Obadiah when he met Dr. Slop.[5] Speaking of Sterne's characters reminds me of his admirer, little Cary. The last news from him was conveyed in a letter he wrote to Ned Dwight, dated at Paris, and full of stories of masked balls, operas, and Grisettes! Of Bill Hunt, I have not heard a word. If you have formed any plans for going to Europe, do not forget to tell me something of them, for I mean myself to cross the pond at no very distant day, and should like nothing better than to behold your jovial countenance in the Tuileries, or the Vatican, or at the Devil's Bridge. (I mean the Devil's Bridge in Switzerland, and must not be understood as insinuating anything with regard to our future prospects.)—We are to have a class-supper in a week, where our scattered remnant will be gathered. —Old Lewis[6] with a quid in his mouth—Hale [*with*] reading the last *English Review*—Ned Dwight with a yardstick in one hand, and Shakespeare in the other—Joe Peabody with Count D'Orsay's[7] *Hints to Gentlemen* in his pocket, and a shillalah in his hand—Gould with a ferule—Wild and Francis[8] with lancets—your humble servant diligently studying Coke upon Littleton,—etc., etc.—Give my best love to old Lev. with my best wishes for the welfare of his legs. Perhaps the same process which removes a pound of flesh from a man's backside, may be of use in diminishing the increased bulk of his crural members. But Lev. is much too wise to try such an imprudent course of practice. Once more, Charley, forgive my involuntary omission, and believe me, Most faithfully Yrs.

FRANK PARKMAN

ADDRESSED: Mr. Chs. W. Dabney, Jr. Fayal, Azores.
MS: Alsop Papers, Historical Manuscripts Room, Yale University Library.

[1] Charles William Dabney, born in the seaport commune of Horta in the Azores on the southeastern coast of Fayal Island in 1823, was a classmate of FP. He served in the Union Army as a major during the Civil War and died in England in 1870, "Class of 1844," HA.

[2] See note 3, FP to C. E. Norton, June 15 [1850].

[3] Here FP has drawn a figure thumbing his nose.

[4] The words "caught" and "grumbling" are partially illegible because of a torn MS.

[5] Dr. Slop, a bigoted awkward physician, "a little squat, uncourtly figure," in Laurence Sterne's *Tristram Shandy*.

[6] This name is almost illegible. FP prob-

ably refers to Samuel Parker Lewis (1824–82), of Pepperel, Mass., class of 1844, graduate of the Harvard Law School, and later an attorney in Boston and in Pepperel. "Class of 1844," HA.

[7] Probably Count Alfred Guillaume Gabriel d'Orsay (1801–52), French society leader who was also a painter, sculptor, and author of an entertaining little book entitled, *The Follies of the Day by a Man of Fashion* (London, 1844).

[8] Tappan Eustis Francis (1823–1909), class of 1844, later obtained an M.D. degree at Harvard and practiced in Brookline, Mass. "Class of 1844," HA.

To Lt. Col. Henry Whiting[1]

Dear Sir: Cambridge March 6th '45

I write to acknowledge your favor in sending me M. Du Buisson's Report.[2] The account it contains is very interesting and quite new to me, and helps to illustrate the outbreak under Pontiac, by showing some points of the French policy in their relations with the Indians, which helped to procure the high estimation in which they were held, compared to the English. If Gen Cass's other papers are of a similar character, he has certainly done great service to the history of Michigan.

ADDRESSED: Lt. Col. Whiting Detroit.
MS: Draft, Parkman Papers, Massachusetts Historical Society.

[1] FP was probably corresponding with Lt. Col. and later General Henry Whiting, longtime resident of Detroit and member of the Historical Society of Michigan. General Whiting, however, had a son, Henry M. Whiting (1821–53), who was brevetted first lieutenant in the army for gallantry at Buena Vista. For this information I am indebted to Mrs. Ellein H. Stones, chief, Burton Historical Collection, Detroit Public Library.

[2] Report of Du Buisson, French commander of Fort Detroit, deals with an attack made by the Fox Indians in 1712. Justin Winsor (ed.), *Narrative and Critical History of America* (8 vols., Boston, 1884–89), V, 561; hereafter cited as Winsor, *History*.

To His Mother

Philadelphia,
Dear Mother, July 14, '45

Though I have been several days here, I have been compelled to remain quiet and passive by the furious heat, which has been steadily increasing at the rate of two degrees per day, for a week past. It has now got up to °100 of the Thermometer. We have nothing like it, thank heaven, at home; and as I have no inclination to stay and bear it, especially as it has driven half the population out of town, I shall set out for the country tomorrow. There is positively no place tolerably comfortable but the bath, where I spend most of my time.—Yesterday I was at a Quaker meeting, where as it was too hot for the spirit to move anybody, the whole congregation slept in perfect quiet for an hour and then walked off, without a word said. The courts and the waterworks alone are in full activity—the former densely crowded and hot as a furnace, for Philadelphia always furnishes a sufficient supply of cases to exercise the wits of her lawyers.

In New York, I called on Dr. Elliot[t],[1] who protested that Carrie's medicine required time for its preparation, but should shortly be forwarded to Boston. I am comfortably established here, taking my meals at a restaurant, which gives me complete command of time, and selection of viands ad libitum.—Dr. Elliot[t], I forgot to say, is earnest to have Carrie come and stay with him at Staten Island this summer; but I represented that she was probably fixed for the season at Medford. The Philadelphians have shrunk away to the dimensions of Frenchmen, by the effects of the climate. People lounge about at corners and around pumps, rapidly cooking in the sun. William Penn ingeniously contrived such a plan for the city, that the sun pours down from morning to night upon all the principal streets, during the hot season; while in winter, it looks upon them sideways, so that they are in complete shade for the greater part of the day. Philadelphia, was once, they tell me, well shaded by trees; but the people, it seems, got a crotchet into their heads, about the roofs of the houses being injured by it, so that many of the trees have been cut down. Still, the city would be a very pleasant one in any weather but such as the present; which, to say the truth, is intolerable, and I am not ass enough to stay and bear it. I go to Lancaster tomorrow—thence to Harrisburg—thence to Pittsburg[h]—thence give a look at Ohio—and thence go to Detroit, from which I propose to return by Niagara and Albany.[2] My love to Carrie and the rest, and believe me

Affectionately Yours.
FRANK

ADDRESSED: Mrs. Francis Parkman Care of Robert G. Shaw, Esq. Boston, Mass.

MS: Parkman Papers, Massachusetts Historical Society.

[1] Samuel Mackenzie Elliott (1811–75), an oculist, graduated from the College of Surgeons in Glasgow, Scotland, and in 1833 emigrated to the U. S. After studying medicine in Cincinnati and Philadelphia, he opened an office in New York,

where he soon gained a wide reputation as an oculist. Longfellow and General Winfield Scott were among his patients. His fellow oculists, however, regarded him as "an irregular practitioner" because of his unprofessional conduct in keeping his "discoveries" secret. As a result of this pressure, Elliott took an examination at the New York Medical College, gained a diploma, and then gave a series of lectures to explain his method of practice. During the Civil War he was wounded at the first Battle of Bull Run, and was mustered out of the army as a brigadier general. *Appleton's Cyclopaedia of American Biography* (6 vols. New York, 1887), II, 331; obituary editorial, *New York Sun*, May 1, 1875.

There is evidence in FP's letters that Elliott tried to convince FP that he would never recover his sight unless he remained in New York under Elliott's care. FP to C. E. Norton, Dec. 6, 1848. FP rebelled at such "threats," and his sister, Carrie, mentions in one of her letters that he had a "blow up" with the doctor. In his letter to E. G. Squier, Jan. 18, 1866, FP declared that it was "Elliott, who nearly blinded me."

[2] See *Journals*, I, 298 ff., for an account of this journey.

To Lyman C. Draper[1]

Boston
Oct. 8 1845

Sir,

Professor Sparks tells me that you have given much attention to the frontier history of Virginia, and have made collections of documents relating to it. I have been, for some time, investigating the Indian War of 1763 and '64, which, as you know, was felt severely in Virginia and Pennsylvania. As I do not know what object you have in view, I cannot tell whether I am making a request that you can grant, in asking information of you on this point. I certainly would avoid interfering with any pursuit of yours; but I think it likely, as my researches are confined to the period mentioned, that you may be able to give me valuable information without injustice to yourself. If you can show me any clue to manuscripts, or any sort of authorities, that may throw light on Bouquet's campaigns in '63 and '64,[2] (in which Col. Lewis[3] of Va. bore a prominent part) or refer me to any sources of information relating to that war, or the causes and circumstances that led to it, no matter how trivial they may appear, you will confer a great favor on me. Anything that might show the state of the frontier, the character of the people, etc., at that period, would be very acceptable. Possibly, I may be of some service to you in your pursuits, in which case you may command me to the best of my power—for we antiquarians are bound to yield mutual assistance.

I hope my request will not incommode you, and am,

Respectfully,
Your obedient,
Francis Parkman, Jr.

ADDRESSED: Lyman C. Draper, Esq. Baltimore.
MS: Draper Correspondence, State Historical Society of Wisconsin.

[1] Lyman Copeland Draper (1815–91), historian and editor, was convinced that the historic figures of the western borders had not received just recognition, and accumulated a vast collection of notes and documents to save the pioneer heroes from oblivion. He is best remembered as a founding father of the State Historical Society of Wisconsin and editor of the society's first ten volumes of *Collections.* His biographer, William B. Hesseltine *(Pioneer's Mission, The Story of Lyman Copeland Draper* [Madison, 1954]), tells us that in some parts of the South, Draper is recalled as the man who took all the documents and carted them off to Wisconsin. Draper was exceedingly generous in permitting Parkman to use his materials, although he exhibited some reticence in allowing others to consult them. Theodore Roosevelt, in writing to FP (July 13, 1889, PP, MHS), complained that "Mr. Draper unfortunately thinks one bit of old MS just exactly as good as any other." See also Introduction.

[2] Colonel Henry Bouquet, the Swiss officer in the British service who led the forces that relieved Fort Pitt during Pontiac's uprising. *Pontiac*, II, 38 ff. FP wrote the preface and revised the translation of a sketch of Bouquet for William Smith's *Historical Account of Bouquet's Expedition Against the Ohio Indians* (Cincinnati, 1868).

[3] The Colonel Lewis who obtained Virginia replacements for Bouquet's deserters *(Pontiac*, II, 105, 220) was probably the Major Andrew Lewis whose men constructed Fort Loudoun at Winchester, Va., before the outbreak of the Indian war. Wilbur R. Jacobs (ed.), *Indians of the Southern Colonial Frontier* (Columbia, 1954), xxviii. From the evidence in *Pontiac* and in Howard H. Peckham's *Pontiac and the Indian Uprising* (Princeton, 1947), it appears that Lewis had no prominent part in Bouquet's campaigns.

To The Postmaster, Wilmington, Delaware[1]

Boston
Oct. 12, 1845

Sir,

I wish to get a copy of a book published at Wilmington—the *Delaware Register*[2]—devoted principally to preserving historical facts and documents. As I do not know any person in your city, I venture to apply to you to learn the name of the publisher, or—if you cannot find *that* out—of any prominent bookseller in Wilmington who would be likely to have the work.

By giving me this information, you very much oblige

Yrs. Respectfully,
F. PARKMAN, JR.
Boston, Mass.

ADDRESSED: To the Postmaster Wilmington Delaware.
MS: Parkman Papers, Massachusetts Historical Society.

Caroline Hall Parkman, Parkman's mother. "Last week, my mother's long and painful illness was calmly and peacefully ended, and a life of rare affection, disinterestedness, and self-devotion came to its close on earth."

From a miniature.

Photographs courtesy of the Massachusetts Historical Society

The Reverend Dr. Francis Parkman, Parkman's father.

Lyman C. Draper, founding father of the Wisconsin State Historical Society and Parkman's lifelong friend.

From a portrait accompanying an undated New York *Daily Graphic* article on Draper.
Courtesy of the Harvard College Library

[1] W. N. Sellers, postmaster, placed FP's request in the hands of Messrs. Wilson and Heald, booksellers. Sellers to FP, Dec. 3, 1845, PP, MHS.

[2] *The Delaware register; or farmers' manufacturers' and mechanics' advocate, containing a variety of original and selected articles* (A. & H. Wilson, Wilmington, Delaware, 1828–29).

To Lyman C. Draper

My Dear Sir, Boston, Dec. 23rd 1845

I thank you for your obliging letter, and am very glad to learn from it that you are so deeply and zealously engaged in pursuits in which I can completely sympathize with you, and for which the country will be so much your debtor. The lives of our frontier heroes—and they *were* heroes—have never been properly written; and, indeed have hardly been touched by anyone combining the requisites of literary attainment with patient unflinching research. The frontiers of Virginia, in particular, can furnish many excellent subjects for biography. I shall look very eagerly for the appearance of your books.

You enquire as to the extent and design of my own investigations: —I mean to write the history of the Indian War of '63–'64, in all its bearings, and especially as connected with the famous Ottawa chief *Pontiac*. My first idea was to make something like a biography of him; but you know how meagre is the information that one gets concerning the life of an Indian chief,—and I resolved to embrace the whole war in my design, and give a minute and complete account of its causes, progress, and results, chiefly with the view of exhibiting the traits of the Indian character. It is about a year and a half since I took up this plan; though I have given my attention to similar subjects—studying them principally in our excellent college library—for a much longer time. I collected last summer a number of MSS some of which are very interesting, relating chiefly, however, to the events of the war in the vicinity of the Upper Lakes. The papers of which you so generously promise me the use, will be very acceptable as they will help to fill what has hitherto been an hiatus in my collections. Everything, even the most minute, that relates to the war of '63–'64 will be welcome to me—my appetite, when I am upon those times, is omnivorous; for though I may not actually make use of all these materials, they will be of great advantage in giving me a just and lively notion of the whole period.

I have seen the "Muskingum Expedition,"[1] which I find quite unsatisfactory. The papers in the P^{a}. state offices give a much better view of the matter. Mante is in the college library;[2] and contains, as I believe, the most complete account of the Indian War that has appeared. It is, however, but a poor affair on the whole; ill digested, and rather clumsily written, though I think you might find it of service in giving a general view of the wars of '54–'64. I have not met with the *History of the Valley of Virginia*,[3] and if you could lay hand on a copy, it would be very acceptable. Have you seen Wither's *C[h]ronicles of Border Warfare?*[4]—or Doddridge's *Notes?*[5]—or a little book by Loudon,[6] published at Carlisle Pa.?—You probably have; but if not, you will no doubt find in them much that is to your purpose. I understand that Mr. Force,[7] at Washington, has a copy of the last work, which is rare. I found at Lancaster Pa. a book called "Incidents of Border Warfare"[8] containing sketches of Capt. Wells, the Whetsels, Kenton, Brady, etc. with a good deal that is new to me. I have it, and shall be happy to lend it to you, should you not have seen it.

I propose making a historical trip southwards in the course of three weeks or more. Shall you be in Baltimore about the middle of February? I am anxious to see you and converse with you, as a congenial spirit, upon these subjects; and shall esteem it a favor if you will write to me acquainting me with your address and when you will be at home. Meanwhile, with many thanks for your politeness, I remain

Sincerely and Respectfully, Yrs,

FRANCIS PARKMAN, JR.

P.S. You no doubt have seen *Hazard's Pa. Register*.[9] The articles in it upon Capt. Jack and some similar subjects are from the pen of Redmond Conyngham Esq.[10] of Paradise, near Lancaster Pa.—a gentleman well versed in Border antiquities, and who no doubt will be happy to assist you to the best of his power. Do you correspond with Hon. Chas. Miner[11] of Wilkesbarre, and do you know when we are to expect his long promised *History of Wyoming?* It occurs to me that I may perhaps be of service to you in informing you as to the contents of books in the college library, and to which you may not have access in Baltimore—or in sending you extracts from them. If in this way or any other I can aid your researches, it will give me the greatest pleasure.

F. P.

ADDRESSED: Lyman C. Draper, Esq. Baltimore.
MS: Draper Correspondence, State Historical Society of Wisconsin.

[1] Bouquet's expedition of 1764 (*Pontiac*, II, 213) entered the valley of the Muskingum River in Ohio. FP possibly refers to a work concerning this expedition.

[2] Thomas Mante's *History*. See Introduction.

[3] Possibly this refers to John D. Burk, *History of Virginia* (4 vols., Petersburg, Va., 1804–1816).

[4] See R. G. Thwaites's edition of Alexander Scott Withers, *Chronicles of Border Warfare* (Cincinnati, 1895).

[5] Joseph Doddridge, *Notes on the Settlement and Indian Wars of the Western parts of Virginia and Pennsylvania from the year 1763 Until the Year 1783 Inclusive* (Winchester, [Va.], 1833).

[6] Archibald Loudon, *A selection of the most interesting narratives of outrages committed by Indians . . .* (Carlisle, Pa., 1811).

[7] Peter Force (1790–1868), archivist and historian, collected and published four volumes entitled *Tracts and Other Papers, Relating Principally to the Origin, Settlement and Progress of the Colonies in North America* (Washington, 1836–46), but is chiefly known for his monumental series on the colonial period and the Revolution, *The American Archives*.

[8] FP probably refers to [Joseph Pritts], *Incidents of Border Life . . .* (Lancaster, Pa., 1841).

[9] *Hazard's Register of Pennsylvania . . .*, edited by Samuel Hazard (Philadelphia, 1828–35).

[10] Redmond Conyngham (1781–1846), an antiquarian who specialized in the history of Lancaster County, Pennsylvania, contributed authoritative papers to the American Philosophical Society and the Historical Society of Pennsylvania. *Appleton's Cyclopaedia* (New York, 1887), I, 713. Conyngham published an early account of the massacre of the Conestoga Indians in 1763 which Parkman used in his *Pontiac*, II, 131 ff.

[11] Charles Miner (1780–1865), editor, legislator, and author. His *History of Wyoming*, published in 1845, dealt with the massacre of July 3, 1778, and with the long-disputed land claims of Connecticut and Pennsylvania.

To Lyman C. Draper

Philada.
My Dear Sir, Wednesday, Jan. 21 '46

I am now on an historic expedition, gathering materials wherever I can, to carry out the objects I described to you. I am just arrived here, where I find in the Historical Society's Collection, some papers of considerable interest; though I was disappointed of getting anything at Trenton. As soon as I get through here, I shall come to Baltimore, where I promise myself the pleasure of seeing you, and we can talk together of these matters to our hearts' content.—Your plan, as I see by the circular,[1] is indeed an extensive one, enough to appal anybody but an enterprising man; however, you have already dispatched the laborious part and have got nothing but the pleasure before you; while I, for my part, have the greater part of the delving and rummaging still to look forward to. Have you got wind of that Bouquet Journal

DOMINICAN COLLEGE
LIBRARY
SAN RAFAEL

yet? Bouquet was a jewel of an officer, and makes a most favorable contrast with Braddock[2]—that epitome of all the worst traits of John Bull.

Bartlett & Welford, New York, had Hutchins' *Narrative*,[3] both in the original English and in the French translation. (to the latter of which a sketch of Bouquet's life is prefixed)—but they have now disposed of them. Mante is quite rare and dear. I found this morning a copy of Rogers's *Concise Account of North America*,[4] which I purchased.

Have you seen Miner's book? I have read his introductory remarks about the Indians, which surprised me by their inaccuracy; though I suppose the rest of the book is of strict authenticity. The *Connecticut* party,[5] at least, speak highly of it.

I shall be in Baltimore in the beginning of the week; and shall take the earliest opportunity to make you a visit. Meanwhile, dear Sir, believe me

Faithfully Yrs.
F. PARKMAN JR.
(Washington Hotel, Philad[a].)

ADDRESSED: Lyman C. Draper, Esq. Baltimore.
MS: Draper Correspondence, State Historical Society of Wisconsin.

[1] Draper sent out printed circulars describing his collections and announcing his intentions of publication. His *Circular* of July 1, 1846, for example, includes this kind of information in addition to testimonials concerning the value of his work. FP is identified in this *Circular* as "an able and industrious antiquarian," and his letter to Draper of Dec. 23, 1845 is quoted.

[2] Edward Braddock (1695–1755), commander of the ill-fated British expedition against Fort Duquesne in July, 1755. See *Montcalm and Wolfe*, I, 195 ff.

[3] FP probably refers to Thomas Hutchins, *A Topographical Description of Virginia, Pennsylvania, Maryland, North Carolina* (London, 1778). A French translation was published in 1781.

[4] By Robert Rogers (1731–95), published in London in 1765.

[5] See note 11, FP to Draper, Dec. 23, 1845.

To Charles Christopher Trowbridge[1]

Sir, Boston, March 7th 1846

I requested my friend Dwight to furnish me with the accompanying introduction[2] in hopes that your intimate acquaintance with the Indians would enable you, without trouble, to aid me in the undertaking which he mentions. I have collected a large mass of materials for the history of the Indian War that immediately followed the conquest of Canada, and in which Pontiac played so prominent a part. I look upon him as one of the most remarkable men that have appeared among the Indians; and upon the events of his time as affording the best opportunities for representing the Indian character and modes of life—as a sort of focus, moreover, in aboriginal history, where the relations and position of the tribes may be very conveniently exhibited. I have been occupied for six or eight years in the study of Indian history and character, both by means of the large collections of books in Cambridge and elsewhere, and such limited observations as I could make in several journeys that I have undertaken for the purpose.

By the kindness of Genl. Cass and Lieut. Col. Whiting, I have obtained some valuable original papers relating to the events of the War on the Lakes: I also found, not long since, the journal, in his own handwriting, of Lieut. Gorell,[3] who commanded at Green Bay in '63 and '64, and as you may recollect, was rescued and brought off safe by the Sioux and Folles Avoines. These materials will enable me to give a tolerable complete account of Pontiac's northern operations—and yet these are so interesting and so valuable as illustrating Indian character and policy, that the smallest additional details would be very welcome to me. I was much disappointed, on applying to Col. McKenney, to learn that the interesting papers with which you furnished him, and which he has used in some of his works, have been unfortunately lost.

I am anxious to obtain as many particulars as possible of Pontiac's life, character and death. If you could furnish me with any [*particulars*] information of this sort,—or, indeed, any other that relates to the events of that day,—I shall esteem it the greatest possible obligation. He seems to be looked back upon as a hero, by the Indians—is it not possible that something might be gathered by personal inquiry among them? Such authority, to be sure, would be very apocryphal, but then one may retain the right of judging for himself, and as I propose to visit the northern and western tribes, I shall have good opportunity for such investigations. Are there no surviving members of his family?

I shall not fail gratefully to acknowledge any assistance you may find it convenient to give me, and am,

With much respect
Your obedient Servant,
F. Parkman, Jr.

(care of Rev. Dr. Parkman, No. 5 Bowdoin Square, Boston)

ADDRESSED: C. C. Trowbridge Esq. Detroit.
MS: Burton Historical Collection, Detroit Public Library.

[1] Charles Christopher Trowbridge (1800–83), a prominent Detroit banker and railroad president, in 1820 had accompanied Lewis Cass on his exploring expedition to Lake Superior and while still a young man had acted as Indian agent and interpreter at Green Bay and Detroit. His "Account of some of the Traditions, Manners and Customs of the Twaatwaa or Miami Indians" has been published by the University of Michigan. [S. D. Bingham (compiler)], *Early History of Michigan with Biographies* (Lansing, 1888), 643–47; Silas Farmer, *History of Detroit and Wayne County and Early Michigan* (2 vols., New York, 1890), II, 1034–35.

An indication of FP's indebtedness to Trowbridge is found in Lewis Cass's letter of Jan. 21, 18—, to Trowbridge (Burton Historical Collection, Detroit Public Library): "Parkman has done well and has used much of your language."

[2] Edmund Dwight to Trowbridge March 6, 1846, *ibid.*

[3] "Lieut. James Gorell's Journal," covering the period 1761–63, *Collections* of the State Historical Society of Wisconsin (Madison, 1855), I, 25–48, was printed by Draper after FP sent him a transcript.

To Lewis Cass[1]

Sir, Boston, March 19th '46

I have already been so much indebted to you for assistance in my investigations into Indian history, that I am scrupulous as to troubling you again.[2] I am, however, on the point of setting out for the Indian country, in order to see and study them in person; and if, among your constant engagements, you can find a moments' leisure to write me a few lines of introduction to persons on the frontier who would be likely to facilitate my undertaking, I should esteem it the greatest favor. I propose to visit the posts on the Missouri, and the Upper Mississippi. The great weight and value of an introduction from you tempts me to take this liberty. Letters may be directed to me at *St. Louis*, where I can take them from the Post-office.

I am, Sir,
Your Most Obliged
and Obedient Servant
F. PARKMAN, JR.

MS: Cass Papers, William L. Clements Library.

[1] For a sketch of Cass, see note 1, Unaddressed, Feb. 1, 1845.

[2] Cass permitted FP to borrow transcripts of documents. Cass to Trowbridge,

Jan. 21, 18—, Burton Historical Collection; *Pontiac,* I, xi. Most important, it was through Cass that Parkman was able to obtain a copy of the "Pontiac Manuscript," now regarded as one of Michigan's most valuable historical documents, a part of the Burton Historical Collection of the Detroit Public Library. The "Pontiac Manuscript" is the very meat of Parkman's whole *Conspiracy of Pontiac.* It is a minute, detailed account of the siege of Fort Detroit, attributed to one Robert Navarre, a Canadian. For a discussion on Parkman's use of this important document, see Wilbur R. Jacobs, "Was the Pontiac Uprising a Conspiracy?" *The Ohio Archaeological and Historical Quarterly,* Vol. LIX (January, 1950), 26–37; Peckham, *Pontiac and the Indian Uprising,* 108 n. The complete and entertaining story of the "Pontiac Manuscript" is told by Helen H. Ellis in "A Mystery of Old Detroit," *Bulletin* of the Detroit Historical Society, Vol. IX (October, 1952), 11–12.

To His Mother

Dear Mother, Cincinnati, April 9th 1846

Since writing my last, I have positively had not a single moment to spare, or at least an available moment, for though I have had abundance of leisure, it has been on board of coaches and steamboats, which don't permit much use of the pen. Riding over the Alleghanies, I got so tanned and dusty as scarcely to know myself in the glass; and on reaching Pittsburgh in this plight on Sunday morning, I saw in the entry of the hotel no less a person than Charley Dabney, whom I had not met for more than a year. As you may believe, the recognition was welcome on both sides; and though our future course lay in different directions, we had one merry day together. He was just arrived from Fayal, and making a western tour for some purpose or other.

Today I reached Cincinnati, after a two days' passage down the Ohio. The boat was good enough, though filled with a swarm of half civilized reprobates, gambling, swearing, etc. among themselves. I, however, found one pleasant companion,—a New York gentleman, who will go on to St. Louis with me. The great annoyance on board these boats is the absurd haste of everybody to gulp down their meals. Ten minutes suffices for dinner, and it requires great skill and assiduity to secure a competent allowance in that space of time. As I don't much fancy this sort of proceeding, I generally manage to carry off from the table enough to alleviate the pangs of hunger without choking myself. The case is much the same here at the best hotel in Cincinnati. When you sit down, you must begin without delay—grab whatever is within your reach, and keep hold of the plate by main force till you have helped yourself. Eat up as many potatoes, onions, or turnips as you can lay hands on; and take your meat afterwards, whenever you have a chance to get it. It is only by economizing time in this fashion that you can avoid starvation—such a set of beasts are these western men. Their principal diet is tobacco; by which they contrive to fill up the [de]ficiency[1] of other viands.

In three or four days, I s[hould][2] be at St. Louis, stopping a short time at Louisville, Kentucky. My eyes are decidedly improved, and my health excellent.—In going about Cincinnati this morning, I found a most ridiculous piece of architecture, in utter defiance of taste or common sense; and learned that it was built by *Mrs. Trollope* during her stay here.[3] She, it seems, set up a theatre and a bazaar, which proved a very bad spec. You will hear from me again, when I get an opportunity. My address is, as I said in my last, Chouteau & Villé [Vallée] St. Louis.

I am, dear Mother,
Very affectionately yrs
F. P.

ADDRESSED: Rev. F. Parkman, DD. (for Mrs. Parkman)
Boston, Mass.
MS: Parkman Papers, Massachusetts Historical Society.

[1] Conjectural reading, MS torn.
[2] Conjectural reading, MS torn.
[3] Frances Trollope (1780–1863), British novelist and wife of Anthony Trollope (1774–1835), an attorney and speculator, accompanied her husband to Cincinnati where he set up a bazaar for the sale of fancy goods. The business venture was a failure; but Mrs. Trollope during the time she was in America (1827–30) gathered material for her famous *Domestic Manners of the Americans* (London, 1832), a fascinating portrayal of American society which does not overlook what she considered the vulgar habits of the people she observed.

To His Mother

Dear Mother, Fort Leavenworth,[1] May 12th 1846

We arrived at this place day before yesterday, riding up, with our whole equipment from Westport.[2] Our tent is pitched under the fort close by that of our English friends. We are a little in advance of the main body of the caravan, which will shortly arrive and follow on our track. Our companions are Captain Chaunley [Chandler],[3] of the British army and his brouther[4] and Mr. Romain[e].[5] They are all men most excellently fitted for companions on such a journey, as they have all travelled very extensively and Romain has been on this route before—in 1841. We find them exceedingly intelligent and agreeable and consider ourselves very fortunate in meeting with such a party, and so avoiding the necessity of too close contact with a very different sort of men who compose the trading parties. Our own *engagés*, Henry Chatillon[6] and Delorier[7] are as good as can be found anywhere on the frontier. Chatillon, in particular, is everything that could be wished. Within a few weeks, there has been a great deal of rain but for a day or two the weather has been very fine, and promises to continue so.

I hear that two or three men intend to accompany the Oregon emigrants[8]—with whom we do not come at all in contact—part of way on their route, and then return. If this is true, we may have an opportunity of sending letters.

Chatillon proclaims that the chocolate is made, and, as I must ride to the Fort to visit Col. Kearney[9] and deliver this, I have no more time to spare this morning. A soldier came to us last night, wishing to desert and join us, but we gave the fellow no encouragement. My best love to Father, Carrie and all—tell Elly I shan't forget his whip—and believe me, dear mother,

Very affectionately yours
FRANK

ADDRESSED: Rev. F. Parkman, D.D. Boston Mass. (Mrs. Parkman).
MS: Parkman Papers, Massachusetts Historical Society.

[1] Constructed on the Missouri in 1827 by Colonel Henry Leavenworth, this fort became an important base for a number of military expeditions in the Far West. Before 1846 its troops usually included parts of the Sixth Infantry or First Dragoons, accustomed to fighting under western conditions. In the Mexican War, Fort Leavenworth rose to national prominence as an outpost when the Army of the West started its long march to the Mexican frontier.

[2] Westport, now a residential and business district of Kansas City on the edge of the Missouri River, had become a center for outfitting Santa Fe traders and California-Oregon travelers. Independence, some six miles from the river, gradually lost ground to Westport as a starting point for western emigrants and traders.

[3] Captain Bill Chandler, an Irish soldier formerly in the British Army, encumbered himself with the greatest possible load of luggage and proved to be an apprehensive and annoying companion. His "eternal motto: 'Anything for a quiet life,'" grated on FP's ears, and on June 10, FP and his group parted company with the Englishmen after encamping along the Platte. *Journals*, II, 436.

[4] Jack Chandler, the captain's brother, was good natured and more acceptable to FP and Shaw.

[5] Romaine had traveled in the Rocky Mountains in 1841 with Father Pierre Jean de Smet (De Smet, *Travels in the Far West, 1836–1841*, in R. G. Thwaites

[ed.], *Early Western Travels*, [32 vols., Cleveland, 1904–1907], XVII, 198, 236), who said of him: "He was of good English family, and like most of his countrymen, fond of travel: he had already seen four quarters of the globe." Both in his *Journals* and in the original *Knickerbocker* account, FP objected to Romaine's highhandedness and "glaring want of courtesy and good sense." Mason Wade is of the opinion that Romaine might have been a secret agent for the British government. *Journals*, II, 616.

[6] Chatillon became a lifelong friend of FP's and wrote that he was tremendously flattered by the way he was portrayed in the *Oregon Trail*. In 1867, FP visited him in St. Louis and obtained a daguerreotype of Chatillon, which he hung in his study. Since Henry was illiterate, the Chatillon letters in the Parkman Papers were written by a scribe. See his letters to FP and Shaw (Feb. 17, 1853, St. Louis, PP, MHS). Recalling the trip of 1846, Henry said, ". . . do you remember what you said to me in the tent, it was better to be *poor* than to be *Rich* [?] I believe your right because I have got about fifty or sixty thousand dollars and I am in trouble all the time. I am agoing to the mountains this April if you would like to come I would be glad if you Both can come."

In the *Knickerbocker Magazine* version of the *Oregon Trail* (Vol. XXXIII, [February, 1849], 114–16), FP leaves a charming picture of his friend: "If sincerity and honor, a boundless generosity of spirit, a delicate regard of the feelings of others and a nice perception of what was due them, are the essential characteristics of a gentleman, then Henry Chatillon deserves the title. . . . In spite of his calling, Henry was always humane and merciful; he was as gentle as a woman though braver than a lion. . . . The polished fops of literature or fashion would laugh with disdain at the idea of comparing his merits with theirs. I deem them worthless by the side of that illiterate hunter."

[7] Or Deslauriers, FP's muleteer. Delorier was capable, cheerful, and loyal; but he did not hesitate to declare that he would run if FP's party were attacked by the Pawnees. *The Oregon Trail*, ed. by Mason Wade (New York, Heritage Press, 1943), 51; hereafter cited as Wade (ed.), *Oregon Trail*. This edition of FP's classic contains excerpts from his journals and original selections from the *Knickerbocker* version which have been deleted from later editions.

[8] As FP and his party moved westward, they found emigrant parties in front of them, in back of them, and on their side. Edwin Bryant's *What I Saw in California, Being a Journal of a Tour* (ed. by Marguerite E. Wilbur; Santa Ana, Calif., 1936) tells the story of one of the groups FP met at Fort Laramie.

[9] Colonel Stephen Watts Kearny (1794–1848) had been to the mouth of the Yellowstone River in 1825 and to the South Pass in 1845. He was an experienced frontier officer and known for his stern discipline. In May, 1846, he was placed in command of the Army of the West, and shortly thereafter elevated to the rank of brigadier before leading his troops on his celebrated march to Santa Fe and then to Los Angeles in January, 1847.

To His Mother

June 12th 1846
Emigrant Waggon,[1]
Near Ft. Laramie
River Platte

My Dear Mother,

This is rather a queer place to write from, and, if you should see me, you would think my *tout ensemble* rather extraordinary. However, I am extremely comfortable, and both Quincy[2] and myself in excellent health. Nothing has occurred contrary to our wishes—day after tomorrow we shall be at Ft. Laramie, where we have letters, and shall find friends. We are singularly fortunate in finding this opportunity of writing, as well as that which occurred a few days since, when we met Papin's trading boats,[3] descending the river. We are living chiefly on buffalo and antelope—a diet which thrives with us astonishingly. Our hunter, Chatillon, of whom I have spoken, is probably the best man whom we could have got in all this region—he is to be implicitly relied on—intelligent, experienced, and knocks over buffalo whenever he chooses.[4] He is married to the daughter of the head chief of the Indians,[5] among whom he has great influence. For a man of no education—(he cannot read or write) he is by far the most complete gentleman I ever saw.

Ft. Laramie is the farthest point we aim at. After satisfying our curiosity there, we shall return by way of Ft. Pierre[6] and the Missouri, reaching the states about the first of October, and then returning directly home. As for incidents of our journey, we have not many to tell, nor time to tell them. The men are gone forward with our cart, to find a proper camping ground, and the five traders who will carry this down are smoking their pipes around one of the fires in the emigrant encampment. We pass these people almost every day—men, women, and children, of whom the latter don't enjoy the journey much. Poor things! they have a long and difficult route between this and Columbia River, and, as they are but poor hunters, they have to burden themselves with a ton of provisions. Their cattle cover the bottoms for a mile or more.

Remember me very affectionately to all—Carrie in particular, and tell father that even my prairie journey furnishes me with some hints that may be useful in the law. I won't forget Elly nor his Indian whip. Remember me, too, to Aunt Mary,[7] and tell her I mean to taste some of her tomato sauce before the fall is over.

And believe me, dear Mother,

Very Affectionately
YOUR SON FRANK

P.S. I shall write, if possible—but the possibility is very remote.

ADDRESSED: F. Parkman, D. D. (for Mrs. Parkman) Boston, Mass.
MS: Parkman Papers, Massachusetts Historical Society.

[1] FP's *Journals*, II, 437, for June 12 read: "Road to Lawrence Fork and nooned. . . . Chimney Rock in sight [Morrill County, western Nebraska]. . . . Overtook a company of emigrants . . . five men from Laramie going down [possibly Joel Palmer's party returning from Oregon]. Crept into one of the waggons—wrote letters—and gave them to these people."

[2] Quincy Adams Shaw (d. 1908), Harvard class of 1845, FP's cousin, came west for sport and adventure, and did not have, as FP put it, "the same motive for hunting Indians that I had." Wade (ed.), *Oregon Trail*, 135. In his letter to Frederic Remington, Jan. 7, 1892, FP described Shaw "as one of the handsomest men in Boston, though he seemed quite unconscious of being so, having no vanity whatever. He was tall, lithe, and active, and even in the roughest dress, had an air of distinction." In 1871, Shaw was instrumental in organizing the Calumet and Hecla Mining Company and became one of the wealthiest men in New England. He lived with his wife, the former Pauline Agassiz, at the old Shaw house at Jamaica Plain, and always was to FP, "the comrade of a summer and the friend of a lifetime." See Quinquennial folder on Shaw, HA.

[3] Pierre D. Papin, an experienced fur trader, took charge of Fort Laramie in 1845 after an active career in the "French Company" on the upper Missouri. In the summer of 1846 he left Bordeau as acting *bourgeois* at the fort and took eleven boats down to Fort Leavenworth, where the crew and cargo (including FP's letter) were transferred to the steamer *Tributory*, which arrived in St. Louis on July 6. LeRoy R. Hafen and Francis M. Young, *Fort Laramie and the Pageant of the West, 1834–1890* (Glendale, Calif., 1938), 113–15. When FP and Shaw arrived at Fort Laramie, they were lodged in Papin's apartment.

[4] Chatillon had acted as a hunter for Captain Joseph La Barge, Missouri steamboat captain. Of Chatillon's work under La Barge, Hiram M. Chittenden writes: "He [Chatillon] was a fine man, an excellent hunter, and sensible and gentlemanly in all his relations." *History of Early Steamboat Navigation on the Missouri River* (2 vols., New York, 1903), I, 126.

[5] Chatillon's Indian wife, Bear Robe, who died during this summer, was the daughter of Bull Bear (Mahto-Tatonka in the *Oregon Trail)*, called by FP one of the most influential chiefs of the Oglala Sioux. Chatillon, FP states in a letter to F. Remington, Jan. 7, 1892, married again about 1855, and as late as 1867 was living in a suburb of St. Louis.

[6] Fort Pierre developed from a small trading post established in 1817 by Joseph LaFramboise at the mouth of the Bad River on the west bank of the Missouri. In 1832 the Astor interests constructed a new post on the site and named it Fort Pierre Chouteau, but the Chouteau appellation never took hold and was eventually dropped.

[7] Sister of FP's mother. See note 5, FP to Mary B. Parkman, Jan. 13, 1859.

To His Mother

My Dear Mother, Fort Laramie[1] June 19th 1846

We have been for three days at this place, and find plenty to entertain us. The Oregon emigrants are arriving in large parties every day, and remain for several days to refit, buy supplies, etc; and the Indians are coming in from all quarters to meet them, and get presents, so that the whole fort is surrounded by waggons, tents, and Indian lodges. As for us, we are well lodged in the fort itself, and though the fare is none of the most luxurious, the *bourgeois*, Mr. Bordeau,[2] takes the greatest pains to make us comfortable. The traders and trappers are daily coming in from the mountains, so that the area of the fort is crowded with them and their men—all in half-Indian dress—besides a swarm of Indians, squaws, and children. Every moment a group of rough looking fellows from the emigrant camps, escorting a bevy of scraggy-necked women, appears at the gate. They go peering about in every direction, without scruple or reserve—no place is sacred from them—twenty times a day a crowd of women, with prying curious eyes, come pressing into our apartment, which generally contains, besides, half a dozen or more of Indians sitting smoking on the floor.

Tell Carrie that more than half of the Indian women suffer wretchedly from bad eyes—some of them are much worse than she has ever been, and, indeed are quite blind. This probably comes from dirt and direct exposure to the sun. We have visited a great many of their lodges, and been treated in a very friendly manner, as our hunter is married to the daughter of a prominent chief, and represents our greatness and dignity among the whites in a very strong light. His squaw is dangerously sick, and his youngest child is just dead—the latter rather a fortunate circumstance, as in case of the mother's death, it would be sure to suffer. After visiting her father's village, which is at the distance of a few days' journey, we shall return to this place, and thence move across the country towards Ft. Pierre, and, after remaining there a little while, descend the Missouri River to the settlements, which we mean to reach early in October.[3]

This country is no doubt one of the most healthy in the world. Both Q. and myself find our health improved, though the necessity of living chiefly on meat produces some temporary disorders. As for my eyes, they are better, though not entirely well, I hope, however, that they will be so in a few weeks. The opportunities for accomplishing the objects for which I came here are greater than I expected.—the emigrants bring the Indians around them, and give us an excellent opportunity of seeing them. The emigrants themselves are a very curious set of people. We have passed on the road eight or ten large companies of them, bound for Oregon or California, and most of them ignorant of the country they are going to, and the journey to it. They have immense droves of cattle and horses, which they turn loose at night, range their waggons in a circle, and build their fires around it. Sometimes a thunder-storm will come up, and frighten their cattle, or the wolves will make a noise and startle them, and the whole body will break off and [run][4] for fifteen or twenty miles upon the prairie.

[It][5] takes a day or two to collect and drive them back, and meanwhile the women will get impatient and cry to go home again, and the men will quarrel and complain, till the party splits up into two or three divisions that in future travel separately. This is a specimen of their vexations upon the easiest part of their journey—what they will do when they get beyond the Mountains, lord knows. Here at the fort, they are very suspicious and mistrustful, and seem to think the traders their natural enemies. We are invariably taken for traders in disguise, and find the most effectual way to persuade them to anything, is to advise them to something directly the contrary.

How soon this letter will reach you, I cannot tell. The clerk of the Fort takes charge of it, and promises to give it in charge to the first person that passes down. Whether this may be in one month or three, nobody can say. Perhaps I shall see you before you see this. I often wonder where you are, and whether you are spending the summer at Medford. I wish Carrie could ride the prairies for a few months—she would become as stout as a squaw. Give my love to her and Sarah, not forgetting Mary, Eliza, or Elly. Father will be gratified to learn that my thoughts often revert to old Harvard, though I am now a scholar in a rougher school, and that here on the prairies, I keep in view his wishes with regard to the future course of my life.

Believe me, dear Mother,
Most affectionately yrs.
FRANK

ADDRESSED: Rev. F. Parkman, D.D. (for Mrs. Parkman)
Boston, Mass.
MS: Parkman Papers, Massachusetts Historical Society.

[1] Fort Laramie, near the confluence of Laramie Creek and the North Platte, was the center of a trading empire of the West rivaled only by Bent's Fort on the Arkansas. In 1834, William Sublette and Robert Campbell constructed a post there and named it Fort William after Bill Sublette. This log and adobe stockade was purchased by the American Fur Company in 1836 and christened Fort John. About 1845, Fort John was torn down and replaced by an enlarged adobe structure nearly a mile up the Laramie on a knoll overlooking a bend in the creek. The new post was known as Fort Laramie in the fur trade, and in 1849 was sold to the government. With the addition of new wooden and adobe buildings it became the center of a military establishment.

Joel Palmer reported that Fort John was still standing as late as June, 1845. *Journal of Travels over the Rocky Mountains,* in Thwaites' *Early Western Travels,* XXX, 60–61. J. C. Frémont in July, 1842, called the post "Fort John or Laramie," and mentioned "its lofty walls, white-washed and picketed." *Report of the Exploring Expedition to the Rocky Mountains* (Washington, 1845), 35.

FP described the new Fort Laramie in his *Journals*, II, 439–41, and in Wade (ed.), *Oregon Trail*, 87. It was shaped like a hollow square with fifteen foot adobe walls, and, as at Bent's Fort, the entrances had a double gate so that Indians who wished to trade could be safely handled in small groups.

[2] Bordeau (otherwise Bordeaux, Boudreau, Boudeaux, Bourdeau, etc.) is mentioned in the notebooks of many travelers. Bryant reported: "Mr. Bourdeau, the principal of the Fort, who is a man about thirty, informed me that he left the settlements of the United States fifteen years since, and had never returned to them." Bryant, *What I Saw in California*, 92. FP described him as "a stout bluff little fellow much inflated by a sense of his new authority." Wade (ed.), *Oregon Trail*, 86. Frémont in 1842 stated that "Mr. Boudeau," received him with "great hospitality and efficient kindness." *Report*, 36.

[3] Parkman never visited Fort Pierre. After leaving Fort Laramie, his party moved southward toward Bent's Fort, following an old trading route that took them via Cherry Creek and Pikes Peak, east of the main Rocky Mountain ranges. From Bent's Fort he followed the Santa Fe Trail back to Westport.

[4] Conjectural reading, MS torn.

[5] Conjectural reading, MS torn.

To His Father

Fort Laramie,
June 28th, 1846

My Dear Father,

Several days ago, I wrote home, and, hearing of a party of homesick emigrants on the return, I have just despatched a man with the letter—whether it reaches you is very doubtful, but the chance is too promising to be neglected.

We are very pleasantly situated here; not in the fort, but at camp on Laramie Creek,[1] eighteen miles distant. I rode in this morning to get the news, and see the fresh arrivals of emigrants. I found a party of the latter; from Kentucky, chiefly drunk, at a little trading-fort not far from this.[2] They were busy in exchanging horses for mules, and were being handsomely imposed on by the *bourgeois*[3] of the fort and the trappers and hunters. Their captain[4] was the most drunk of the party, and, taking me by the button, he began a long rigmarole about his "moral influence" over his men. But, in fact, they have no leader—each man follows his own whim, and the result is endless quarrels and divisions, and all sorts of misfortunes in consequence. A party that passed yesterday, left at the Fort a woman, who, it seems, had become a scandal to them, and, what had probably much greater weight, caused them trouble to feed and take care of her. She is now lodged among the squaws of the traders—in a most pitiful situation; for it is quite impossible that she will be able to get to the settlements before many months at least, and, meanwhile, she is left alone among the Indian women, and the half-savage retainers of the Company—for there are no white women, and very few civilized white men in the country. Everybody here is directly or indirectly a subject of the Fur Company,[5] who sway everything at their sovereign pleasure, and hold a most tyrannical monopoly. They employ multitudes of hunters, trappers, and traders, who are chiefly French, and both from their breed and their mode of life, utterly careless of tomorrow. They dress like the Indians, and live on dried meat and tallow when nothing else is to be had. Give them but flour, sugar, coffee, and tobacco, and they are happy; and these articles they will have, if possible, at whatever cost—and the Company supply them at the modest rates of a dollar and a half for a pint-cup of sugar or coffee, and the same price for a pound of tobacco that costs at St. Louis from three to five cents.[6] Add to this, that almost all of these men have squaws to maintain, and you can give a guess how much money they lay up in the course of a year.

The Indians look upon us as great chiefs and entertain us with feasts of young puppies, which they consider the summit of luxury; and which, in fact are very good. One old fellow was very anxious yesterday, that I should become his son-in-law; and offered his daughter at the cheap rate of one horse; but I explained to him that I loved my horses too well to part with them; with which excuse he seemed satisfied.

This country is remarkably healthy. Quincy has improved wonderfully, and I am in very excellent health.—We are now encamped with one of the traders, Raynale a Frenchman,[7] who has been about twenty years in the country, and is an excellent fellow, with a large circle of Indian acquaintance. He is particularly skillful as a cook, and as a hunter, is second only to Henry Chatillon; between these two our table is well supplied, and as Raynale has his squaw (with whom he has lived nine years) and her two nephews along with him, we can get at short notice anything we want from the river or prairie. Tunica, the Whirlwind,[8] one of the most noted chiefs, and an old friend of Chatillon's and Raynale's had attached himself particularly to us, and wants us to live with him.

Our next move will be across the country to Fort Pierre, and thence down the Missouri to the settlements where we shall probably arrive about the first of October, and soon after, I hope to see you,

Parkman at Fort Laramie in 1846

From an illustration by Frederic Remington in the de luxe 1892 edition of *The Oregon Trail.*

Courtesy of the Remington Art Memorial

Henry Chatillon, Parkman's guide on the plains in 1846. "I shall take liberties with H. C. which the good soul would resent were he alive. He would number me with the bears and his other natural enemies."—Frederic Remington.

From an illustration by Frederic Remington for *The Oregon Trail.*
Courtesy of the Remington Art Memorial

with my objects effectually accomplished. Mother and Carrie will read this and be assured of my best love, and I am, dear Father

Very affectionately Yr. Son
F. PARKMAN

ADDRESSED: Rev. F. Parkman, D.D. Boston Mass. [*Care of Chouteau & Villé St. Louis*]. Postmarked July St. Louis.[9]
MS: Parkman Papers, Massachusetts Historical Society.

[1] At the mouth of the Chugwater on Laramie Creek. *Journals*, II, 446.

[2] Richard's Fort Bernard, a crude, partially built structure was located some eight miles below Fort Laramie. Prices, according to FP's account book of this year, were lower at Fort Bernard. Henry Chatillon purchased flour there at fifteen cents a pound, while at Fort Laramie the price was ten cents higher. *Journals*, II, 494.

[3] Probably John Richard, described by FP as "a little, swarthy black-eyed Frenchman" whose "black curling hair was parted in the middle of his head, and fell below his shoulders." Wade (ed.), *Oregon Trail*, 82.

[4] Colonel William Henry Russell (1802–73), or "Owl Russell," was "drunk as a pigeon" (*Journals*, II, 447), and had recently been deposed as captain of Edwin Bryant's party. Bryant wrote that Russell had been suffering from an attack of "bilious fever" and had resigned. *What I Saw in California*, 76–77. Russell was later an attorney in San Jose, California, and in 1861 was appointed U. S. consul at Trinidad, Cuba.

[5] By the summer of 1846, Fort Laramie had passed from the hands of the American Fur Company to a combination of interests, Pierre Chouteau, Jr. & Company. FP's "passport" for the Indian country, a note signed by J. M. Clapp for "P. Chouteau Son & Co.," St. Louis, April 25, 1846 (PP, MHS), directed company representatives to furnish Shaw and FP with "every aid in your power, of which they may stand in need."

[6] Many travelers complained about Fort Laramie prices. An interesting manuscript journal of 1849 in the University of California's Bancroft Library ("Journal of a trip across the plains," by Dr. T., May 20–June 23) states: "Good waggons here [Fort Laramie] bring from 4 to 30 dollars, mules from 100 to 150 dollars. That is you sell your waggons to the traders at the Fort and buy from them their mules. Everything you buy costs four times as much as it is worth and everything you sell brings perhaps one tenth its value."

[7] "A vagrant Indian trader named Reynal joined us, together with his squaw Margot and her two nephews. . . . Reynal the trader, the image of sleek and selfish complacency" Wade (ed.), *Oregon Trail*, 99.

[8] The Whirlwind was the leader of a group of Oglala warriors who planned to avenge scalps taken by the Snakes (Shoshonies) in the previous summer. Wade (ed.), *Oregon Trail*, 97.

[9] FP's letter missed his father, who had attended "a meeting" in St. Louis. See FP's letter to his mother, Oct. 7, 1846.

To His Father

Westport, Mo.
Sept. 26th '46

Dear Father,

I have but a moment before the mail closes to give you notice of my safe return. We have just come in, and are selling off our equipment—horses, etc. We set out from Bent's Fort,[1] on the Upper Arkansas, towards the end of last month—lay by on the journey five days to hunt buffalo—and reached the settlements in the short space of thirty days. We apprehended some molestation on the way from the Pawnee Indians who have been mischievous of late, but we set a careful guard at night, and they gave us no trouble. All along the road we met detachments of troops and military stores passing to Santa Fe.[2] We encountered one large Indian village—Arapahoes—who gave us no trouble, having been well frightened lately by the threats of Gen'l. Kearney.

As for our journey, we have enjoyed it exceedingly. Shaw's health is most thoroughly and completely restored, though, after leaving Fort Laramie, I was violently attacked by a bilious complaint which continued for more than two months and very much reduced my strength. During this time, however, I did not lose sight of the objects that brought me here. I took a Canadian attendant and rode across the Black Mountains[3] to the neighborhood of the Rocky Mountains, where I found a village of Sioux Indians,[4] with whom I remained two or three weeks, and got a pretty intimate acquaintance with them. Shaw was obliged to remain at the Fort, in consequence of being poisoned with ivy. I was at this time so weak that, for a while, I could not saddle my horse without assistance, and an Indian village is no place for an invalid. I saw what I wanted to, however, and returned to the Fort in comparative health; and am now completely well.

In conclusion, we have been most amply repaid for considerable trouble and some danger, by what we have seen on our expedition—things whereof the men of the East have little idea. I have enjoyed myself in spite of temporary illness (which, by the way, I am none the worse for)—and the experience of one season on the prairies will teach a man more than half a dozen in the settlements. There is no place on earth where he is thrown more completely on his own resources.

I cannot say too much in favor of our hunter, Henry Chatillon, and our driver, Delorier; they have both served us as faithfully and skillfully as one need desire. Chatillon has the reputation of being the best hunter in the Mountains, and he is certainly one of the best men.

I have deputed Shaw to act as salesman of our outfit while I write this; and I hear him bargaining most vigorously below. We are in haste to embark for St. Louis. He will wri[te] as soon as he gets an opportunity, but as the boat leaves tomorrow morning, and the mail closes in five minutes, only one of us can be spared to the pen at the present. I shall not tarry by the way, but come to Boston with all possible speed, only staying to see Mrs. Stone at Saratoga,[5] and call on Dr. Elliot[t] to give a finishing touch to my eyes, which, though improved, are not quite well. Give my best love to mother, Carrie and all—I am very anxious to see them, and can tell them, better than I can write, my "travel's history." The Law has certain claims on me also which will be fully answered, now that I have returned from my last journey—the last I suppose it will be for the present, though not so if I consulted my inclination only.

I am, Dear Father
Very Respectfully
Your affectionate son
F. PARKMAN

ADDRESSED: Rev F Parkman, DD Boston, Mass. Postmarked Westport Mo. Sept. 30.
MS: Parkman Papers, Massachusetts Historical Society.

[1] Some 530 miles out of Westport, Bent's Fort, the crossroads of the West and headquarters for a vast "adobe empire" of the Indian trade, stood on the north bank of the Arkansas. There were four Bent brothers, but Charley and William were best known to the Santa Fe traders. Céran and Marcellin St. Vrain were also business partners, and through these men Bent's Fort became the outstanding trading post of the Southwest. It was originally known as Fort William, founded about 1832, a rectangular gray adobe structure, of approximately 180 by 135 feet. Its central patio enclosed a complete factory, and the Bent and St. Vrain brothers employed as many as 150 men as permanent hands. FP reached the Fort on August 22, *Journals*, II, 474. He mentions "its high clay walls in the midst of the scorching plains" in Wade (ed.), *Oregon Trail*, 242. A good description of Bent's Fort is in Lewis H. Garrard's *Wah-to-ya and the Taos Trail* (Cincinnati, (1850), 42 (reprinted by the University of Oklahoma Press, 1955).

[2] See Wade (ed.), *Oregon Trail*, 250, for FP's description of the Santa Fe traders with their military stores.

[3] The Laramie Range. Frémont called this range "the Black hills," *Report*, 46, and subsequent travelers through the 1840's used the same name.

[4] FP's lonely trail took him through the Sybille Canyon of the Laramie Range into the basin of the Medicine Bow and southwest to the lodgepole-pine-covered foothills of the Medicine Bow Range of the Rockies. See also Introduction.

[5] Undoubtedly the widow of William Leete Stone (1792–1844), New York journalist and historian. Stone wrote a *Life of Joseph Brant* (1838); *Life and Times of Red Jacket* (1841); and on the border wars of the American Revolution. Stone also accumulated a collection of papers for a projected life of Sir William Johnson which was eventually written by his son (W. L. Stone, Jr.), and published in 1865. The son became one of FP's correspondents, for Johnson was a prominent figure in the *History*, especially in *Pontiac*.

To His Mother

My Dear Mother, St. Louis, Oct. 7th '46

I am here after a vexatious passage of seven days down the Missouri from Westport. The distance is but five hundred miles; and we might have arrived here three days ago, but for the folly of the captain, who insisted on receiving load after load of freight, till his boat would not pass the more shallow places, and was aground *full half the time.* Meanwhile the passengers took their revenge by eating up the provisions and drinking the liquors; so that instead of gaining by his rapacity, he lost.

Everybody here speaks of the intense heat of the past summer. We—Q and I—may congratulate ourselves on having escaped it, besides gaining a great [dea]l[1] of sport, and a cartload of practical experience. I feel about ten years older than I did five months ago. Today, for the first time, I have mounted the white shirt, tight dress coat, etc. my garb, for some time past having consisted of a red flannel shirt, a pair of pantaloons of dressed deer-skin garnished with long fringes down to the foot, and a sort of frock[2] of similar material and befringed in the same style, and a pair of very dusky Sioux moccasins. Thus equipped, mounted on an Indian horse, with a rifle laid before me on the saddle, and a blanket strapped behind, I have ridden considerably more than two thousand miles.

I find no letters here for me.—none, that is, from the family, which I attribute to your thinking me beyond the reach of correspondence. Today, I found a notice in the Post of the 25th Sept. of father's attending a meeting a day or two before, from which I infer that he is well. I hope that the hot weather has not injured Carrie's health; and I wish the prairie was the place for women to visit, as I think hers is the very case to receive benefit from the mode of life. If there is only strength enough to support the fatigue—which need not be great —the air and exercise are sure to strengthen a weakly constitution. My temperament is bilious, and a meat diet, I suppose, acts unfavorably on it; and hence the particularly uncomfortable state to which I was reduced when in the Indian country; but, in spite of this, they tell me here that I look better than when I set out for the Mountains. I have brought thus far one of the inhabitants of the Rocky Mts.—to show to Elly.—I caught him near the foot of Long's Peak,[3] one of the highest summits; made a box of buffalo hid[e] for his accommodation, and have now kept him for more than two months, without food or drink. Yet he seems hale and hearty as ever. He is a nondescript reptile, something like a chameleon, and goes among the trappers and traders by the name of *crapaud à corne*, or *horned frog*.

If you will write immediately, and direct to [*me at the*] Buffalo, N. Y. I shall get the letter. I have arrangements to make which will detain me here a day or two. Then I shall go, by stage, as the rivers are all low, to Chicago, thence by railroad to Detroit, and thence to Buffalo. Ask Carrie to write, as I want very much to hear from her. You will hear from me often, and meanwhile believe me, Dear Mother,

Respectfully
Your affectionate
FRANK

ADDRESSED: Rev. F. Parkman, D.D. (for Mrs. Parkman)
Boston, Mass. Postmarked St. Louis Mo. Oct. 7.
MS: Parkman Papers, Massachusetts Historical Society.

[1] Word illegible, conjectural reading.

[2] FP's deerskin shirt, remarkably preserved, is in the possession of his grandson, Mr. John T. Coolidge of Milton, Mass. Further description of FP's garb on the plains is in his letter to Frederic Remington of Jan. 7, 1892.

[3] Named after Stephen H. Long (1784–1864), military explorer and engineer, who discovered the peak in July, 1820, while leading an expedition in the Rocky Mountains.

To Charles Christopher Trowbridge

Sir, New York. Nov. 11th 1846

Mr. H. R. Schoolcraft[1] informs me that there is in the possession of Gen. B. F. Witherell of Detroit,[2] a book containing documents relating to the transfer of power from the French to the English in the West. The title page has been torn away, so that Mr. S. is ignorant of the name and date of the volume; it contains, however, among the rest, papers relating to the surrender of Detroit to Major Rogers.[3] My friend, Edmund Dwight, has informed you of the work on which I am engaged—the history of the period of Pontiac—and as this book must contain matter of importance in that relation, I take the liberty of requesting your interest to get me the loan of it for a short time. If Gen. W. will send it to me, by express or otherwise, directed to the care of Bartlett & Wellford, Booksellers, no. 7 Astor House, New York, I will take pains to return it at an early opportunity.

I shall be much indebted to you if you can procure me this favor and remain

Respectfully,
Your Obedient Servant,
FRANCIS PARKMAN, JR.

MS: Burton Historical Collection, Detroit Public Library.

[1] Henry Rowe Schoolcraft (1793–1864), pioneer ethnologist, specialized on the subject of the American Indians and their culture. Schoolcraft had been Indian agent in the Lake Superior region (1822–36) and superintendent of Indian affairs for Michigan (1836–41). As a college student FP purchased Schoolcraft's *Algic Researches* (1839) and probably read everything Schoolcraft published. In the *North American Review*, Vol. CIII (July, 1866), 1–18, FP attacked Schoolcraft's monumental *Indian Tribes of the United States* (1851–57) as ". . . taxing to the utmost the patience of those who would extract what is valuable in it from its oceans of pedantic verbiage."

FP records his early visits with Schoolcraft in his *Journals*, and the ethnologist apparently had considerable influence upon him. In a letter to Mary [Howard], of Nov. 14, 1846 (Mellen Chamberlain Collection, Boston Public Library), Schoolcraft writes: "I have been visited today [in New York] by a Mr. Parkman, a young gentleman from Boston, who went out to the Rocky Mountains last summer by my direction and advice. He proposes to write on a period of history, which involves a knowledge of Indian character, & I told him it would not do to rely upon books alone. He must bring some personal knowledge to such a task."

[2] Benjamin Franklin Hawkins Witherell (1797–1867), Detroit judge and brigadier general, was president of the Michigan State Historical Society and wrote a number of articles on Michigan history. Farmer, *History of Detroit*, II, 1133–34.

[3] Robert Rogers (1731–95), colonial ranger, was, for FP, one of the most romantic figures of the frontier. For the surrender of Detroit, see *Pontiac*, I, 176.

To Lyman C. Draper

New York
Nov. 20th 1846

My Dear Draper,

I cannot tell whether this will reach you or not, but hoping that you may be still in Baltimore, I venture to direct a letter there. I am anxious to hear from you and learn what progress you have made in your researches. For my own part, I have lately returned from the Rocky Mountains, where I have been all the summer among the Indians. After so long an absence, I have lost the run of antiquarianism, and it takes some time to get again in the track. Pray let me hear from you, and all about you. My own researches get on very well, *considering*. I found, on my return, a cart-load of papers—most of them useless, however, waiting for me, together with some twenty letters. Having skimmed the cream of this mass, I found enough to reward me for my trouble, and rejected the rest.

I saw Prof. Sparks only for a few minutes. He now lives in Salem, and is as kind hearted, and as well disposed to assist historians in embryo, like you and I, as ever.—Let me know what journeys you have been making, and with what success. I heard of you in the spring from Mr. Biddle of Pittsburg,[1] who said that you meant to come in that direction on a tour of investigation. Let me know, too, if you have picked up anything that will suit my purposes—anything at all concerning the space between the years 1760 and 1765.

Believe me, my dear Sir,
With great regard,
Yrs. truly
F. PARKMAN, JR.

N. B. My present address is
Delmonico's Hotel
25 Broadway
New York.

ADDRESSED: Lyman C. Draper Esq. Baltimore.
MS: Draper Correspondence, State Historical Society of Wisconsin.

[1] Lyman C. Draper published James W. Biddle's "Recollections of Green Bay, 1816–17" in the first volume of the *Collections* of the State Historical Society of Wisconsin, pp. 49–63. Draper states that Biddle was editor of the *Pittsburgh American.* This James (or John W.) Biddle was apparently related to Richard Biddle; both are mentioned in FP's *Journals,* II, 408, 487, 490. The first letter in the PP, MHS, R. Biddle to FP, April 1, 1838, Washington, D. C., describes a series of tracts relating to the French Huguenot settlement in Florida that Biddle promised to send FP.

To Lyman C. Draper

My Dear Draper, Boston, May 29th 1847

I am exceedingly obliged to you for your last kind letter; and the only reason that has hitherto prevented active correspondence on my part is the extremely bad state of my eyes. I am wholly unable to use them, either for reading or writing.—I write this without looking upon the paper, guiding the pen by a framework of wire. Yet I manage to get on by employing a person to read to me; so that my researches are not wholly at a stand.

Your account of Pontiac's death is very welcome. I saw old Mr. P. Chouteau who is almost superannuated,[1] though he gave me some valuable information, and I got more at second hand, from his son. The papers in the N. Y. state offices are of the greatest importance. I have many of them, and shall procure them all. Meanwhile, I shall wait with great interest the appearance of your own work, for which you have chosen a most interesting subject. I wish that circumstances would permit me to write to you more at length, but I must close, only hoping to resume and continue our correspondence under more favorable auspices at a future time.

With sincere regard
very Faithfully
Yr. Friend.
F. PARKMAN, JR.

ADDRESSED: Lyman C. Draper Esq. Baltimore.
MS: Draper Correspondence, State Historical Society of Wisconsin.

[1] FP visited Pierre Chouteau (1758–1849), pioneer founder of a St. Louis fur trading dynasty, on April 27, 1846. *Journals*, II, 415. Chouteau, to FP's delight, remembered Pontiac distinctly "as a man six feet high, of very commanding appearance, and, whenever he saw him, splendidly dressed." *Ibid.* In a note in *Pontiac*, II, 274, FP recalled Chouteau's splendid memory and the pleasure of meeting "this venerable man" personally.

To Charles Eliot Norton[1]

Staten Island July 13th 1848

My Dear Charley,

I am exceedingly obliged to you for your kind letter, and the expressions of friendship which it contains. I assure you, I set the highest value on the sympathy and goodwill of your family, and could not desire a more powerful stimulus to exertion, than the consciousness of acting under the eye of such spectators. My health, is now, I think, decidedly changing for the better. My position is anything but comfortable, but I begin to flatter myself that I have only to hold fast for a while, and the world will brighten once more around me.

I suppose that by this time you must have returned from Niagara. I envy you the trip, especially as I believe you were not quite Yankee enough to do up the job in two hours, one for dinner and one for seeing the Falls. If I get out of this scrape, I should like to go up to Lake

George and thereabouts with you some time, and spend a week or two in fishing among the islands there.—Give my compliments and truest regards to the members of your family

and believe me, very truly Yrs
F. PARKMAN

ADDRESSED: Mr. Charles E. Norton, Cambridge, Mass. Postmarked July 13 New-York.
MS: Letter book copy, Norton Papers, Harvard College Library.

[1] The MS discloses FP's difficulty in writing legibly during this period of semi-blindness. Charles Eliot Norton (1827–1908), Harvard class of 1846, unfortunately cut much of the lively, interesting detail from FP's *Oregon Trail,* although FP himself deleted some fascinating details from later editions. Norton, after graduating from college, entered the "counting-house" of the East India merchants, Bullard and Lee, and in an autobiographical letter described his work on the *Oregon Trail:* "During my years in the counting-house a casual acquaintance with Frank Parkman developed into a friendship which lasted through life. He was then printing in the "Knickerbocker Magazine," if I remember rightly, his first book, "The Oregon Trail," and when it was to be published as a volume he asked me to revise the numbers, and many an evening, when there was not other work to be done, was spent by me and him in the solitary counting-room in going over his work." *Letters of Charles Eliot Norton, with Biographical Comment,* by Sarah Norton and M. A. DeWolfe Howe (2 vols., Boston, 1913), I, 27–28.

In 1849, Norton, still associated with Bullard and Lee, made a grand tour that took him through portions of the Near East and a large part of Europe. He returned in 1851, continued his business career, but in 1855 went to Europe at the advice of doctors; and in Rome he began his long literary career with studies of Dante. In 1857 he returned to the United States, wrote articles for the *Atlantic Monthly* and in 1864 joined Lowell as an editor for the *North American Review.* From 1873 to 1897 Norton was a teacher at Harvard, during which time his cousin, Charles W. Eliot, was president of the university.

FP valued Norton's friendship, although, as he wrote E. G. Squier, Norton's education had been of "the strict and precise sort." Norton, he told Squier, was "an acquaintance worth having, not only as a good fellow but because he stands among a set of literary men whose opinions and influence are worth having." See letters to Squier: [1849]; March 15, 1849. FP was correct, for Norton became one of the leading literary figures of his day. "The Norton Era" in the history of fine arts as a subject of instruction at Harvard is described in Samuel E. Morison (ed.), *The Development of Harvard University* (Cambridge, Mass., 1930), 130 ff.

To Charles Eliot Norton

Staten Island,
Sept. 12th 1848

My Dear Charley,

Thank you for your two kind letters, to the first of which I should have answered some time ago, had I not been out of town—up at

Catskill, where I went to get rid of an attack akin to my old enemy of the prairie. I met with partial success, but my system has been greatly deranged again, and old symptoms revived with most unwelcome activity. The condition of my head has in consequence caused me at times suffering almost intolerable, so that I have found no relief except in lying on my back without thought or motion. My best chance of recovery is in perfect idleness, for every effort of mind increases the difficulty.—Patience I suppose, is the only medicine; and a most hateful one to me it is.

With regard to your very friendly offers to read the proofs of the *Oregon Trail,* I think I may very thankfully accept them. Putnam will publish, in January or February, a good edition with illustrations by Darley,[1] who is now at work upon P's new edition of Irving.[2] He would bring it out sooner, but his hands are more than full at present. This month I sent no chapter to the *Knickerbocker,* because I want the book to be out before the appearance of the last chapter, for fear of piracy. If P. can make a satisfactory arrangement to that effect, there will be an English edition also.

I am glad to hear that you have not abandoned your literary pursuits, and hope before long to see the result upon the pages of our ancient and respectable quarterly.[3] Put a little pepper and allspice into it—it will not harm its respectability, and perhaps will make it more welcome to the taste of some of its readers.

I have heard with much regret that your sisters have been suffering from illness, and am glad to learn of their improved health. Pray give my best compliments to them and to your father and mother; and assure them of my respectful regards. Don't let Ned Dwight work himself to death. He is engaged in a great scramble after usefulness, which he can reach with much less effort. Can I do anything for you here? If so, you may command my services,—and believe me,

With sincere regard
Yrs. truly
F. Parkman

ADDRESSED: Mr. Charles E. Norton, Cambridge, Mass.
MS: Norton Papers, Harvard College Library.

[1] Felix O. C. Darley (1822–88), the illustrator, was commissioned in 1848 to illustrate Washington Irving's works. He was the artist who produced the curious, awkward Indians on horseback for the frontispiece of FP's 1849 edition of *The*

California and Oregon Trail. Later his illustrations for the works of Cooper, Hawthorne, Longfellow, and Dickens brought him a degree of fame.

[2] FP regarded Washington Irving (1783–1859), author of *History of New York . . . by Diedrich Knickerbocker* (1809), *Alhambra* (1832), and many other works, as one of the three greatest American writers. FP to Frank Parsons, May 21, 1890.

[3] *The North American Review.*

To Charles Eliot Norton

Staten Island—
Wednesday Decr. 6th 1848

My dear Charlie,

Your letter reached Brattleboro[1] I am sorry to say, after I left, so that I did not receive it until a day or two since when it was forwarded to me from Boston.—I was obliged to leave Brattleboro post haste; on account of the cursed condition of my eyes which suddenly relapsed into a state quite as bad certainly as they have ever been, & so painful that it was folly to endure it when there was any chance of being relieved, so I came on here where I have been about a month. Dr. Elliott has removed the pain to some extent and now tells me my eyes are out of danger so long as I remain under his care. I am sick of the business however, & shall go on to Boston; my eyes may go to the devil if they like, but I'm tired of this place & no threats of consequences will keep me here longer.—

You'll see me I think within a week.—"Squire" is just back from a new exploring tour [*in the*] within the state of N. York. He is full of enthusiasm & in my opinion is a most enviable fellow, having free scope to exercise it.

I'm sorry that Emerson[2] has undertaken to study law, for which he is not half as well fitted as for the ministry, & I wish that his too delicate conscience would have permitted him to adhere to his original intentions. I have heard nothing from Ned Dwight for some time, but presume he is in a thriving condition—please remember me to him when you see him, tho' perhaps I shall see him as soon as you do—Shaw is going to Europe in a few days,—but—it is useless to protract a letter when I shall see you so soon, & excuse [*the*] my unavoidable delay in answering your letter, & believe me my dear C—— very sincerely yrs

FRANK PARKMAN

ADDRESSED: Mr. Charles E. Norton Cambridge Mass. Postmarked New York 7 Dec.

MS: Entire letter, including signature, is dictated. Norton Papers, Harvard College Library.

[1] Where FP visited a water-cure establishment. He also returned to Brattleboro in 1849. See Introduction.

[2] FP probably refers to one John Winslow Emerson (1830–99), LL.B., Harvard, 1849. Quinquennial folder on J. W. Emerson, HA.

To Ephraim George Squier[1]

Dear Squier [1849][2]

I am much obliged to you for the pamphlet which you sent me with a sketch of the New York earth works. I read it with much interest, but hope before long to see a fuller account embracing all the plans, etc. I was glad to see the Delaware picture writing in the last *American Review*. By this time, I suppose you have changed your quarters as you told me you were going to do, on the morning when I smashed a bottle of Elliott's damnable compound in your room. A friend of mine, a Mr. Charles Norton, who is going to review you in the next *North American*, is coming to New York and will call on you. He takes an interest in ethnology, and though I do not think your ideas and his are in all respects congenial—as his education has been rather of the strict and precise sort—yet you will find him a most capital fellow and well able to appreciate all that you have done. Who published Denonville's Expedition?[3] Was it Marshall?[4] If so I want to know him. Believe me,

Very faithfully yours,
F. PARKMAN, JR.

MS: Huntington Manuscripts, Henry E. Huntington Library.

[1] Ephraim George Squier (1821–88), archaeologist and diplomat, in 1847 published *Ancient Monuments of the Mississippi Valley* (Smithsonian *Contributions to Knowledge*, No. 1), and in 1849 opened correspondence with FP by sending him an offprint of his "Aboriginal Monuments" of New York, published by the New-York Historical Society. His chief work on this subject was published in 1851. In 1849, largely through the efforts of William H. Prescott, the historian, Squier was appointed chargé d'affaires to Central America, a post he held for about a year and a half. Here he negotiated and signed an agreement (which was never ratified by the U. S. Senate) for the construction of an interoceanic canal by the United States.

About 1860 Squier became associated with Frank Leslie (1821–80), the New York publisher, famed for his *Frank Leslie's Illustrated Newspaper*. Squier apparently did editorial work for a number of Leslie's publications. He also traveled in many parts of Latin America and was a prolific writer, publishing works on Peru, Honduras, and Nicaragua, and dozens of his lengthy, beautifully penned letters are among the Parkman Papers.

Squier's tremendous energy and ambition excited the admiration of the youthful FP. As the years went by, however, Squier had difficulty with his eyes, and eventually his mind became clouded as a result of what appears to have been a hopeless illness. With Albert Gallatin, H. R. Schoolcraft, John R. Bartlett, and Brantz Mayer, he was one of the founders of the American Ethnological Society.

[2] The contents of the letter indicate that it was written early in 1849.

[3] For the story of Denonville's campaign against the Senecas, see *Frontenac*, 156 ff.

[4] In 1848, Orsamus Holmes Marshall (1813–84) edited and translated a French account of Denonville's campaign. Marshall, a distinguished civic leader and attorney of Buffalo, New York, was a founder of the Buffalo Historical Society, and published a number of monographs on the early history of the New York frontier. Like FP, he based his research on a personal inspection of the sites described in his writings. FP carried on a lifelong correspondence with Marshall and acknowledged his debt to Marshall's researches in the *History*. See, for example, *Frontenac*, 163 n. Marshall became a friend of Pierre Margry, as evidenced by the dozens of letters by Marshall in the Margry Correspondence at the Bibliothèque Nationale. Dozens of Marshall's letters are also preserved in the Parkman Papers, but unfortunately only two of FP's letters to Marshall have been found in the collections of the Buffalo Historical Society: those of May 6, 1849, and of March 27, 1882. The *Buffalo Commercial Advertiser* of July 10, 1884, has an informative obituary notice on Marshall, describing his accomplishments as a local historian.

To Charles Eliot Norton

My Dear Charley Boston, March 3[d] 1849

I am much obliged for your letter, and the information in it. Nothing new is stirring here. I am very glad that you like Squier so well and intended that you should from the first, [*which*] with which view I held up to your notice the rough side of him, so that the admirable qualities which form his essential substance might strike you the more from the contrast. I have got nothing in particular to say. Putnam has sent me the cuts which I think are excellent, and he promises me six copies which you kindly ordered, next Tuesday.

If as you return, you see Bartlett[1] and Squier give them my best regards and tell them that Copway the Indian[2] presented their letters, though not until the day before he went away. I was sorry for this as I liked him much and wanted to see more of him, but he had his hands full of letters and everybody was running after him. Eugene Batchelder[3] acted as a sort of cicerone to him and looked more like a baboon than ever.

This I suppose will reach you just after the agonies of inauguration,[4] on which great occasion I wish you joy. As for myself, my eyes are very [*bad*] fair though otherwise I am rather below par. Let us see you again as soon as you can and believe me

Very faithfully yours
F. PARKMAN, JR.

ADDRESSED: Mr Charles E Norton Care of Capt. W. H. Swift Washington D. C. Postmarked Boston Mar 3.
MS: Norton Papers, Harvard College Library.

[1] Probably John Bartlett (1820–1905), editor and publisher, who edited some of FP's early work. In 1849, Bartlett became owner of the University Book Store in Cambridge, where he had been employed and had acquired his love of books and interest in quotations which led to the publication of his *Familiar Quotations* in 1855.

John Russell Bartlett (1805–86), bibliographer and librarian associated with John Carter Brown, was among FP's correspondents (FP to J. R. Bartlett, Oct. 12, 1880), and should not be confused with the above John Bartlett.

[2] George Copway (1818–c. 63), Chippewa (Ojibway) Indian Methodist missionary, lectured and wrote about his people, and in 1850 visited Europe, attending the Peace Congress at Frankfurt. Copway was for a time a journalist in New York and was the author of an autobiography, *The Life, History, and Travels of Kah-Ge-Ga-Gah-Bowh* [Copway's Indian name] (Philadelphia, 1847); *Recollections of A Forest Life* (London, 1850); *The Traditional History and Characteristic Sketches of the Ojibway Nation* (London, 1850); *Organization of the New Indian Territory East of the Missouri River* (1850); and other works. Copway was tall, handsome, and altogether a fine figure of a man. Undoubtedly FP was attracted to him; but he felt that Copway's writings were based too much on a "discursive imagination." FP to Squier, Nov. 18, 1849.

[3] Eugene Batchelder (1822–78), Harvard class of 1845, had been in law school with FP, who characterized him as a man who "will talk on forever." *Journals*, I, 295.

[4] The inauguration of President Zachary Taylor.

To Ephraim George Squier

Dear Squier — Boston, Thursday March 15, 1849

I beg you will excuse my being silent so long, which was in consequence of being a good deal below par in point of health as well as an occurrence of some interest to myself which has just taken place.[1] I was very sorry that I did not hear from Copway until he was on the point of leaving. I liked him very much and wanted to see more of him. Some time ago, I told Putnam to give you, in my name, a copy of the redoubtable *Oregon Trail*, which is just out. This is rather an awkward way of conveying it to you and perhaps after all you have not got it yet—if so, pray drop in upon Putnam the next time you pass there. I have been writing a little, but only a very little. Let me have the particulars of the Guatemala scheme—that is, what position it is you are anxious to reach, as it is possible that I may be able to make some influence in your favor. Norton wrote me that he had seen you. I think you will find him an acquaintance worth having, not only as a good fellow but because he stands among a set of literary men whose opinions and influence are worth having—The unfortunate *Trail* seems likely to be choked under a mass of California books. If you can give it a push, you will do it a favor.

I am at present grubbing into the history of the collision of the French and English in America, and tracing the effects which resulted therefrom to the Indian tribes, all this being considered as a sort of introduction to the history of the subsequent wars among the Indians themselves.

I think I shall be in New York before the Spring is out, and till then

Believe me,
Very faithfully,
F. PARKMAN, JR.

MS: Huntington Manuscripts, Henry E. Huntington Library.

[1] FP's engagement to Catherine Scollay Bigelow. See Introduction.

To Orsamus Holmes Marshall[1]

Dear Sir: Boston May 6th 1849

I have the honor to enclose to you a letter of introduction from Mr E. G. Squier, as I cannot promise myself at present the pleasure of an interview, I take this means of transmitting it; being very unwilling to omit so excellent an opportunity of gaining the acquaintance of a gentleman who has engaged so deeply and successfully in studies which for many years have been my favorite pursuits.

For some time past, I have entertained the plan of writing, at some future period, a general history of the Indians. At present however my investigations are restricted to a much narrower compass. I have collected a great mass of materials, illustrating the period immediately succeeding the Old French War—at which time, as you are well aware, a general rising of the northern tribes against the English took place. Those events are not only highly interesting in themselves, but by the aid of the materials in my hands, afford an admirable opportunity of representing Indian manners and character.

My studies have been almost wholly interrupted, for more than two years, by the state of my health, and the useless condition of my eyes, which are quite unavailable either for reading or writing. The disorders from which I suffer are of a character which render mental exertion of any kind highly injurious, and often impossible—so much so, that I have been compelled to wait for several days to find an opportunity even for [*writing*] dictating this letter. There is no probability of escaping for some time at least, from this very uncomfortable predicament, so that, as you may suppose, my schemes are not in a very progressive state. I lay on my oars, and wait for better times, doing a little meanwhile in the way of collecting and arranging materials in which work my friends' eyesight supplies the place of my own.

I am very happy to hear from Mr Squier, that some of the results of your researches are likely to appear before the public, accompanied by a map of the Iroquois cantons. Next to labouring upon a favourite field yourself, is the satisfaction of seeing it cultivated ably and successfully by others, and I hope to see from your hands many more papers of equal interest and value with your observations on De Nonville's expedition. I envy you your opportunities of local inquiry among the remnants of a people, more worthy of study than all the other Indian tribes united.

Can you direct me to any sources of information in regard to the condition of the Iroquois about the year 1763. At that time and for some years previous the Senecas seem to have held singular relations with the Delawares—to have been mingled with them in several of their more southern villages, and to have acted in conjunction with them on many occasions. I should be much indebted to you for any information upon this subject or for anything that may throw farther light upon the general relation of the Iroquois with the tribes to the south of them.

Hoping to be able to meet you hereafter in person

I am with much respect
Your obedient
F. Parkman, Jr.

Henry Chatillon in 1848

"For a man of no education—(he cannot read or write) he is by far the most complete gentleman I ever saw."

From a daguerreotype which hung in Parkman's Chestnut Street study.
Courtesy of the late Elizabeth Cordner

Fort Laramie, June 28th, 1846

My Dear Father,

Several days ago, I wrote home, and, hearing of a party of homesick emigrants on the return, I have just despatched a man with the letter — whether it reaches you is very doubtful, but the chance is too promising to be neglected.

We are very pleasantly situated here; not in the fort, but at camp on Laramie creek, eighteen miles distant. I rode in this morning to get the news, and see the fresh arrivals of emigrants. I found a party of the latter, from Kentucky, chiefly drunk, at a little trading-fort not far from this. They were busy in exchanging horses for mules, and were being handsomely imposed on by the bourgeois of the fort and the trappers and hunters. Their captain was the most drunk of the party, and, taking me by the button, he began a long rigmarole about his "moral influence" over his men. But, in fact, they have no leader — each man follows his own whim, and the result is endless quarrels and divisions, and all sorts of misfortunes in consequence. A party that passed yesterday, left at the Fort a woman who, it seems, had become a scandal to them, and, what had probably much

The first page of Parkman's letter to his father written from Fort Laramie, June 28, 1846.

Courtesy of the Massachusetts Historical Society.

P.S. I beg your acceptance of the volume of sketches mentioned by Mr Squier which I have sent to Buffalo by Express.

MS: Dictated, Buffalo Historical Society.

[1] See sketch, note 4, FP to E. G. Squier [1849].

To Ephraim George Squier

My dear Squier — Boston, May 13 [18]49

I was very glad indeed to get a line from you before your departure for the land of El Vomito, not however, that I augur for you any unpleasant visitations from that source. I have heard of your visitation from the measles, an infantile weakness, of which I should hardly have suspected you. This infliction together with the cares of science and of state which are weighing upon you, would be enough to smash any man who was not bound to go ahead. This latter destiny is, I flatter myself, the one marked out for you, though I infer that you will have need of all your grit, as I am led to presume that Uncle Sam has burdened your shoulders with a greater load than you had bargained for, —that you will carry it through in safety, I do not doubt, nor do I doubt that the result of success will be such as to repay you for all your toil and trouble. Only don't let Politics swallow up science. They will pull together well enough and make a strong team—one however, which will require a hand as strong as yours to manage it. I hope you will find an opportunity to send me a line now and then, though I, poor devil, am compelled to lay disabled in port, while others are prosperously voyaging on the high seas. Damn the luck—perhaps my turn will come some time.

I have sent your letter to Mr. Marshall and am expecting his answer. Norton sails in a week or two, to my great regret. I hope that the map of the Iroquois country is not spoiled by your departure, if so, I shall mourn over it as a lamentable casualty. Perhaps by the time your volume on the Guatemala is out, I shall come down with a narrative of backwood scrimmages—but that all depends on my luck. My eyes I don't mind. I can get along without them, but to have one's brains stirred up in a mush, may be regarded as a decided obstacle in the way of intellectual achievements. Give me a tithe of a chance, and I will do it.

If I can do anything for you here, you will of course, make use of me, and meanwhile believe me, with the warmest wishes for your success.

Very faithfully yours,
F. Parkman, Jr.

ms: Dictated, Huntington Manuscripts, Henry E. Huntington Library.

To Ephraim George Squier

My dear Squier Boston, Oct. 15, 1849

I heartily congratulate you on the reception you met with at Leon, and particularly on the distinguished success of your negotiations[1] with the government—a noble beginning for your diplomatic career, and a pledge of future success, should your ambition lead you deeper into Politics. The affair is much talked of here and seems to excite very general attention everywhere as indeed it necessarily must. As for those fellows who have obligingly taken the kingdom of "Musquetia," under their protection, I trust you will lose no opportunity of snubbing them on every possible occasion. I am very glad that your political work has not suspended your researches and I shall look anxiously for a forthcoming volume on the Antiquities of Central America. As for me, I am rather inclined to envy you less for your success and your prospects, than for your power of activity. From a complete and ample experience of both, I can bear witness that no amount of physical pain is so intolerable as the position of being stranded and doomed to be rotting for year after year. However, I have not abandoned any plan, which I have ever formed and I have no intention of abandoning any until I am made cold meat of. At present I am much better in health than when you last saw me, and I do not suffer from that constant sense of oppression on the brain which then at times annoyed me beyond endurance. I find myself able to work a little although my eyes are in a totally useless state, and excessively sensitive. The eyes are nothing to the other infernal thing which now seems inclined to leave me alone, good riddance to it; so I contrive to dig slowly along by the aid of other people's eyes, doing the work more thoroughly, no doubt, and digesting my materials better than if I used my own. I have just obtained the papers which were wanting to complete my collection for the illustrative work on the

Indians which I told you about. The manuscripts amount to several thousand pages. I am inclined to think the labor of collecting them might have been better bestowed, but I was a boy when I began it, and at all events it will be done thoroughly.

The commission which you charged me with will be duly attended to, at an early opportunity. Charley Norton is I suppose by this time at Madras. I saw his family the other day. They have several times spoken about you and will be very glad to hear of your luck. Mr. Gallatin's death is a blow to the Ethnologicals,[2] and they will hardly find such a rallying point as his house was.

If I can serve you in any way of writing or otherwise, I wish you would let me know and I shall be very glad to do anything in my power. By some practice I have caught the knack of dictating and find it as easy as lying. Drop me a line when you get a chance, and believe me.

Very truly yours,
F. PARKMAN.

MS: Dictated, Huntington Manuscripts, Henry E. Huntington Library.

[1] See note 1, FP to Squier [1849].

[2] Albert Gallatin (1761–1849), secretary of the treasury under Jefferson, left public life in 1827 and in 1836 published his celebrated *Synopsis of Indian Tribes* . . . in the second volume of the *Transactions* of the American Antiquarian Society. With FP's correspondents, J. R. Bartlett, E. G. Squier, H. R. Schoolcraft, and Brantz Mayer, Gallatin founded the American Ethnological Society. He has often been called "the father of American ethnology." Gallatin's name is scratched on the endpapers of FP's "Old North-West Journal" of 1844–45 (*Journals*, I, 284), and he is mentioned in the notes in *Pontiac*, I, 9 n., where FP alludes to a personal conversation with him.

To Ephraim George Squier

My dear Squier — Boston, Nov. 18th [1849]

Your last note reached me a few days ago, and I shall certainly keep a bright look out for the publications which will throw any further light on your proceedings. I was in New York the other day where I saw at the Historical Society's rooms, a number of boxes of antiquities marked with your name and apparently sent there by Mr. Cotheal.[1] Your communications published in the *Literary World* and elsewhere have attracted considerable attention. Copway has recently come back from his Western tour and is now in New York preparing to publish the Traditional History of the Ogibhewas, and a collection of their legends.

Between you and me I shall have no great faith in them. Copway is endowed with a discursive imagination and facts grow under his hands into a preposterous shape and dimensions. His scheme of settling the Indians is a flash in the pan, or rather he has no settled scheme at all, and never had any. I had a letter from him dated at Council Bluffs which was I believe the fartherest limit of his travels. He had a great deal to say about the forest gentlemen, nature's noblemen, etc., but very little about the regeneration of the tribes.

I enclose you a paragraph containing an account of some remarkable discoveries in the Navahoe country which was once as I remember the field of your own proposed researches, and where a vast deal doubtless, yet remains to be discovered. You will be rather surprised to hear that Hoffman,[2] poor devil, became engaged to Schoolcraft's daughter and took a fancy into his head that he was bound in consequence to avenge the wrongs of the Red race against the white men. This idea got such possession of him that his friends rightly concluded him to be mad and the match was broken off. He then threw up his government employment and has not resumed it, in fact he is hardly capable. He made a desperate effort to act on Mrs. Emberg's advice and after such a result, it is not likely that he will try again.

The Nortons desire to be kindly remembered to you, the ring was smilingly accepted and I am requested to return many thanks for the gift. Mrs. Norton has been very dangerously ill, but seems now in a fair way to recover, especially since two days ago letters were received from Charley, announcing his safe arrival in Madras.

Believe me,
Very truly your friend,
F. Parkman, Jr.
by C. S. B.[3]

P.S. When you write me again, which I hope will be very soon, tell me what was the upshot of your plan of publishing in conjunction with Mr. Marshall, a map of the Iroquois country. I hope you have not abandoned it. Mr. M. has been delivering a lecture touching on early Jesuit missions, etc., which has been published in *The Western Literary Messenger* and of which he sent me a copy. O'Callaghan's first volume of the *Documentary history of New York,*[4] is full of interest. You remember that you asked me by what authority it is stated that the Iroquois secured their palisades by an embankment of earth thrown up around the bases. By one of my notebooks, I find that the fact is mentioned by Cartier in his account of the village of Hochelaga[5] which probably belonged to the Hurons and not the Five Nations though I have no doubt that the military structures of both were on the same plan.

MS: Dictated, Huntington Manuscripts, Henry E. Huntington Library.

[1] Squier's mail was sent through "Cotheal & Co. 49 Water St. [N. Y.]" while he was in Nicaragua. Squier to FP, Oct. 12, 1849, PP, MHS. MS dated by contents.

[2] Charles Fenno Hoffman (1806–84), editor, poet, and novelist, was an editor of the New York *American* and, for almost a year, editor of the *Knickerbocker Magazine*. In 1833 he toured the Northwest on horseback, and his travel letters were published in 1835 under the title of *A Winter in the West* (1835). In 1847 he became editor of the *Literary World*, but his health failed, and in January, 1849, he was treated for mental disorders. In that year he entered a state hospital at Harrisburg, Pa., where he remained a patient for the rest of his life. Henry R. Schoolcraft had married the daughter of an Ojibway chief, and Hoffman had written in 1839 a novel, *Greyslaer, a Romance of the Mohawk*. Schoolcraft's daughter, with her Indian background, and Hoffman's own interest in Indians were undoubtedly involved in the incident FP describes.

[3] Catherine Scollay Bigelow, FP's fiancée.

[4] Edmund Bailey O'Callaghan (1797–1880), physician, historian, and Irish emigrant to Canada, participated in the 1837 Papineau rebellion and fled to New York, where his study of the history of anti-rent agitation led him to early New York history. He mastered Dutch in two years and from 1848 to 1870, as New York state historian, devoted himself to the study of documentary history. He is justly remembered for his excellent editing of *The Documentary History of the State of New York* (4 vols., 1849–51) and the first nine volumes of the monumental *Documents Relative to the Colonial History of New York* (1853–61) which were invaluable to FP in writing his *History*. FP expressed his deep appreciation on more than one occasion to editor O'Callaghan, who responded by saying that he enjoyed reading FP's *History*. Of the *Pioneers*, O'Callaghan wrote: "It is a charming work; authentic and exhaustive in research; glowing and enticing in style, so that when I had once taken it up, I was compelled to read it through." Letter to FP, Sept. 26, 1865, PP, MHS.

[5] See *Pioneers*, II, 26 ff.

To Henry R. Schoolcraft[1]

Dear Sir, Boston, March 1st [1850][2]

I much regret to hear of your illness & sincerely hope that when this reaches you, you will be in a condition to resume your labours. I have sent you by express, a copy of the book I mentioned,[3] which is, as you will see, merely of a popular character. I am now at work upon a history of the period immediately succeeding the conquest of Canada, an interesting era as you are well aware, in the history of the Indians. I have gathered manuscript authorities in France, England, & this country, to the amount of several thousand pages, & [*have*] am already far advanced in the composition of the book a copy of which I shall send you on its publication.

What are the sources from which a view may be best obtained of the policy of the American government towards the Indian tribes? I have had occasion to dilate upon the course adopted by the French, & the English, & wish to have the means of incidentally comparing them with the American policy since the Revolution. If you think of any book, pamphlet, or record which would give this sort of information you will much oblige me by sending me the title. Believe me

with much respect
yours truly
F. PARKMAN, JR.

ADDRESSED: Henry R. Schoolcraft Esq. Washington, D. C.
MS: Dictated, Schoolcraft Papers, Library of Congress.

[1] See note 1, FP to C. C. Trowbridge, Nov. 11, 1846.
[2] Letter is endorsed in Schoolcraft's hand "F. Parkman 1 Mar. 1850."
[3] *The California and Oregon Trail* (New York, 1849).

To Ephraim George Squier

My dear Squier Boston April 2d, 1850

The spirit moves me to write from having read your personal narrative, sent to the Ethnological Society—a document for which by the way, I owe you a grudge, as it kindled in me a burning desire to get among fevers and volcanoes, niggers, Indians and other outcasts of humanity, a restless fit which is apt to seize me at intervals and which you have unmercifully aggravated. I hear frequent mention of the idols, extremely curious and unspeakably ugly, which you have sent to Washington, and I hope some day to see the originals of those whose portraits figure in a late number of the *Literary World*. For my own part, I am usually kept a prisoner by the sensitive state of my eyes, which only permit me to come out like an owl after dark, but with the aid of an amanuensis I contrive to do a little reading and writing, and if nothing happens will probably finish the job in hand within a year, on which great occasion you will receive a presentation copy. There is nothing here of much importance in the literary way. Your friend Ticknor has come down with his three volumes on Spanish literature.[1] Pickering's book is published in admirable style with fine engravings.[2] It has been noticed in the *Prospective Review*, and other English journals, but I hear that the method and arrangement are objected to as obscure. He goes for the derivation of the races of mankind from one source. Agassiz[3] has written an article in which he aims at proving that both men and animals originated from different acts of creative power at different parts of the earth's surface. The Orthodox are at him in consequence, raising a great outcry about impiety, and attacking him with texts of Scripture. If they could, they would serve him as the Church served Galileo.

Norton has been up to Delhi and is now probably in Egypt, having done up his undertaking in very handsome style. He will probably remain abroad some time longer. It has been a winter of excitement here, what with the threats of disunion and the consequent panic among the cotton spinners, and other events of a more domestic nature. Prof. Webster of Cambridge, whom perhaps you know, was sentenced to death yesterday for murdering my uncle in his laboratory at the Medical College, in order to prevent the exposure of numerous frauds and swindling transactions of which he, Webster, had been guilty.[4] All the town has been in commotion, and the feeling of satisfaction at the result of the trial is, I believe universal.

In the course of this Spring I expect to become domiciliated at Milton, within a few miles of here, where I hope some day or other to welcome you as my guest. Meanwhile wishing you all possible success, and an escape from fevers, snakes, dirks, revolvers and all other evils which may beset your path, I remain with warm regard,

Very faithfully yours,
F. Parkman, Jr.

P.S. I had a letter from Schoolcraft the other day; he seems to be very busy about something but what the deuce it was, I could not tell. The second volume of the *Documentary History of New York* is already out.

MS: Dictated, Huntington Manuscripts, Henry E. Huntington Library.

[1] George Ticknor (1791–1871), one of Harvard's leading teachers in modern languages, spent some ten years in writing his *History of Spanish Literature* (New York, 1849). In 1864 he published a biography of his friend, William H. Prescott. A number of interesting side lights on Ticknor as a teacher are found in Samuel E. Morison, *Three Centuries of Harvard, 1636–1936* (Cambridge, 1946), 225 ff.

[2] FP probably refers to Charles Pickering (1805–1878), physician and naturalist, who in 1848 published his *Races of Man and Their Geographic Distribution.*

[3] Louis Agassiz (1807–73), Harvard's celebrated naturalist whose daughter, Ida, FP later hoped to marry.

[4] Dr. George Parkman, brother of FP's father, was last seen mounting the steps of Harvard's medical school building about two o'clock on Friday afternoon, November 23. He was missing for a week thereafter, until a janitor found the remains of his body in a brick vault in Professor John White Webster's laboratory. A professor in the medical school and a pioneer in the treatment of the criminally insane, Dr. George Parkman was also a man of great wealth, known for his philanthropy, his business acumen, and his ability to collect outstanding debts. Professor Webster, a colleague who taught chemistry and mineralogy in the medical school, had borrowed heavily from Parkman in order to maintain a luxurious manner of living far beyond his means. At his trial Webster claimed that after an argument he had struck his creditor with a stick of wood and accidentally killed him. He then disposed of the body in his laboratory.

This tragic murder became one of the most celebrated and publicized crimes in the history of Harvard University. The story has been told many times, but Cleveland Amory's "Dr. Parkman Takes a Walk," in William Bentinck-Smith's *The Harvard Book* (Cambridge 1955), 119–34, is probably the most vivid and dramatic version.

A blow by blow description of the trial appeared in the Boston newspapers. Edward Everett told of meeting FP's father on January 14, 1850 (Diary, Massachusetts Historical Society), and noted that "The means of disposing of the body is itself horrible beyond anything in the annals of crime."

FP's father's letters are filled with distress caused by his brother's tragic death. "During that terrible week of his mysterious disappearance," he wrote a friend, "when we knew not where to look or what to fear, no method that human thought could devise was left untried to discover the awful secret." Rev. Dr. Francis Parkman to Rev. William B. Sprague, Dec. 24, 1849, MSS Collection, Parkman Folder, New-York Historical Society. The murder had a lasting effect on young George Parkman, son of the Doctor and FP's classmate and cousin, who became a recluse for the rest of his life.

To Charles Eliot Norton

Milton—June 15th [1850][1]

My dear Charley—Meeting Mr Bullard the other day,[2] he told me that you probably would not come back until a year from next October, a piece of information which excited my strongest discontent and disapproval. In staying away so long you overrun your furlough and give your friends a just right of indignation & complaint & a clear title to an emphatic remonstrance. I for one hoped, & still hope to see you back sooner. You have had a noble chance of seeing the world & I don't doubt have turned it to as good an account. You had better let [. . .] & Nineveh alone & make tracks homeward.

I had a letter the other day from Quincy Shaw dated at Marseilles. He was just returned from a five month's tour in the East, with which he was evidently highly pleased, though he expresses an unmeasured contempt for the people & considers the whole affair as rather tame & unadventurous. He returns in July, an example which I commend to your consideration.

I am at the tag end of the honeymoon. This spring has turned out a numerous crop of marriages among which Fred Cunningham's[3] figures as one to say nothing of others which touch you more closely. About a dozen have started or are on the point of starting in the matrimonial race & it will be edifying to watch their various careers. I have a place near Milton Hill small, snug, & comfortable, where I can offer entertainment for man & beast, of which I hope you and your steed will one day avail yourselves. We have woods about us dark enough for an owl to hide in; very fair society, not too near to bore us, & what is quite as much to the purpose a railroad to place us within arm's reach of town. This kind of life has one or two drawbacks, such as the necessity of paying bills, and the manifold responsibilities of a householder, an impending visit from the tax-gatherer, and petitions for the furtherance of charitable enterprises which as I am informed, the son of my father will not fail to promote. The last who came was a yellow cadaverous fellow who introduced himself as Mr [Speat?] commonly known as the "prisoner's friend" produced a magazine to which he wished me to subscribe & several books of his own, out of a green satchel which he wished me to buy. I told him that I was an enemy to philanthropists & with great difficulty forced him out of the door, for he stuck to his chair like a leech.

I have a reader for an hour or two, and when it is not too bright, play the amateur farmer, to the great benefit of my corporeal man. Kate is generally my amanuensis,[4] as perhaps you may see by this handwriting. *Pontiac* is about three quarters through, & I hope will see the light within a year. I think it will make two volumes with maps, plans, et cet. I calculated at starting it would take four years to finish it, which at the pace I was then writing, was about a straight calculation, for I was then handsomely used up, soul & body on the rack, & with no external means & appliances to help me on. You may judge whether my present condition is a more favourable one. I detest being spooney or an approximation to it, so I say nothing, but if you want to understand the thing take a jump out of hell-fire to the opposite extreme, such a one in short as Satan made when he broke bounds & paid his visit to our first parents.

A telegraphic dispatch has just come on from Louisville, announcing the divorce of Bigelow Lawrence & his wife.[5]—That was a bad business all round. He has got rid of his wild cat, but with miserable damage to his reputation. The writ of error brought by Webster's counsel was yesterday under consideration of the judges, & is not yet decided on, though it is said that there is no chance of its saving the fellow's neck from a collar of hemp which he deserves as richly as [*ever*] any scoundrel who ever drew breath. You have heard of Mary Dwight's illness.[6] I wish I could tell you of her convalescence, but yesterday we heard that she was still extremely weak. That it may be no worse, I most sincerely trust. Kate had a note from Sophia who seemed in a highly contented state at Chicopee—

with the greatest regard. Very truly yours

F. PARKMAN JR.

ADDRESSED: Mr Charles E Norton, Bullard & Lee—India Wharf. Rec. 19 June too late for Steamer.

MS: Dictated, Norton Papers, Harvard College Library.

[1] Dated from contents of letter.

[2] During Norton's absence, his sister, Louisa, married William S. Bullard (d. 1897) of the firm of Bullard and Lee. Bullard became one of Boston's leading shipping merchants. Norton and Howe, *Letters of Charles Eliot Norton,* I, 47 n., II, 28.

[3] Frederic Cunningham (d. 1864), Harvard class of 1845. Quinquennial folder on F. Cunningham, HA.

[4] FP's wife. See Introduction.

[5] Lawrence Timothy Bigelow (1826–69), Harvard class of 1846, consul-general of the U. S. to Italy. Bigelow was twice married, first to Miss Sally Ward of Louisville, Kentucky, Dec. 5, 1848, and second to Miss Elizabeth Chapman of Doylestown, Pennsylvania, on March 16, 1854. Quinquennial folder on L. T. Bigelow. HA.

[6] Mary Eliot Dwight, who married FP's cousin, Dr. Samuel Parkman, a physician. See note 1, FP to Mary Dwight Parkman [1852].

Unaddressed[1]

My Dear Sir — Milton July 16th [1850][2]

You may tell the Harpers that the form and type in which I should prefer to have the book published [*is that*] are those, of Prescott's *Mexico*[3]—two vols, instead of three. Perhaps it would be better to make it a trifle smaller.

If you can negotiate from the Harpers the same terms which

they gave to Prescott, I should be much gratified. If on the other hand you should not succeed in gaining terms so favorable or approximately so favorable, I think it would be better to stipulate only for a number of copies sufficient to pay the expense of stereotyping. In this case after the first edition is sold, it will not be so difficult, should the book prove successful, to gain a fresh bargain on better terms; and in any event I am safe from loss.

I am not rigidly bent on any particular form of publication; provided the book appears in a decent and scholarlike dress; but I am strongly in favor of two volumes.

The Harpers will understand that all arrangements are subject to my approval. Perhaps it would not be amiss to tie the M.S. in a close parcel and direct it to yourself or Crosby & Nichols, so that in case of accident it may return to you. As to the title the following occurs to me, which however I don't greatly admire.

A History of the War with Pontiac & the Indian Tribes of North America in their combined attack upon the British Colonies after the Conquest of Canada—

I like best the one that first occurred to me; & I think that Johnson's dictionary will bear me out in the use of the word conspiracy.—"A History of the Conspiracy of Pontiac & the struggle of the North American Indians against the British Colonies after the Conquest of Canada."

How will this do—"The War with Pontiac (or Pontiac's War). A History of the outbreak of the Indian tribes of America against the British colonies after the Conquest of Canada."

Believe me with the greatest regard. Yours faithfully—

F. PARKMAN, JR.

MS: Dictated draft, Parkman Papers, Massachusetts Historical Society.

[1] Although this draft is addressed to "My Dear Sir," is was probably written to Dr. George Edward Ellis (1814–94), the Unitarian minister who was, perhaps, FP's most intimate male friend. Little correspondence took place between FP and Ellis, for the minister spent most of his days in Boston or in near-by Charlestown, where he was pastor of the Harvard Church for nearly thirty years. There are a number of undated notes in the Parkman Papers indicating that Ellis read the MS copy of most of FP's books before they were published.

It was appropriate that one of FP's long autobiographical letters was addressed to Ellis, who as president of the Massachusetts Historical Society read it at a special meeting of the society on November 21, 1893, called to honor FP. Ellis during this period (1849–55) was an editor of the *Christian Examiner*, and later wrote *The Red Man and the White Man in North America* (Boston, 1871), *The Puritan Age and Rule* (Boston, 1880), and other works, including memoirs of Jacob Bigelow (FP's father-in-law) and Jared Sparks.

Ellis submitted FP's MS to Harper's and on August 1, 1850, received this reply: Rev. and Dear Sir:

Our reader has just returned to us Mr. Parkman's MS. His opinion, as regards the literary execution of the work, etc is very favorable,—but he is apprehensive that the work, highly respectable as it is, will not meet with a very rapid or extensive sale. (PP, MHS)

[2] MS dated by contents.

[3] Willam Hickling Prescott's *History of the Conquest of Mexico* (3 vols., 1843). FP borrowed books from Prescott, as indicated by several undated letters from Prescott in the PP, MHS. Unfortunately none of FP's letters are to be found in the large collection of Prescott Papers, MHS.

To Ephraim George Squier

Dear Squier [Milton, July 16, 1850][1]

I hear through the papers that you are in New York. If you come to Boston, which I hope you will, you will find me established in a domicile of my own at Milton, where I hope you will take up your quarters during your stay. The advantages are, country air and a railroad conveyance morning and night and through the day, to and from the City. Go to the Old Colony Depot near the U. S. Hotel in Boston, and get a ticket for Milton Lower Falls, and when there inquire for my house which is within five minutes walk of the Station house.

I shall finish my book in a month or two. The subject is wholly new, and I am told it will take. Proposals for its publication are now before the Harpers—two vols., octavo.

Come in person, if you can, and if not, let me hear from you.

Yours very truly
F. Parkman, Jr.

MS: Huntington Manuscripts, Henry E. Huntington Library.

[1] MS dated by postmark.

To Henry R. Schoolcraft

Boston July 21st 1850

Dear Sir—I venture to intrude on your patience in order to inquire upon a matter concerning which your authority is better than that of anyone else. Can you inform me whether in the totemic system as existing among the Ojibwas and other Algonquins who have come under your observation the children followed the totem of the father or that of the mother? Among the Iroquois, as you well know, the mother always transmitted her totem to the offspring,[1] and my impression has always been that the same was the case among the Algonquins. I am inclined to think that the totemic system prevailed among all or nearly all of the tribes east of the Mississippi, and that the prohibition of marriage between persons bearing the same totem was an essential feature of the institution.

I need hardly say that any information with which you may favor me on these points will not be made use of without ample acknowledgment.

I remain with great respect

Yours faithfully
F. PARKMAN, JR.
(5 Bowdoin Sq.
Boston)

MS: Dictated, Schoolcraft Papers, Library of Congress.

[1] Many primitive tribes are divided into sibs (clans or gentes), and the sib name is derived from an animal, plant, or natural object. The sib mates display special attitudes towards these creatures or objects, designated by ethnologists as totems. FP's researches on this subject are discussed in *Jesuits,* I, 41 ff. That part of Schoolcraft's reply (July 24, 1850, PP, MHS), which his abominable handwriting permits us to decipher reads: "My dear Sir, You are entirely right, agreeably to my observations, in supposing that the descent was traced politically, among the Iroquois, through the mother. Some other tribes did the same. But it did not extend to the Ojibways or other Algonquian tribes."

To Ephraim George Squier

My dear Squier — Milton, Sept. 6th [1850]

I owe the Washingtonians a grudge for their scandalous behavior in carrying you off from my expectant eyes. So you've given up Nicaragua. All the better, I fancy, for yourself, as well as your friends. Four years among Greasers and Indians with a touch of snakes, alligators and el vomito, would be unpalatable to the best stomached antiquarian. I don't wonder your Artist grew homesick, more especially as I fancy he hadn't much leisure time given him to swallow quinine and calomel.

I don't despair of seeing you yet. After October, by the way, I shall be in town where you will find me at my father-in-law's, Dr. Bigelow,[1] but I hope to see you before that time at what you are pleased to call my classic retreat.

Yours very faithfully,
F. PARKMAN, JR.

MS: Dictated, Huntington Manuscripts, Henry E. Huntington Library.

[1] Dr. Jacob Bigelow (1787–1879), one of Boston's leading physicians and professor of materia medica and clinical medicine at the Harvard Medical School 1815–55. Bigelow is also remembered as the founder of Mount Auburn Cemetery, where FP is buried. MS dated by contents.

To Charles Eliot Norton

My dear Charley — Milton, Sept. 22[d] 1850

It is a fortnight since your letter came to hand, and I have been too busy to answer it; rather a new condition of things for me, but the fact is all the time I could prudently give to work has been taken up in carrying forward my book so as to be ready for [*next*] publication next spring. I see that you are a true hearted American, and have too much sense to be bitten by the John Bull mania which is the prevailing disease of Boston in high places and in low. A disgusting malady it is, and I pray Heaven to deliver us from its influence. We can afford to stand on our own feet and travel our own course without aid or guidance, and my maxim is that it is about as well to go wrong on one's own hook, as to go right by slavishly tagging at the heels of another. But in the present case the thing is reversed. It is we that are going right, and John Bull may go to the devil. Fine Yankee bray,—isn't it? In spite of Taylor's death we have come out right at last.[1] There is no danger, thank God, of the Union breaking up at present in spite of all the efforts of Garrison[2] and his coadjutors. Q. Shaw has often been here and speaks with pleasure of having met you. He comes out nobly after his European travels, and is about the finest fellow in these parts. I am extremely disappointed at hearing from your own pen the confirmation of what Mr Bullard told me about your not coming home for a year. You don't treat your friends well, and will never be allowed to leave home again. Squier has come back from

Nicaragua and I believe don't intend to return. He was to have spent a few days with me, but a call to Washington prevented him and I received instead a letter brimfull of wrath and malediction against the politicians, together with two pamphlets about the volcanos of Nicaragua. What he means to do next I don't know. I went to Charlotte Everett's—now Wise's—reception. All very gay with the exception of Mrs. Everett's face, which was dolorous enough. Mr. E. was inscrutable as usual.[3] The feeling in Cambridge against the inconstant bride is not of an amiable nature.

I wish with all my heart that you could be here as you kindly wish at the forthcoming of my book; but a copy shall be put by for you. I find it seriously no easy job to accomplish all the details of dates, citations, notes et. cet. without the use of eyes. Prescott[4] could see a little—confound him he could even look over his proofs, but I am no better off than an owl in the sunlight. The ugliest job of the whole is getting up a map. I have a draught made in the first place on a very large scale. Then I direct how to fill it in with the names of forts, Indian villages &c. all of which I have pretty clearly in my memory from the reading of countless journals, letters et. cet. and former travels over the whole ground. Then I examine the map, inch by inch, taking about half a minute for each examination, and also have it compared by competent eyes with ancient maps and draughts, then I have the big map reduced to a proper size. I have got to the end of the book and killed off Pontiac. The opening chapters howev[er] are not yet complete. I have just finished an introductory chapter on the Indian tribes, which my wife pronounces uncommonly stupid. Never mind, nobody need read it who don't want to. Mr George Ellis stands my friend,[5] has read the manuscript through and likes it. Nobody else has seen it. I shall stereotype it myself and take the risk. Pray Heaven the newspapers & reviews may have tender hearts. All depends on them nowadays. Merit must speak out trumpet tongued or else it's all of no use. Ten men in New York earn their daily bread by the trade of literary puffing; but woe is me I have nothing in my pocket to give them, and wouldn't give it if I had. The clock strikes one—our primitive dinner hour. Don't let your European sensibilities be shocked. I must come to an end—so wishing you every prosperity in your future travels and a safe return to fatherland I remain my dear Charley —Ever faithfully yours

F. Parkman, Jr.

ADDRESSED: Mr Charles E Norton.
MS: Dictated, Norton Papers, Harvard College Library.

[1] Zachary Taylor, who died on July 9, 1850, after only a year and four months as President. Norton, in a letter to FP from England, July 22, 1850 (PP, MHS), wrote of Taylor: "He was the man of all others who was to be looked to at the present time to conciliate the differences of opinion among the parties, and to bring affairs to a good issue. His death is the heaviest loss we could meet with."

[2] William Lloyd Garrison (1805–79), the abolitionist, founder of the *Liberator*, a famous antislavery journal, and a founder and president of the American Anti-Slavery Society.

[3] Edward Everett (1764–1865), Unitarian clergyman, teacher, and statesman, married Charlotte Gray Brooks and was the father of six children. Everett, also known as one of America's greatest orators, had recently resigned as president of Harvard (1846–49), which he characterized as an "ill-disciplined school." Morison, *Three Centuries of Harvard*, 280.

[4] Prescott lost the use of his left eye as the result of "a blow from a large, hard piece of bread, thrown undoubtedly at random," in the Commons Hall when he was a junior at Harvard. For the results of this injury, see George Ticknor, *Life of William Prescott* (Philadelphia, 1863), 18–19, 26 ff.

[5] See note 1, Unaddressed, July 16 [1850].

To Charles Eliot Norton

My dear Charley — Boston, Nov. 10th 1850

Your letter from Constance reached me yesterday, and though you do not say anything in it about a longwinded epistle which I wrote you some two months ago I hope, nevertheless, that by this time it has reached you. I had forgotten that you knew Copway here. One morning at about five o'clock, the fellow called on me at Milton, and finding that I was not up, which you will consider pardonable, as it was scarcely light, he left me a flourishing complimentary note congratulating me on my domestic prospects, and informing me that as my literary fame must be wide spread throughout Europe, he was anxious to obtain letters of introduction to some of my more distinguished correspondents. I wrote him that the only person in Europe with whom I was on writing terms was an American gentleman who would be happy to give him such counsel and direction as a green traveller requires. Accordingly I gave him a note to you which I suppose did not flatter his vanity enough for presentation. I accompanied it with a hint that he was not to trouble you with any applications, direct or indirect, for pecuniary aid. You know his weakness on that point. I myself have experienced its effects. As for Squier he has been removed from his chargé ship by Webster, with a view it is said, of pleasing the English minister Bulwer.[1] Squier's offence was exceeding his instructions and dealing a little too sharply with the English for whom he never had a partiality. He is very indignant, and I should think not without justice, at the treatment which he has received. I hear that he has taken the editorship of the *American Review* which he will no doubt turn to good account. He had an able article in one of the last numbers on the republics of Central America. In the same number [*of*] is a portrait of him, and a notice of his life. He was to have spent a week with me this summer but was prevented by a sudden summons to Washington, and I have heard nothing from him for two or three weeks. I believe he has a book in press. He has shown a little disposition to bluster and make himself too common in the public prints; and of anybody else I should say that he was dissipating his talents by having too many irons in the fire, but [*with*] under all his skirmishing he generally contrives to have some heavy piece of ordnance loading for a grand discharge, and he has a degree of physical stamina which permits him to work day and night without breaking down.

I have just come to town and taken up my abode at Dr. Bigelow's so that I have not yet had the pleasure of seeing your family since their return from Newport. Mr Bullard has received on all hands the congratulations which are due to his signal good fortune; and I can't but think that you ought to come in for a share of congratulations in having so pleasant an addition to your family.

Just now we are on the eve of an election—a great row about the fugitive slave law,[2] and an infinity of nonsense talked and acted upon the subject. A great union party[3] is forming in opposition to the abolitionists and the southern fanatics. For my part I would see every slave knocked on the head before I would see the Union go to pieces and would include in the sacrifice as many abolitionists as could be conveniently brought together. My book gets on rather slowly. Shouldn't wonder if the final delivery should not take place before next autumn. My wife desires her best regards, and I needn't assure you that mine are most emphatically yrs and that I am with most cordial good wishes Yrs.

F. PARKMAN

ADDRESSED: Mr Charles E Norton.
MS: Dictated, Norton Papers, Harvard College Library.

[1] Daniel Webster (1782–1852) in July, 1850, became President Fillmore's secretary of state. Sir Henry Bulwer (1801–72) came to Washington as British ambassador in 1849 and negotiated the Clayton-Bulwer Treaty of 1850, a compromise agreement between the United States and Britain resulting from conflicting interests in Central America. The treaty provided that the two countries should jointly control and protect the canal which was to be built somewhere on the isthmus. Squier's treaty, never ratified by the Senate, provided for the construction of a canal independent of the British and was hence distasteful to Bulwer. See note 1, FP to Squier [1849].

[2] The Fugitive Slave Law, part of the famous Compromise of 1850, replaced earlier fugitive slave laws by provisions for federal commissioners and federal courts in apprehending runaways. Citizens were forced to aid in executing the new law, and those harboring, concealing, or rescuing fugitives were liable for six months' imprisonment and a fine of $1,000.

[3] The principle of the nonextension of slavery of the Free Soil party of 1848 became the main party platform of the new Republican party, composed of Whigs, Northern Democrats, and Free Soilers. The name "Republican" was first adopted at a local meeting held in Ripon, Wisconsin, on February 28, 1854, and John C. Frémont was the first Republican candidate for President in 1856.

To Ephraim George Squier

My dear Squier, Boston, May 14th, '51

Not long since, I met Rev. Mr. Osgood, pastor of I don't know exactly what church in New York, who, hearing that I was to be delivered of a volume, obligingly offered his services as a Wet Nurse and proposed to exhibit the book at a meeting of the Ethnological Soc. that receiving their approval, it might figure in the reports of their proceedings and thereby gain glory and renown. I have accordingly sent him a bundle of the proofs. But for his offer, I might have inflicted them upon you, and you owe the reverend gentleman thanks for having saved you from a bore. If you have any curiosity to look them over, he will lend them to you. At all events give them your vote at the meeting, and when you chance to meet any of the editors with whom your voice is potential, speak a word in their ears in behalf of the forthcoming *Conspiracy of Pontiac.*

Among the tribulations of your life, you have not yet numbered the crowning evil called par excellence "moving." I have just tasted it in all its bitterness but am snugly shaken down at last, and divide my time between antiquities, agriculture, and educating a dog. My box is in Brookline, four miles from town.

Very truly Yrs.
F. Parkman, Jr.

MS: Huntington Manuscripts, Henry E. Huntington Library.

To Charles Eliot Norton

My dear Charley Boston, June 25th, 1851.

Bowen[1] wrote me this morning that you intended, on his application, to review 'Pontiac' for the N. A. This is a kindness somewhat unexpected. I took the book to Bowen, upon which he observed that he must have a review of it and mentioned you as the person best fitted to do it. I don't know how it was but I had a sort of instinct that you were busy this summer in writing something or other and accordingly I demurred at his troubling you with the proposal. The other day after seeing you, finding that my conjecture was right, I wrote to Bowen not to propose this job to you as you had other work in hand. It appears however that he had already written. I owe you, my dear Charley, double thanks for your friendly intentions, and only hope that it will not interfere with any other plans.

As for the remaining proofs, maps, etc. I shall be able to forward them in a few days. The execrable job of stereotyping[2] is not yet quite through but I am looking forward to a speedy deliverance from the printers' devils on which occasion I shall sing Oh be joyful. Give my kind remembrances to your family and believe me.

Your obliged friend
F. Parkman, Jr.

MS: Dictated, Norton Papers, Harvard College Library.

[1] Francis Bowen (1811–90) was editor and proprietor of the *North American Review* from 1843 to 1853 and then accepted the post of Alford Professor of Religion, Philosophy, and Civil Polity at Harvard, a position he held for thirty-six years. Bowen eventually reviewed the book in the *North American Review*, Vol. LXXIII (October, 1851), 495–529, stating that "this work has been a labor of love" and praising FP for his "lively style and judicious observations."

Bowen had also reviewed *The California and Oregon Trail* favorably in *ibid.*, Vol LXIX (July, 1849), 176–96, and found it superior to Edwin Bryant's *What I Saw in California*. However, he wrote: "Mr. Parkman, indeed, hardly went within a thousand miles of the inhabited part of California, and the addition of the name of the country to the title of his book was merely a publisher's trick, in which he had no share, to catch unwary purchasers."

[2] Jared Sparks suggested this method of publication to FP through George Ellis: "As to printing, the best way for Mr. Parkman is to procure the Stereotype plates [a plate made by using a mold or matrix of a printing surface in plaster of Paris, and making from this cast a plate in type metal] at his own charge, & sell the right of printing from them, at a fixed sum per volume as Ticknor, Prescott, & others have done;—making a bargain with the publishers to take & pay for a certain number of copies at the outset, & take the risk of their sale." (Enclosed in a letter from George Ellis to FP, June 25, 1850, PP, MHS.) See also FP to Draper, Jan. 16, 1854.

To Ephraim George Squier

My dear S,　　　　Boston, July 9th '51

A friend of mine reading my proof sheets, volunteered to write a preliminary puff. I assented and told him to enclose it to you, and you would put it in the *Am. Review*, or some other Journal. This was a fortnight ago. Meeting him to-day he told me that he had already manufactured and sent the puff. I had not expected—he being a dilatory gentleman, such prompt execution, and so did not warn you. I really don't care whether the thing is published or not—so if it will give you the least trouble, pray let it alone, enough has been done already to answer the purpose. If it is quite in your way, and if, in reading the paper, you think it will serve its end—I myself have not seen it—you can give it to your old friends of the *American*—to Ripley,[1] or anybody you like. Otherwise fling it into the fire.

When I last wrote, I had not seen the very kind notice in the *International*, which I presume to be yours. Be assured, I highly value your commendation—no man's more so—and nothing could be more acceptable than such a token of your friendship.

You got my note of a few days since? I hope you will find it worth while to attend to the hints contained in it. As for the matter I have been speaking of, it is not of a farthing's consequence. If the paragraph is published at all, it had better be a month hence than now. "Pontiac" won't be out till September. Some delay is caused by waiting for an English edition, which Bentley[2] is to father.

Your obliged friend,
F. PARKMAN, JR.

MS: Huntington Manuscripts, Henry E. Huntington Library.

[1] FP undoubtedly refers to George Ripley (1802–80), a Unitarian minister who left his pulpit in Boston to become one of the leading literary critics of his day. In 1849 he became critic for the *New York Tribune*, a post he held for thirty-one years; and in 1850 he was one of the founders of *Harper's New Monthly Magazine.*

[2] Richard Bentley (1794–1871), who published the English edition of FP's *Pontiac*, also brought out editions of the writings of Benjamin Disraeli, Charles Dickens, and many other prominent figures. Letters from Bentley in the Parkman Papers indicate that the book had a poor sale.

On the whole English reviews were favorable, as indicated by excerpts printed in *Littell's Living Age* (Vol. XXXI [Oct. 18, 1851], 137–40; Vol. XXXII [January 17, 1852], 143–44). The *London Spectator*, however, came down on FP with both feet: "The landscape is described, not to possess the reader with the features of the country so far as they are essential to the due apprehension of the historical event, but as a thing important in itself, and sometimes as a thing adapted to show off the writing or the writer. . . . the probable or possible feelings of the actors are laid before the reader." This scathing criticism applied to American writers like Irving, Prescott, and Bancroft as well as to FP's *Pontiac*. *Harper's New Monthly Magazine*, Vol. III (Nov., 1851), 857, printed the excerpt with the comment: "The obtuseness of John Bull can no farther go."

To Lyman C. Draper

My dear Sir — Boston, July 13th 1851

I received your kind letter yesterday and am very glad to hear from you again. In fact I have intended for some time past to renew a correspondence with you, but have not been able to get your address. I am very sorry to hear of your illness. You do quite right to try the water cure. It is much better than drugging yourself with medicines. Fresh air, cold water, and exercise will, I hope, set you up in time, and enable you to go forward actively with your investigations. When are your collections to see the light. I look for a series of Pioneer biographies from you, and hope that the day will not be far distant.

As for myself I am quite well, with the exception of my eyes which do not behave themselves as they should, so that my writing and reading is done by proxy—a tolerably easy plan when you once get used to it. My book will be out in September if no further delay occurs.

I see Mr. Turner has made mention of you in his *History of the Holland Land Purchase*.[1] I cordially hope that returning health will enable you to take the field and bring forth all your accumulated treasures.

I am living now at Brookline, four miles from Boston, and if you ever travel this way, I hope you will not forget to favor me with a visit. Believe me

My dear Sir
Very faithfully yours
F. Parkman, Jr.

P.S. My letters are addressed to *Boston*.

MS: Dictated, Draper Correspondence, State Historical Society of Wisconsin.

[1] O[rsamus] Turner, *Pioneer History of the Holland Purchase of Western New York* (Buffalo, 1849).

To Lyman C. Draper

My dear Sir Boston, July 19th '51

I have just received your very kind letter, containing hints concerning MSS, etc. You would greatly oblige me by sending copies of such newspaper extracts as contain any facts with regard to the *death of Pontiac*—for though I believe I have searched the newspapers pretty thoroughly, something may very probably have escaped me.

"Ponteach" the tragedy,[1]—I have a copy of; and various MSS and newspaper extracts relating to Johnson's exploits against the hostile Indians in 1764.[2]

Of Pontiac's son Shegenaba,[3] I am sorry to say, I know very little, —can you point to any authorities concerning him?

My chief authority with regard to Pontiac's death is old Pierre Chouteau of St. Louis, whom I saw in '46. For anything on this subject, I shall be greatly indebted to you.

Thank you heartily for your kind interest in my researches. Can't I help you here in any way? If so I shall be very glad.

I am, Dear Sir, in great haste,

Yrs very Faithfully
F. PARKMAN, JR.

P.S. My book is already stereotyped, but I should recast the plates if any new facts turned up. The printing begins in a week.

ADDRESSED: Lyman C. Draper Leverington Phila. City Pa.
MS: Draper Correspondence, State Historical Society of Wisconsin.

[1] FP obtained the copy from Henry Stevens, the London bookman. The full title of the work is *Ponteach: Or the Savages of America. A Tragedy* (London, 1766). This work was published anonymously, but Robert Rogers is probably the author. See *Pontiac,* II, 343 ff., for extracts of the play.

[2] Sir William Johnson (1715–74), northern superintendent of Indian affairs and a prominent figure in *Pontiac* and *Montcalm and Wolfe.* An appraisal of Johnson's career is found in Jacobs, *Diplomacy and Indian Gifts,* 76 ff.

[3] See *Pontiac,* II, 331 n.

To Charles Eliot Norton

My Dear C. Boston, July 25th 1851

Thank you heartily for the pains you have taken in my behalf. I appreciate them, I assure you—proof reading is the climax of bores.

I am only sorry that the necessity of getting out the English edition before the 1st Sept. made it indispensable to send the whole budget out by last Wednesday's steamer. Nevertheless, some of your corrections will figure in the American edition, and for the English it is no great matter, as I am glad to see you detected no very bad blunder.

Infernally hot, isn't it?—or don't you feel it at Newport. If you don't you are lucky. I wish to heaven I were a fish or a lobster,—anything to get out of a warm air bath at a temperature of ninety. Three toads perished today in my garden stewed to death under the stones where they ensconced themselves.

Yrs very truly
F. PARKMAN, JR.

ADDRESSED: Charles E. Norton Newport, R. I.
MS: Letter book copy, Norton Papers, Harvard College Library.

To Lyman C. Draper

My dear Sir — Boston July 28th 1851

I am exceedingly obliged to you for the great pains you took in sending me copies of newspaper extracts, and other interesting matter. Both your inclosures reached me safely. I wish that every one engaged in such researches would show the same generosity and readiness to aid his brethren which you have shown—virtues rather rare among the historical and antiquarian fraternity. A considerable part of what you sent was quite new to me, and I have added the substance of it in notes appended to the text, giving your name as having aided me in my inquiries. I am very sorry that the earlier part of the volume being already in the printer's grasp, I cannot insert your name in the preface, and thus give myself the pleasure of acknowledging my obligation in the most suitable manner.

Old M. Chouteau gave me his story in a more circumstantial manner than to M. Nicollet,[1] or to your correspondent. M. Pascal Cerré[2] told me the same story in substance though with much less detail. I am inclined to believe Chouteau's locality correct. The letter in the *Penn. Gaz.* mentioning Fort Chartres as the place of Pontiac's death, speaks, you observe, from hearsay evidence. The Indian who brought the report seems not to have been there at the time.

I inquired of Drake what was his authority for his date of 1779.[3]

He could not give me any and confessed that the date was wrong. With regard to Pontiac's son, he could not remember where he got his information. I have seen Sheganaba's name in several treaties but the eloquent speech in Force's Archives was new to me, and had I seen it at an earlier date, I should certainly have placed it in the appendix. I was very glad to get the extracts from the Gazettes of 1769 concerning Pontiac's death since the files of the *Penn. Gaz.* which I have had access to, did not extend beyond 1688 [1788?] and the authorities which you sent contributed more than anything which I had before seen to clear up my doubts respecting the time of Pontiac's death. I was before much perplexed by a letter of Gen. Gage's dated July 15th 1688[4] in which he speaks of Pontiac as dead; but I am now convinced that this date is [a] mistake of the copyist.

Again my dear Draper I thank you for your kindness and hope I shall soon find an opportunity of repaying it. Have you yet begun to try the water cure. I cordially hope the experiment may succeed, and that before long you will give the fruits of all your interesting researches to the country.

Believe me ever

With great regard yours
F. PARKMAN, JR.

MS: Dictated, Draper Correspondence, State Historical Society of Wisconsin.

[1] Joseph Nicolas Nicollet (1786–1843), French mathematician and astronomer, emigrated to America in 1832, and in 1836–37 headed an expedition in search of the source of the Mississippi. A year later he was sent out on a government surveying expedition up the Missouri. J. C. Frémont accompanied him on this latter journey. Nicollet's *Report*, published in 1843, is cited in *Pontiac*, II, 268, 330.

[2] Pascal Louis Cerré, whose sister married Auguste Chouteau, was the son of Jean Gabriel Cerré (1734–1805), frontiersman and trader of the Middle West. About 1755 the father established a fur-trading post at Kaskaskia, Illinois, where he maintained close relations with the Indians and "was well acquainted with Pontiac." *Pontiac*, II, 329 n. FP visited the son in St. Louis in April, 1846 and found him "nearly eighty—lively, bright, and active—" *Journals*, II, 411.

[3] Samuel Gardner Drake (1798–1875), antiquarian and historian, wrote *Book on the Indians* (1841), a number of works on early New England history, and, beginning in 1847, edited the first ten volumes of the *New England Historical and Genealogical Register*. FP mentions Drake's Indian book in *Journals*, I, 325.

[4] The MS unmistakably reads 1688, and Draper has inserted a question mark after the date. FP dictated this letter to his wife, and it is undoubtedly her error. In *Pontiac*, II, 330 n., FP cites a letter written by Gage on Pontiac's death as "July 10, 176–." FP, however, concluded that Pontiac died in the summer of 1769.

To Lyman C. Draper

My dear Sir Boston, Aug. 16th 1851

I hope you received my letter in reply to your very kind communication respecting Pontiac. I was glad to see by the International and some of the papers, that your life of Clark which I have long been looking for is not far from publication. The subject is an admirable one—the best, as it seems to me of all the pioneer series. It can't fail to be well received, especially in the West. The country owes you a great obligation for the devotion with which you have given yourself to preserving so much matter of interest which, otherwise would have been lost forever. When the book appears, I hope to be able to do something towards making it known to the public in this quarter.

Is your health improving? I trust so. No impediment on earth is so formidable as the prostration of chronic disease—but time and good courage work wonders

With great regard, your friend
F. PARKMAN, JR.

MS: Draper Correspondence, State Historical Society of Wisconsin.

To Lyman C. Draper

My dear Sir Boston September 5th/51

Your letter reached me yesterday. I am rejoiced to hear that your health improves & hope that your western tour will set you up effectually. Only look out for fever & ague.

Dr. Oliver Wendell Holmes the poet[1] is the son of Dr. Holmes the annalist,[2] & will I don't doubt be happy to answer any historical enquiry which you may make. His present residence is Pittsfield, Mass.

I like exceedingly the thoroughness with which you pursue your enquiries. It is the great secret of success, & you cannot fail to produce a work of national interest & value. I wish you would let me know where to direct letters & parcels to you during your absence.

Wishing you a successful tour

I remain dear sir
yours with great esteem
F. PARKMAN, JR.

ADDRESSED: Lyman C. Draper Esq. Leverington Phila City, Pa.
MS: Dictated, Draper Correspondence, State Historical Society of Wisconsin.

[1] Oliver Wendell Holmes (1809–94), Parkman Professor of Anatomy and Physiology (a chair endowed by Dr. George Parkman, FP's uncle) at Harvard, was one of the celebrated literary figures of his day. Holmes wrote a poem about FP which was read at the Special Meeting of the Massachusetts Historical Society held on November 21, 1893, to honor FP. Holmes and FP knew each other intimately, and there are several undated letters from FP in the Holmes Papers, Library of Congress.

[2] The Reverend Abiel Holmes (1763–1837), Congregational clergyman, who in 1805 published his *American Annals, or a Chronological History of America*, 2 vols.

To Ephraim George Squier

My Dear Squier, Boston, Sep. 12, 1851

I have just sent you a copy of my book—Adams's Express care of Putnam. When will your own ship be launched? I saw in Norton's *Advertiser* or some where else that you would be off again this fall and no mistake for Central America, accompanied by an artist who I hope will serve you better than the last. With regard to the present affair, can I do any thing for you? The literary gentleman who concocted the puff of which I wrote you, has marvelled greatly at its nonappearance at which his vanity is touched. I profess ignorance as to what has become of it and advise him to a diligent examination of the contemporary New York papers. Wherever it is I don't doubt it's in the right place; but whether you threw it into the grate or devoted it to Cloacina[1] you need not tell me, for I expect further queries before long and prefer to retain the plea of ignorance. Give me a hint of your movements, and believe me,

Yours very truly,
F. PARKMAN, JR.

P.S. A young heiress is yawling in the next room. Mrs. P. quite well.

MS: Huntington Manuscripts, Henry E. Huntington Library.

[1] Goddess of Rome who presided over the *cloacae*, the sewers of the city.

To Brantz Mayer[1]

My Dear Sir, Boston Sep. 12, 1851

I have just sent you by [*Adams's*] Harnden's express, a copy of the "Conspiracy of Pontiac," as a slight acknowledgment of the assistance and sympathy for which you made me your debtor during the progress of the work. I trust your eyes are better than when I last heard from you. Mine are behaving badly and keep me a prisoner in bright weather—the effect of too much exposure. I have grown used to it however like the eels in the proverb. One of our chief lawyers here Judge Sprague has managed to distinguish himself in his profession without them,[2] and walks the street with blue spectacles and a green umbrella. Hoping to hear good accounts from you of the condition of your sight, I remain my dear sir,

yours with great regard,
F. PARKMAN, JR.

MS: Photostat in the Parkman Papers of an original letter. Photostat given to the Massachusetts Historical Society by Clarence M. Warner, October, 1923.

[1] Brantz Mayer (1809–79), lawyer, antiquarian, and historian, was instrumental in the founding of the Maryland Historical Society in 1844, and from 1867–71 was the society's president. FP had talked with Mayer in Baltimore in 1846, by which time Mayer had started to accumulate his large collection of original MSS on Colonial and Revolutionary America. Much of Mayer's correspondence is in the Maryland Historical Society's collections, but no letters from FP have been preserved.

In 1841, Mayer went to Mexico as secretary of the U. S. legation, and three years later he published his *Mexico as It Was and as It Is*, a popular work that went through three editions. He is also author of *Baltimore Past and Present* (1871), and other works. His writings on local history are considered the most authoritative of his works.

[2] Peleg Sprague (1793–1880) in 1841 was appointed U. S. district judge for the District of Massachusetts, a position he held until 1865. Despite his blindness, Sprague was regarded as an exceedingly capable judge. He delivered his opinions orally, demonstrating an exceptional mind and a remarkable memory.

To Evert A. Duyckinck[1]

My Dear Sir, Boston, Sept. 13th. '51

Thank you for the extract from "Pontiac," published in the *Literary World*, a week or two since. I have directed the publisher to send you a copy, which I hope has reached you safely. If you do not receive it, a line to me will set the matter right. Hoping to profit by your criticism, I remain

Faithfully Yrs.
F. Parkman, Jr.

P.S. The above "damned cramped piece of penmanship" attributable to lack of good eyesight.

MS: Duyckinck Papers, New York Public Library.

[1] Evert Augustus Duyckinck (1816–78), editor and biographer, was a descendant of a seventeenth-century Dutch family of colonial New Amsterdam. From 1847–53 he was editor of the *Literary World, A Journal of American and Foreign Literature, Science, and Art*, regarded as one of the best literary journals of its time. In his editorial work, Evert was associated with his brothers, especially George Long Duyckinck (1823–63). Together they edited the *Cyclopaedia of American Literature* (2 vols., 1853) and other works.

To Ephraim George Squier

My dear Squier — Boston, Sept. 17th [1851]

Yours of the 13th came to hand yesterday; I commiserate your situation and wish you a prosperous deliverance. Quill driving in the Tartarian weather of last week is too serious a matter for a joke, and as for the thirty pages of proofs, they will serve to expiate all your numerous past sins, and form a handsome balance against any which it may please you to commit in future. I think Littell[1] will insert extracts. I met him the other day and with your matter in view, dropped a hint to that effect, so send along your sheets, and if he won't listen to reason, I will find some editor who will.

Being just out of one scrape, I am plunging into a worse one. "Pontiac," thank Heaven, is off the stocks. When the next will be, I don't know, but suppose my hair will be grey first. Go to work at consulting fifteen hundred books in five different languages with the help of a school girl who hardly knows English and you will find it a bore; add to this the infantile music in the next room and you will agree that my iniquities have as good a chance of being atoned for as yours,

Yrs. very faithfully
F. Parkman

P.S. A word in the ear of the *American Review* would not be amiss. He has my book. Just give him a hint to use it with propriety.

MS: Dictated, Huntington Manuscripts, Henry E. Huntington Library.

[1] Eliakim Littell (1797–1870), editor and publisher, who in 1844 founded *Littell's Living Age*, a publication primarily devoted to reprinting materials from British journals. MS dated by contents.

To Ephraim George Squier

My Dear S. Boston, Sept. 20th 1851

Why, the deuce, are you fagging yourself to death. Take a trip to England or anywhere else that will set you up. Nature has made you tough as a pine knot, but a pine knot won't stand fire. As for the matter of *Pontiac,* clear your conscience of that business. I have done nothing to serve you that I am aware of more than you have done for me, and if I had, it would not have been on the quid pro quo principle. The sheets have come to hand and shall be submitted to Littell on Monday. Perhaps I shall write again in a day or two, until then believe me, in haste,

Yrs truly,
PARKMAN

MS: Dictated, Huntington Manuscripts, Henry E. Huntington Library.

To Jared Sparks

Dear Sir, Brookline, Sept. 26th, 1851.

You may perhaps remember that you have several times spoken to me of a collection of documents in your possession relating to the life and enterprises of La Salle.[1] The papers, as you informed me, you design at some future day, if your engagements permit, to digest, throw into form, and publish. Will you excuse me if I venture to make a proposal which may not seem a very modest one. If it is consistent with your views to place these documents in my hands, I will compose from them, together with the standard authorities and such additional MSS as I may be able to collect, an elaborate life of La Salle, your name as well as my own to appear on the title page, and such an account to be given in the preface as I think would fully meet your wishes.

With respect to the sales & other particulars, the work would have the character of a joint publication. References would be made to your previous biography of La Salle, as in some measure the foundation of the succeeding narrative. The manuscript and proofs would be [*inspected*] submitted to your examination and your wishes concerning them studiously consulted. I should not have been emboldened to make such a proposal, had you not on one occasion most kindly intimated that should you not find time to prepare these papers for the press, you might at some period place them at my disposal. The life and character of La Salle are to me objects of especial interest and I should spare neither time nor labor to produce a work valuable to the public. Believe me

With high esteem
Respectfully yours
F. PARKMAN, JR.

P.S. I hope you received the copy of "Pontiac" which I sent you about a week since. A note directed to me at *Boston* will reach me.

MS: Dictated, Sparks Papers, Harvard College Library.

[1] For FP's expressed gratitude for the favor of being allowed to use these documents, see *Discovery of the Great West* (Boston, 1869), viii–ix.

To Ephraim George Squier

My Dear Squier — Boston, Nov. 3d 1851

Let me congratulate you on having got through with your book[1] which I hope will prove a Californian gold mine. With respect to England, I was there only six weeks, seven years ago, and made no acquaintances except travelling ones, who by this time have forgotten me as I have them. The only man I know in London who can do anything except invite you to a stiff necked, white cravated dinner party, is an American who is, or has been connected with the British Museum, one of the sort commonly called "smart fellers" with a considerable knowledge of the world, a great knowledge of books and libraries, and an eye to the main chance. I should think you might find him a good acquaintance. Possibly you know him already—his name is Henry Stevens,[2] but in case you don't I enclose a note to him. I don't know his London address, but you'll easily find it by inquiring at the American Minister's or probably at Chapman's book store.

As for Paris, since the death of my revered Uncle who dwelt there, and who was truly a jewel to the bewildered traveller, I can think of no acquaintance I have there except one old classmate, a good-natured eccentric fellow who walks the hospitals, and to whom I will gladly introduce you if you think it worth while.

Can you take care of a parcel as big as an octavo volume to be delivered to Poussin,[3] late French Minister to the U. S. The parcel may be left with Hector Bossange, the Paris book seller. I am sorry I can't do more for you.

Yours very truly,
F. PARKMAN, JR.

P.S. It just occurs to me that one of my six score of cousins and a good whole souled fellow is in the firm of Baring & Brothers.[4] It's queer enough that I didn't think of him before. You'll find a line to him enclosed.

MS: Dictated, Huntington Manuscripts, Henry E. Huntington Library.

[1] In 1851 Squier published his *Aboriginal Monuments of the State of New York*, and the next year saw the appearance of his *Nicaragua: Its People, Scenery, and Monuments*, and the *Serpent Symbol*. His *The States of Central America* was published in 1858.

[2] Henry Stevens (1819–86), American-born bibliophile and London bookseller, attended the Harvard Law School in 1844 when FP first made his acquaintance. In 1845, Stevens went to London on a book-hunting expedition and remained to make this city his permanent home. In the Parkman Papers are dozens of letters from Stevens and drafts by FP ordering rare books and transcripts of MSS, but only one original recipient's copy of FP's letters to Stevens has been found (Nov. 27, 1855, Stevens Papers, William L. Clements Library). Stevens collected Americana for the British Museum, the John Carter Brown Library, the Lenox Library, the Smithsonian Institution, and the Library of Congress. He is also known for his catalogs of the British Museum's collections of Americana and lists of its famous Bibles. His brother, Benjamin Franklin Stevens (1833–1902), joined him as a bookseller in 1864, and left him two years later to set up an independent London bookselling business. B. F. Stevens was also one of FP's agents and made extensive collections of transcripts for the Library of Congress.

[3] Guillaume-Tell Poussin, envoy extraordinary and minister plenipotentiary from June 8, 1848, to October 3, 1849. A. Guyot (ed.), *Almanach National Annuaire de la République Française* (Paris, 1850), xv.

[4] Russell Sturgis (1805–87), senior partner of Baring Brothers, London bankers, was the son of Susan Parkman Sturgis and Nathaniel R. Sturgis, and the grandson of Samuel Parkman (FP's grandfather), the Boston merchant. "Parkman Genealogy," by Mary Bigelow Coffin, MS in the possession of the editor.

II

1852-1865

II

1852-1865

DEPRESSION AND DISILLUSIONMENT, TRAVEL AND RESEARCH, LETTERS TO THE PRESS DURING THE CIVIL WAR, COMPLETION OF *THE PIONEERS*

THERE WAS NOT a marked improvement in Parkman's health and spirit, although *Pontiac* by 1852 was in book form and had been enthusiastically reviewed by many critics. The intimate letters he wrote Mary Dwight Parkman, his cousin-in-law, reveal that he reached a low point of depression and disillusionment in the spring of 1853. Yet, as has been mentioned, his marriage was a happy one and appears to have been chiefly responsible for a measure of recovery immediately after his wedding took place. By November, 1855, Parkman had another upsurge in his health and was back at his desk engrossed in research and writing. His letters to fellow historians Edmund B. O'Callaghan, George Bancroft, and John G. Shea are filled with the business of writing history.

This brief but encouraging recovery was halted, as Parkman's letters show, by two disquieting events: the tragic loss of his three-year-old son in 1857, and his wife's death in the following year. Sick at heart and suffering from other complaints in addition to his old malady, Parkman turned away from labors on his *History* and sought relief in Paris, where he consulted physicians and occupied much of his time by sight-seeing on the city's omnibuses. His illness complicated by inflamed eyelids, his head tortured by pain, and his knees weakened by lameness, Parkman finally sailed for America to battle his infirmity at home.

Parkman's peace of mind was disturbed in these crucial years by other occurrences, details of which are found in his correspondence. In a letter of 1856, he described his anger and astonishment in discovering the duplicity of Benjamin Perley Poore, who performed an amazing hoax by cheating Parkman in making copies of documents. Five years later Parkman had a joust with Joel Tyler Headley, a popular writer, who plagiarized whole sections of *Pontiac.* A third incident had its beginning when Parkman tried to fend off the attentions of a mysterious "Miss B," who attempted to interfere with his courtship of Ida, the daughter of Louis Agassiz. When Ida married another suitor in 1863, a cavalry officer who had been wounded in the Civil War, Parkman's keen disappointment appears to have been responsible for one more severe headache.

Fortunately these events of Parkman's "dark years" did not prevent him from regaining moderately good health and spirits. He even wrote lively letters to the press during the Civil War complaining of the mediocre leadership of the North. Near the end of this period Parkman wrote a long autobiographical letter to his friend, George Ellis, describing these agonizing years of his life and his desire to continue writing. There is reason to believe that his hobby of cultivating flowers, mentioned in a number of his letters, was one factor that diverted him from what might have been a complete collapse. In spite of all his difficulties Parkman managed, with tremendous effort and persistence, to conclude his volume on *The Pioneers of France in the New World.*

To Mary Dwight Parkman[1]

My Dear Cousin, [1852][2]

In your kind note of last Sunday, you wish that you might return me a helpful answer.—Your answer was doubly helpful. Your sympathy is a balm and a cordial—very unlike the condolences that one must sometimes endure from the common herd of kind acquaintances. I have pondered, also, the graver consolations which you offer. You express fully and clearly, views towards which I have long been tending. I believe profoundly in the truth of what you say. It is the only key [*to*] which can explain the mystery of life; and if even this key does not in every instance suffice, I am content to rest in the full assurance of a clear light hereafter. It was, many years ago, my prayer that my lot in life might be such as might tend most to the advancement of my highest interests, irrespective of happiness or suffering. It may be that the prayer is granted. I accept whatever destiny is assigned to me, and shall seek to draw from it whatever germs of good it may conceal. Yet I hold that, where action is possible, passive resignation is no virtue, but a weakness. At present I am fast bound—hand and foot—and there is little probability of my ever regaining even a moderate share of liberty. Yet if by God's mercy, a single finger is unloosed, its feeble strength will not lie idle. In *achievement* I expect to fail, but I shall never recoil from endeavour, and I shall go through life, hoping little for this world, yet despairing of nothing.

You have done me a great service. Truth from the lips of a friend [*is*] brings with it [*a more intimate*] double conviction. Your views are not hard and gloomy, for they embody a glorious hope.—You and I have certain vital aims and feelings in common, and I feel that a friendship founded on such sympathies must be enduring—not wholly dependent on the accidents of intercourse or separation.

Believe me, dear Mary, with earnest wishes for your happiness, most cordially and faithfully yours

F. P.

Bowdoin Sq.
Sunday M'n'g.

P.S. I began this note partly as a leave-taking, for I am off on Wednesday to Northampton, forwarded like a crate of brittle China.—You see that it is not your sex alone who put the essential part of their letters in the postscript.

ADDRESSED: Mrs. S. Parkman Tremont St.
MS: Parkman Family Papers, Harvard College Library.

[1] Mary Eliot Dwight (1821–79) was the sister of FP's classmate, Edmund Dwight, and the wife of Dr. Samuel Parkman (1816–54), FP's cousin. Dr. Parkman died in 1854 as the result of typhoid contracted from a patient. He was the son of FP's uncle, Samuel Parkman, who lived in Paris, the brother of FP's father, the Reverend Dr. Francis Parkman.

FP knew Mary Eliot Dwight in the 1840's through her brother Edmund, or "Ned." From a letter of August 16, 1848 (Parkman Family Papers, HCL), written by Mary Eliot Dwight, now Mrs. Parkman, to her husband, we find that FP was deeply attracted to her beautiful sister Ellen, but his illness appears to have interfered with his courtship. Ellen married Edward Twisleton in 1852 (Mary Dwight Parkman to "Fanny"

[April, 1852], Parkman Family Papers), and moved to England. After her husband's death Mary Dwight Parkman opened a school in Boston, where Grace, FP's elder daughter, was one of her pupils. In 1862, Mary Dwight Parkman went to England because of the illness of her sister Ellen; and in later years she lived a part of the time at Beverly Farms, where she became a close friend of Henry Adams and his wife. Mary Dwight Parkman was a woman of many talents, for she wrote secretly for the *Nation*, as letters to her from Wendell P. Garrison show. See Parkman Family Papers, HCL; Howard Doughty, "Parkman's Dark Years: Letters to Mary Dwight Parkman," *Harvard Library Bulletin*, Vol. IV (Winter, 1950), 53 n.; Harold Dean Cater (comp.), *Henry Adams and His Friends: A Collection of His Unpublished Letters* (Cambridge, 1947), 88–89; Ellen Twisleton Vaughan (ed.), *Letters of the Hon. Mrs. Edward Twisleton* . . . (London, 1928), ix, 146 ff.

[2] The postscript reference to FP's journey to Northampton to undergo several months of water-cure treatment confirms the fact that the letter was written in 1852.

To Lyman C. Draper

My Dear Sir — Boston, Jan 29th, 1852.

Your kind note reached me day before yesterday. I am glad you liked *Pontiac;* and I wish that when you have had time to read it more completely you will let me know whatever errors you may discover, in order that they may be corrected in another edition. I have done my best to secure accuracy, but you know that some mistakes are sure to creep in.[1] I have already discovered one in respect to the marriage of Sir Wm Johnson which I mean to have duly corrected.

For the present at least I shall leave Sir Wm's papers at peace for I am occupied in researches into the early history of Canada & Acadia concerning which I propose to manufacture a book in time. Looking earnestly for your forthcoming biographies I remain

Dear Sir
Very truly yours
F. Parkman Jr.

P.S. Can you direct me to any M.S. authorities relating to the French of Canada etc?

MS: Dictated, Draper Correspondence, State Historical Society of Wisconsin.

[1] For an excellent analysis of FP's "mistakes" and revisions, see "The Sources and Revisions of Parkman's *Pontiac*," by Howard H. Peckham, in *The Papers of the Bibliographical Society of America*, Vol. XXXVII (Fourth Quarter, 1943), 293–307.

To Evert A. Duyckinck

Dear Sir Boston, Jan 30*th*, 1852.

I enclose my subscription for the *Literary World*, 1852, in advance. I am engaged in preparing an historical work upon French Discovery and Settlement in Canada and Acadia, for which I have new and copious material. You may if you please announce my intention in the *Literary World*. With the best wishes for the continued success of your paper, I remain

Yours truly
F. PARKMAN, JR.

MS: Dictated, Duyckinck Papers, New York Public Library.

To Jared Sparks

My Dear Sir Boston, May 1st, 1852

I yesterday received your letter in which you request me to become one of the committee of examination in history. I should be very happy to do so were I not at present disabled by a lameness of the knee, which attacked me in the autumn and though at one time nearly cured, has returned again, so that I am now confined to my room. If the exigency is not pressing I hope I may be able before many months to attend to the duties of the committee. If however the place must be supplied immediately I am very sorry that I shall be obliged to decline it, as I cannot promise any active services earlier than next autumn or winter.

I have continued my historical studies, and made some progress, though of necessity very slowly. Poore[1] is at work for me, and I am not without hopes of securing his agency in Paris. I am now writing a chapter on Cartier's voyages. I shall take my time and do the work thoroughly or not at all.

I thank you for the copy which you sent me of your reply to the strictures on the writings of Washington.[2] I had already read the letters as they appeared in the papers, and it seems to me that they must prove satisfactory to any person who is not blinded by interest or prejudice. I hear them spoken of in this manner, and the *New York Herald* I observed a few days ago contained a remark to the same effect. What you have said in conclusion concerning the manner in which the edition was prepared, and the insight which is thus afforded even to the most ignorant of the vast research embodied in it, must convince every competent person that no edition of the writings of Washington is likely to be published hereafter which can compete in value and authority with that for which the public is indebted to you.

With the highest respect
yours truly
F. PARKMAN, JR.

MS: Dictated, Sparks Papers, Harvard College Library.

[1] Benjamin Perley Poore. See note 1, FP to Poore, April 21, 1856.

[2] For Sparks's editorial methods, see note 1, FP to Jared Sparks, April 29 [1842].

To John Langdon Sibley[1]

Dear Sibley — Boston, June 20th, 1852

I return the books due from me. Please give to the bearer the M.S. Catalogue of books on American History which I placed in your hands, with a view to discovering, in compliance with the President's request, what books were wanting in the American alcove. Will you let me know whether Biard's *Relation de la Nouvelle France,*[2] published in 1612, and also I think in 1615, is in the library. It is the first of the Jesuit writings on this country, and is of great interest. If it is not in the library I shall send for it immediately to Europe and it will eventually find its way to Cambridge.

Yours truly
F. PARKMAN, JR.

MS: Dictated, Autograph Collection, Harvard College Library.

[1] John Langdon Sibley (1804–85), clergyman and Harvard's assistant librarian (1841–56) and librarian (1856–77). Sibley is chiefly remembered for his most important literary work, *Biographical Sketches of Graduates of Harvard University in Cambridge, Massachusetts* (3 vols., 1873–85), and the accumulation of materials left for the continuation of his work.

[2] Father Pierre Biard (c.1567–1622), Jesuit missionary of Acadia and Maine. His *Relation* of 1611 was an important source for FP's *Jesuits*. See Vol. I, 69, 92, 117; II, 78.

To Mary Dwight Parkman

Bowdoin Sq.
Dear Cousin, Friday, Ap. 15, '53

Kate & I hoped, before the week closed, to gain you as a companion on one of our country drives, but the fates are adverse. I am visited by a sharp and sudden return of the original complaint in my knee—or, in other words, I am where I was at the first,—a close prisoner for an indefinite time. As Mercutio observed when Tybalt perforated him, the wound is not as wide as a church nor as deep as a well, but it is enough.[1] It does its work effectually, for, with me, a doom to bodily inaction is sure to become within a few days, a doom to mental inaction also—a bar to reading, thought, and often even to conversation. With a worthy object in view, I have never shrunk from any pain or danger which involved the body only. I have been well trained to endurance, yet I cannot look unmoved at the [*prospect*] future which now opens before me—a weary death in life, with the remembrance of worthy purposes unfulfilled, the consciousness of strong energies paralyzed, high hopes crushed to the dust—a blank of passive endurance, where courage and determination avail nothing.

You may ask why I am writing to you in this strain. It is simply that I am oppressed with reiterated and protracted disaster—that expression is a relief—and that I am in a mood to indulge myself with this relief. Not but that I can confront even the doom that lies before me; but I do so with a feeling which I will not here set down. I know but one other person to whom I would use this kind of language, and she has too much sorrow of her own, for me to increase it by my complaints. Before her, I am bound to assume what pretence of cheerfulness I can. There is something in you which attracts confidence—an influence which soothes, elevates, and strengthens. In a matter of this nature, I need not hesitate to address you, for I speak of a grief which, though strong and bitter, is simple and commonplace—clear in its length and its breadth. But, if it were a question of a higher and finer sorrow, I should more than hesitate, not as doubting in general the fulness of your sympathies, [*but*] true and cordial as I know them to be, but only doubting whether in such a case they would be extended to me. You may have been led to imagine that, [*from*] in such a form of sorrow, my nature would not be apt to find any very deep or lasting suffering. Do not think so. My failings are not those of a light mind or a faint heart. Perhaps it is needless for me to say this, for I have cause to think that you have endeavored to place a friendly interpretation on circumstances of my past life, which seemed to justify and even to demand an unfavorable construction.[2] Believe me, the kinder view is the more correct. If you had been my father confessor and I had then unfolded to you all my springs of feeling and action, you would have wondered at the strangeness and cruelty of the destiny which held me in its gripe, but you would, to say the least, have been no less my friend than now. This is a bare and unexplained assertion; but I am writing to one who will believe it. When I recall that most miserable period of my life, I am tempted to believe, with the Manichaeans, that the world is under the temporary rule of demons, and to admire the malignant ingenuity of their torments. Yet it is some gain to have passed through a complication of agonies, the remembrance of which makes the worst evils of later life seem bearable. The change from then to now is a change from tempest to calm. Out of that tempest, I saw a harbor of refuge; and looking for peace and rest, I found happiness. I owe unbounded gratitude to the source of that happiness, and I feel far more than gratitude.

This is the longest letter I have written with my own hand for seven years, and by far the most communicative I ever wrote. I hesitate even now whether to tear it or to seal it, but you will not fail to read it aright. It is meant for your eye alone. Send me a few lines in answer, and believe me, dear friend and cousin,

Sincerely yours
F. Parkman.

MS: Parkman Family Papers, Harvard College Library.

[1] Mercutio: "No, 'tis not so deep as a well, nor so wide as a church-door; but 'tis enough. . . ." Act. III, Scene 1, *Romeo and Juliet.*

[2] This may be an allusion to FP's former interest in Mary Dwight Parkman's sister, Ellen, in 1848. See note 1, FP to Mary Dwight Parkman [1852].

To Lyman C. Draper

My Dear Sir, Boston, Jan. 16, 1854.

I was very glad to hear from you and learn that you are still in the land of the living and engaged on your old labors. For my own part, I have been of late so much taken up with affairs of business[1]—

my health, too, being poor—that history has been of necessity postponed in great measure to other pursuits. This I hope, however, will not be permanent.

With regard to your proposed publication, I can only tell you the arrangement which I myself made and leave you to follow your own judgment. I had the work stereotyped at my own cost, and copyrighted in my name. I then arranged with a publisher to publish for me, allowing me 65 cents a copy, besides a number of copies for distribution, he to bear all the expense of printing, binding, etc. and to have the right of continuing to publish as long as he sold 500 copies a year. The plates and copyright remain mine.

I shall be happy to send a copy of Gorell's[2] journals and will do so, as soon as I can find an opportunity of looking over my Pontiac MSS which are in most admired disorder.

Very sincerely Yours.
F. PARKMAN

P.S. Many thanks for your kind intention of proposing my name for an honorary membership of the Wisconsin Hist. Soc. I shall value the honor. I hope you received a copy of "Pontiac" which I forwarded to you.

ADDRESSED: Lyman C. Draper Esq. Madison, Wisconsin.
MS: Draper Correspondence, State Historical Society of Wisconsin.

[1] Probably a reference to family financial affairs, which required FP's attention after the death of his father in 1852.

[2] See note 3, FP to C. C. Trowbridge, March 7, 1846.

To Charles Scribner[1]

Dear Sir, Boston, May 8, 1854

In reply to the questions in your circular of May 4th I beg to state that I was born on the 16th of September 1823, and was graduated at Harvard College in 1844. My father was a clergyman of Boston,[2]—my grandfather[3] a merchant of the same place—my great-grandfather[4] a clergyman of Westborough, Mass.

A volume written by me—called "Sketches of Prairie and Rocky Mountain Life"—was published in 1849, the contents having previously appeared in the Knickerbocker Magazine under the title of the

"Oregon Trail." It is a simple narrative of the incidents of a journey to the Rocky Mountains, with descriptions of scenery, Indian life, etc.

The "History of the Conspiracy of Pontiac" published in 1851 was designed as a tableau of forest life and Indian character. The subject was chosen with this view, and not on account of any peculiar historic importance attaching to it. Great pains were however taken to secure fullness and accuracy of historic detail.

These books and a few fugitive papers in reviews and magazines comprise all published writings from my pen. I am now collecting material for a general history of French discovery and colonization in North America.

Yr. obedient Servt.
FRANCIS PARKMAN

MS: Duyckinck Papers, New York Public Library.

[1] Charles Scribner (1821–71) founded in 1846 with Isaac Baker, Baker & Scribner, a publishing house which in 1878 became Charles Scribner's Sons. He was also founder and publisher of *Scribner's Monthly*.

[2] The Reverend Dr. Francis Parkman. See FP's letter to his father, note 1, July 22 [1841].

[3] Samuel Parkman (1751–1824), a wealthy Boston merchant, was father of eleven children, and the Reverend Dr. Francis Parkman, FP's father, was his eighth child.

[4] Rev. Ebenezer Parkman (1703–82), father of the merchant, Samuel, and fifteen other children, seven boys and eight girls. Rev. Ebenezer Parkman's diary was published by the Westborough Historical Society in 1899. Four of the original MS volumes are preserved at the American Antiquarian Society, and one at the Massachusetts Historical Society. FP's ancestry may be further studied in the "Parkman Family MSS," at the Boston Athenaeum; and David B. Hall, *The Halls of New England, Genealogical and Biographical* (Albany, N. Y., 1883), 304, traces FP's maternal ancestors back to Peter Chardon, a Huguenot merchant of Boston. Mary Bigelow Coffin's "Parkman Genealogy," a MS in my possession, is the best single account of FP's ancestral lineage.

To Henry Stevens[1]

Dear Stevens, Boston, Nov. 27, 1855

After a long and unavoidable delay, I am launched again on history—French colonization in N.A.—I sent you some years since a catalogue of books which I needed. Not hearing from you, I supposed that they were not to be had. I now send it in substance again. Several of them, especially those marked *x* are of great importance to me, and I will therefore give any price, not wholly unreasonable, for them. If you still do not know where they are to be had, can you refer me to any source whence I may possibly get information? and will you ascertain for me whether those marked are in the British Museum?

x Chevillard, (André) *Les Desseins de son Excellence le Cardinal de Richelieu pour l'Amerique.*[2]

x Charlevoix (Pierre F. Xavier) *Vie de Marie de l'Incarnation* Paris 1724 Ibid 1724–1725.[3]

xx Marie de l'Incarnation (la Reverende Mère) *Lettres de*— Paris 1681.[4]

x Martin,[5] *Vie de M. de l'Incarnation, première Supérieure des Ursulines de la N. France.* Paris 1677.

Les Veritables Motifs de Messieurs et Dames de la Société de Notre Dame de Montreal pour la conversion des Sauvages. Paris 1643–1644.[6]

xx La Tour, (l'Abbé Bertrand de) *Mémoire sur la Vie de M. de Laval, premier Evêque de Québec,* Cologne 1761.

Juchereau,[7] *Hist. de l'Hôtel Dieu de Québec.* Montauban, Paris, 1751.

Saumer, *Annales de l'histoire d'Institution des Religieuses Hospitalières de St. Joseph sous la regle de St. Augustin,* 1829, 8vo.

Prince (Paul) *Vie de la Mère de St. Augustin,* Paris, 1671.

Here you have the list. I shall be very glad if you can get any of them, or set me on the track. *Any* information relating to my subject, any suggestions of new authorities, printed or MS.—any hints of persons with whom to correspond, will be most welcome. May I beg an answer at yr. early convenience, as I shall have immediate occasion for all that I can get.

Pray where is yr. promised catalogue? It is too good an enterprise to be allowed to sleep. Push it on in your old go-ahead style, and don't forget your Yankee energy among the London fogs. Hoping soon to hear from you, I remain, Very sincerely Yrs.

F. PARKMAN

MS: Stevens Papers, William L. Clements Library.

[1] For a sketch, see note 1, FP to E. G. Squier, Nov. 3, 1851.

[2] Published in Rennes, France, 1659. French publications of the seventeenth and eighteenth centuries did not always include accent marks, and FP sometimes neglected them in his letters.

[3] There is also a third Paris imprint of 1735. FP obtained a copy of this work from the Fordham University Library

through John G. Shea as indicated in two brief notes by FP: to Shea, Oct. 4, 1857, Parkman Letters, Library of Congress; to George Bancroft, Nov. 27, 1857, BP, MHS. A number of other rare items FP borrowed from ecclesiastical libraries in Canada through the assistance of Abbé Casgrain and other Canadian friends. Casgrain later published a life of Marie de l'Incarnation (Quebec, 1864) which FP cites in *Jesuits*, I, 265.

[4] *Lettres de venerable Mere Marie de l'Incarnation premiere Superieure des Ursulines de Nouvelle France* (Paris, 1681), republished in Paris in 1857.

[5] Claude Martin (1619–96).

[6] Published in Paris in 1644.

[7] La Mère Juchereau de St. Ignace. Almost all these works were used by FP in writing the chapter on "Devotees and Nuns" in *Jesuits*, I, 259–80.

To Georges-Barthélemi Faribault[1]

Dear Sir, Boston, Jan. 15, 1856

I have been for some time engaged on a general history of French colonization in America, in connexion with which I have been under great obligation to your labors, more especially in your excellent catalogue of books relating to Canada. I learn that your researches have been continued since the publication of this work, and you will pardon, I hope, the liberty I take in requesting the aid of any suggestions with which you may favor me respecting books or documents not mentioned in your catalogue. My purpose is to investigate very thoroughly the subject I have taken in hand; and, if I find it necessary, I shall go to France to collect manuscripts. I hear that there is a large collection of historical manuscripts at Quebec. Pray what is its extent and character? Does it embrace all or nearly all the documents on Canada in the archives of Paris, or is it only a partial and limited collection? We have in Boston ten folio volumes of Paris MSS.—There are, as you know, still more at Albany, besides those which I have had from the same quarter. These, however, are not enough to spare me a personal visit to France, unless the collection at Quebec is comprehensive enough to fill out the hiatus. If you will furnish me with information on this or any other point connected with French American history, you will add to the obligation under which I already stand to you.

I have the honor to be respectfully yours

FRANCIS PARKMAN

(Boston, Mass.)

MS: Archives, Collège de Montréal, Montreal, Canada.

[1] Georges-Barthélemi Faribault (1789–1866), Canadian bibliographer and clerk of the provincial assembly of Quebec, made two large collections of books and

papers relating to Canadian history. The first was entirely destroyed by a fire of 1849 and the second partially destroyed by another fire of 1854. Faribault's *Catalogue d'ouvrages sur l'histoire de l'Amérique, et en particulier sur celle du Canada* (Quebec, 1837) is considered the first essay on Canadian historical bibliography.

To Edmund B. O'Callaghan[1]

My Dear Sir, [Boston, Jan. 18, 1856][2]

It would be ungrateful in me not to thank you for your labors in editing The Colonial Documents,—especially the last vol. of Paris Documents, to me invaluable. I trust that the legislature will be liberal enough to continue the work.

For my own part, I have been interrupted by a variety of other occupations, which joined with other impediments, have so kept back my historical pursuits that I have accomplished much less than I had hoped. I look forward to smoother sailing in the future; and, at all events, shall spare no effort.

Pray can you tell me of what the collection of French documents at Quebec consists, and how far it is a complete representative of the contents of the Paris archives? I believe that I have nearly all papers necessary for my first volume, but, for the rest, I must go in person to Paris unless the Quebec collections should be much larger than I take them to be. Any further information touching French American matters which may occur to you, will be, I need not say, very welcome.

I am indebted to the Regents of the University for the vols. of Colonial Docs. No one can appreciate better than yourself what an amount of time, labor, and expense their publication saves me.

Very sincerely and respectfully yrs.
Francis Parkman

MS: Papers of Edmund B. O'Callaghan, Library of Congress.

1 For a sketch, see note 4, FP to E. G. Squier, Nov. 18, 1849.

2 Dated by the postmark on the letter.

To Benjamin Perley Poore[1]

Mr Poore, Boston, April 21st, 1856.

I have at length made an examination throughout of the documents in the three volumes prepared for me by you. I find that, reckoning by the number of pages written upon, about three fourths of the whole are duplicates of documents in the ten vols. of MSS. collected by you in Paris for the State of Massachusetts; while of the remaining fourth, a portion are of no value, and several are in the Brodhead Collection[2] of New York.

The account stands as follows:

Vol. 1—Pages written on (by your own reckoning)—		502
In Mass. Collection	350	
Not in Mass. Collection	152	
	502	
Vol. 2—Pages written on		496
In Mass. collection	395	
Not " " "	101	
	496	
Vol. 3. Pages written on		362
In Mass. Collection	271	
Not " " "	91	
	362	
Total of pages written on, as reckoned by yourself		1360
Total of Pages.		1360
In Mass. Collection	1016	
Not " " "	344	
	1360	

You cannot fail to remember that the express basis of the agreement between us was that the documents should be distinct from those in the Massachusetts Collection. The duplicate papers are wholly useless to me. They do not even spare me the trouble of consulting the Mass. Collection since they form but a part of it, selected without special discrimination here and there. Your conduct can be characterized only as deliberately and audaciously fraudulent.

When last year, I settled with you for the work you expressed gratitude for the liberality with which you were treated and also for the unusual indulgence shown you in spite of your long delay.

The work was to have been done in January 1852, in fact it dragged on till the beginning of 1855.

Courtesy of J. Templeman Coolidge

Parkman's "fringed buckskin frock" and powder horn (above), Sioux shield, bow, and arrows, relics from the Oregon Trail journey of 1846.

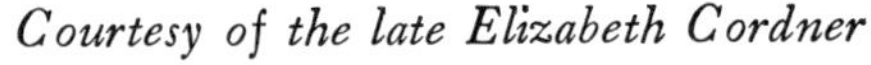

Courtesy of the late Elizabeth Cordner

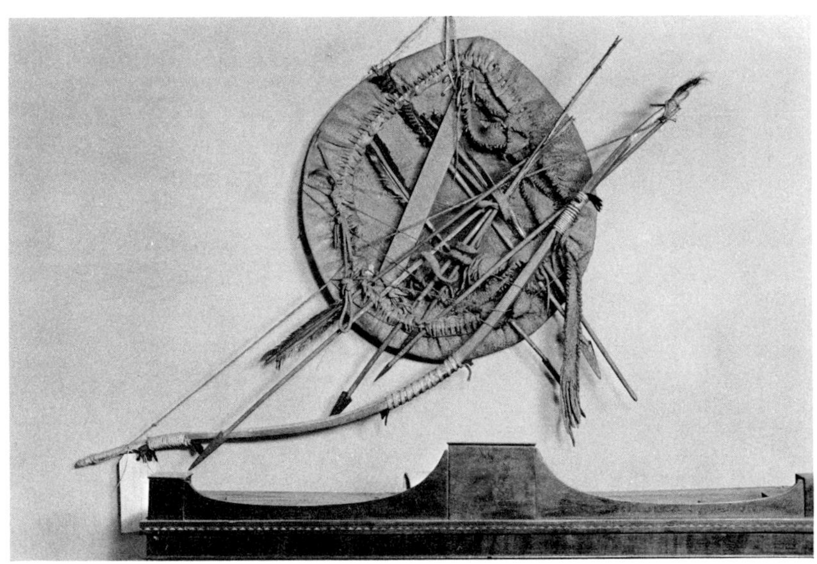

Francis Parkman in the early 1850's

Courtesy of the Massachusetts Historical Society

Four years ago, I advanced you $200. on a security merely nominal; and, on the next year, I lent you $250. without security. Your return for these favors was to avail yourself of the illness which for several years confined me within doors in order to practice on me a fraud which you would not have attempted had I been in a condition to give attention to your proceedings. You must be conscious that your behaviour was peculiarly mean and base.

When I settled with you last May, I allowed you for your work about $428.—an amount much beyond the terms of the compact.—and received from you a note of $97. being the balance, with the interest, of your debts to me. Aside from pecuniary loss, I should be unpardonable if I allowed you to enjoy the results of your artifice without exposure and punishment. I shall therefore pursue such steps against you as the case demands.

Unless you comply with the conditions I shall mention, I shall publicly expose you, and at once proceed to legal means for compelling restitution. At the same time, the note will be placed in proper hands for collection, with instructions to use the most stringent methods within the compass of the law. The conditions are,

1st You will find satisfactory security for the note, in stocks or other property to be placed in my hands, or in a name which shall be unquestionable.

2nd You deposited with me in 1852 a number of books and maps as security—though but a nominal one—for money advanced. They are of some, though not of great value. These you will make over to me.

3rd You will give me your note for $128. payable in three years, with full security for principal and interest.

If these things are promptly and satisfactorily done, I shall not demand payment of your first note till the new one becomes due.

As I am anxious that, under no possibility, you should fail to receive a full remuneration for services rendered, I have taken into consideration the value of notes and other illustrations, as well as every palliating circumstance that I have been able to discover in your course. I have placed the broadest possible interpretation on the agreement between us, and to escape any suspicions of unfairness, have given you so wide a margin, that the conditions offered still leave me greatly a loser. You need, therefore, expect no abatement; and a neglect after reasonable time to answer this letter will be taken as a refusal, and followed up accordingly. Mr. Francis Parker,[3] my attorney, will receive your reply, as I must decline communication with you.

MS: Dictated, duplicate, Parkman Papers, Massachusetts Historical Society.

[1] Benjamin Perley Poore (1820–87), journalist, editor, and author, met FP through Jared Sparks. In 1844 he formed a collection of transcripts of Paris documents for the Commonwealth of Massachusetts, and shortly thereafter assembled a collection for FP. In 1851, Poore contracted to make a larger collection of transcripts for FP; and, although it was to have been completed by the next year, Poore reported his financial difficulties in trying to purchase a Washington newspaper had caused delays. FP began to have misgivings about the whole affair, but finally accepted Poore's books as security for a loan (Poore to FP, Jan. 16, 1852, PP, MHS). Meanwhile, Poore sounded out Henry Schoolcraft as a prospective customer for his transcripts. In spite of Schoolcraft's refusal to buy them (see Schoolcraft's letters to FP of July, 1856, PP, MHS), Poore wrote FP that the ethnologist would surely "take these documents, if you do not." (Poore to FP, Dec. 30, 1852, PP, MHS.) FP also was irritated with Poore's insistence on making "an elaborate & artistic collection" on linen paper. Throughout these negotiations FP's eyesight and health were giving him great difficulty and reluctantly he made more financial advances to Poore. Finally, in 1856, when the collection was completed, FP discovered the duplicity of Poore and put the matter in the hands of his attorney, Francis E. Parker.

Upon receiving FP's letter of April 21, 1856, Poore blandly denied everything, stating, "I cannot but think that ill-health, or some other foreign influence, has prompted the use of such harsh and opprobrious language." Poore then proposed to put the matter before "three competent gentlemen, selected in the usual manner." (Poore to FP, April 25, 1856, PP, MHS.) Apparently the matter was handled in this fashion, for Poore obtained a receipt from FP for his books and in July, 1856, there was an "arbitration." ("R. M." to FP, June 13, 1856, PP, MHS.) Poore later served as clerk for the U. S. Senate Committee on Publication, and was in a position to delay the publication of Pierre Margry's documents. The sketch in the *DAB* describes him as a very popular person in Washington with a never ending stock of jokes and stories.

[2] John Romeyn Brodhead (1814–73), New York historian, who in Europe in 1841–45 collected eighty volumes of MS copies of documents relating to the colonial history of New York.

[3] Francis E. Parker (1822–86), FP's friend and attorney. See FP to W. C. Endicott, Feb. 4, 1886.

To Edmund B. O'Callaghan

My Dear Sir, Boston, June 19, 1856

Though I have not heard from you since my last, & though I have nothing in particular to write about, I don't like to let a pleasant correspondence lie in abeyance,—so snatch a leisure moment to scrawl this. I am devoting all the time and all the very limited eyesight and other needful appliances that I can command, to French American history. I learn from Mr. Faribault, of Quebec, that there are in

Canada 23 vols. of documents. I have a friend at Paris delving for me to find more. Your Ninth Volume is invaluable.[1] May the eyes of your legislators be opened that they may carry on so generous an enterprise to its full consummation! By the way, I thought that the Post Office had played me a trick not very rare with it, and failed to bring me a note from you touching a memoir on Champlain; but I found some time since that I had charged it unjustly. The note was carefully filed away with others upon similar matters. It reached me in the spring of 1853, at a time when I was very ill and in no plight to give it the attention it deserved. During that time—unhappily a long one,—when I was forced to suspend historical studies, I amused myself with writing a story.[2] Possibly you may have seen and smiled at the publisher's advertisement of it.

Pray, what is the address of Mr. Shea,[3] author of the *Catholic Missions?* I wish to correspond with him.

Believe me, dear Sir,

Always sincerely yrs,
FRANCIS PARKMAN

MS: Papers of Edmund B. O'Callaghan, Library of Congress.

[1] O'Callaghan published volume IX of the *Documents Relative to the Colonial History of New York* out of chronological order because he felt "certain scholars" had need of it. Presumably he did this to accommodate FP, as well as his friends among Canadian scholars, but the New York newspapers were highly critical of O'Callaghan's motives. As he wrote FP, he hoped "certain gentlemen" would appreciate the value of his work. O'Callaghan to FP, June 21, 1856, PP, MHS.

[2] FP's novel, *Vassall Morton* (Boston, 1856).

[3] FP did not wait for O'Callaghan's reply, for on this very day he opened correspondence with John G. Shea. See the letter that follows.

To John G. Shea[1]

Dear Sir, Boston, June 19, 1856

I beg to express to you now, as I shall hereafter do more publicly, my indebtedness to your historical labors in the "Discovery of the Mississippi" & the "Catholic Missions." Possibly you may be aware that I am still busied with studies of a kindred kind. I mean to write the history of French Colonization in America, including, of course a condensed view of the subjects which you have treated so excellently in detail. Your own research is so thorough that you will readily understand the time and labor required to explore completely so extensive a field. My aim is that nothing of any importance shall escape me. The Missions are a branch of the subject which I regard with very great interest. The more I examine them, the more I am impressed with the purity of motive, the devoted self-sacrifice, and the heroism of the early missionaries. Some of them seem to me, to fall no whit below the martyrs of the primitive church; and though not writing from the same point of view, my testimony to their virtues will often be no less emphatic than your own.

A friend of mine in Paris is collecting papers for me, besides those which I have already procured there. I wish also to get access to whatever may have value in Canada & elsewhere. M. l'Abbé Faillon[2] has kindly offered me assistance, as well as my respected friend, Bishop Fitzpatrick.[3] Can you give me any hints to aid my researches? You speak of a MS.—"*Mémoires sur la Vie & les Vertus des Pères Isaac Jogues* etc," and another—Buteux, "*la Prise de Père Jogues.*"[4] Pray are these in the hands of M. Viger[5] or of Father St. Martin?[6] Besides these, you mention various MSS of Chaumonot, Garnier, Dablon, Gravier, Villiers, and especially of Ragueneau, to which I would gladly gain access if possible.[7] Can you inform me where they now are, and of the inclination of the owners respecting them? Some of Dablon's, I know, are published, but there seems to be interesting matter from his pen still in manuscript.

You will readily believe that I shall take pleasure in acknowledging future as well as past obligations to you. The story of the Missions ought to be written both by a Catholic & by a Protestant. It is honorable alike to the Church and to mankind. For my own part, I shall spare no pains to make the chapters I shall give to it scrupulously truthful & accurate. You have helped me to discover statements requiring to be corrected or modified in "Pontiac"—a man writing without his eyes, as I then did, must expect to blunder a little—& I shall be glad to receive any farther hints in the matter that may occur to you.

Yrs. very truly,
FRANCIS PARKMAN.

MS: Parkman Letters, Library of Congress.

[1] John Gilmary Shea (1824–92) was almost an exact contemporary of FP's. Son of an Irish teacher and political leader, Shea studied law and was admitted to the bar in 1846 with only a grammar school education. Two years later he be-

came a Jesuit novice as a student at St. John's College, Fordham, and later at St. Mary's College in Montreal. In 1852 he left the order and in 1854 married. Shea has been called America's greatest Catholic historian, although his life is a story of penury and unprofitable scholarly writing. His first important historical work (dedicated to Jared Sparks), *Discovery and Exploration of the Mississippi Valley*, written in 1852, won recognition among historians; but his *History of the Catholic Missions among the Indian Tribes of the United States*, published in 1854, won FP's attention. Shea also edited twenty-six volumes of the Jesuit Relations (the Cramoisy Press series; see Joseph Sabin, *Dictionary of Books Relating to America* . . . [29 vols., New York, 1868–1936], XVI, 541–42), translated Charlevoix's *History and General Description of New France* (1866–72), and published a four-volume *History of the Catholic Church in the United States* (1886–92).

Shea proved to be an invaluable friend to FP, for their correspondence is filled with bibliographical information concerning rare works that Shea was able to borrow for FP from Catholic libraries. It was only after Shea exhibited his dislike for Pierre Margry by a hostile review of Margry's published documents that the friendly Parkman-Shea correspondence came to an end.

[2] Abbé Etienne-Michel Faillon (1799–1870), Sulpician historian who was born in France, visited Canada in 1849–50 and in 1854, and from 1858 to 1862 was a resident of Montreal. He was a voluminous writer, but is primarily known for his *Histoire de la colonie française en Canada* (Paris, 1865–66).

[3] John Bernard Fitzpatrick (1812–66), third bishop of Boston, was an acquaintance of FP's, and in the *Catholic Encyclopedia* is given credit for the conversion of FP's cousin, J. Coolidge Shaw. See also note 4, FP to his mother, April 15, 1844.

[4] The heroic martyrdom of the French Jesuit Isaac Jogues (1607–46) is dramatically portrayed in *Jesuits*, II, 118 ff. Father Jacques Buteux was a companion of Jogues. Buteux's work is cited by FP in *Jesuits*, II, 34 n., 49. Shea informed FP that St. Mary's College in Montreal had a volume relating to Buteux and Jogues made up of extracts from the Jesuit Relations. Shea to FP June 19, 1856, PP, MHS. This date of June 19 is probably an error, for FP's letter to Shea has the same date and was sent from Boston to New York.

[5] Jacques Viger (1787–1858), Montreal antiquarian, devoted his life to the collection of materials concerning Canadian history. FP found Viger's collection useful (*Pioneers*, II, 5, 62 n.), especially for items like Champlain's journal, of which Viger had a copy.

[6] Félix Martin (1804–86), Jesuit founder of St. Mary's College in Montreal and John G. Shea's teacher, wrote biographies of Jogues, Brébeuf, and Chaumonot, translated Bressani's narrative from Italian to French, and from about 1857 to 1862 was rector of the Jesuit residence in Quebec. After 1862 he went to France, the country of his birth, as the rector of a college.

[7] Chaumonot, Garnier, Dablon, Gravier, and Ragueneau, seventeenth-century Jesuit missionaries in Canada, are portrayed in FP's *Jesuits*. The Villiers mentioned here is Coulon de Villiers, French soldier and brother of Jumonville, who received George Washington's capitulation at Fort Necessity. *Montcalm and Wolfe*, I, 159 ff.; Shea to FP, June 19, 1856, PP, MHS.

To John G. Shea

My Dear Sir, Boston, July 17, 1856

It gave me particular pleasure to hear from you and to find you in the number of my correspondents. Though my historical pursuits have been very seriously interrupted, I trust now to carry them on to a satisfactory issue,—that is, to *exploiter* fully the field of French American history. If I find opportunity to assist you in your own researches it will always give me pleasure to do so.

With regard to the "Nicollet" papers,[1] I am by no means sure that I can tell you anything. Possibly they are identical with several letters & memoirs of Jesuits & others, now in the hands of Mr. Force at Washington. These relate chiefly to Louisiana & the West, and bear date from 1683 to 1708. There is one on the affairs of Canada, 1696. I have copies of them, which, on yr. next visit to Boston, will be at yr. service for examination or copying.

As to the Andastes,[2] your suggestion of their identity with the Conestogues[3] took me by surprise when I first observed it in your "Missions." On reflection you seem to me to be right. Their synonym of "Andastogues" has a close affinity with the Pennsylvania name. At all events, it is clear that they were not destroyed so early as has been asserted, or even completely conquered, for Denonville writes in 1686 that the Iroquois were then forming alliances with them. The Pennsylvanians sometimes called the Conestogues, "Mingoes." Dr. O'Callaghan (Paris Docs., 227, note) places the Andastes on the Susquehanna, & refers to a paper in the *Doc. Hist. of N. Y.* in which the position of the "Susquehanna Castle" is indicated. But this is probably nothing new to you.

You tell me that you have copies of Chaumonot's Autobiography & Journal, Perrot's Mem., Dablon's unprinted relations, & Garnier's letters.[4] Will you allow me, at some time within a year, the privilege of examining them? Anything relating to Champlain or to his wife will be of great interest to me.[5] Can you set me on the track of the discoveries concerning them of which you speak?

The vol. containing Ragueneau, Buteux, & the "Memoires" would be in my eyes a jewel of the first water, and I shall be under great obligation to you if you can enable me to see it.

I hope to visit Father Martin & M. Viger [*this*] next autumn; and would gladly embrace an opportunity to correspond with the Abbé Ferland,[6] if I knew his address. I hope to find much that is valuable in the collections made by M. Margry[7] for the Canadian government. Margry was to have written a life of La Salle, but I hear nothing of it, of late, except the faint allusion in Dussieux.

As for your papers on the Abnakis,[8] I must appeal to you against the publisher of the *Pilot;* who told me that you had written but four articles for that paper. These are all in my hands; and include, three chapters on the Church in N. England, together with the interesting letters of Bressani[9] & [. . .]. I have a strong impression that the publisher mistook, and that there are more behind. If so, will you have the kindness to send me a memorandum of them, that I may get them.

Though I am sometimes a tardy, I am, in this instance, by no means a forgetful correspondent. My very limited pittance of eyesight, makes a strict economy of that commodity indispensable, and often obliges me to long postponement. It will always give me pleasure to hear from you, & still more to meet you personally. Meanwhile believe me, Dear Sir,

With sincere esteem,
Yr. Obe't. Servant.
FRANCIS PARKMAN.

MS: Parkman Letters, Library of Congress.

[1] According to Shea's letter of June 19, 1856, to FP, PP, MHS, Joseph Nicolas Nicollet, the nineteenth-century explorer, borrowed a number of MSS from a church in Vincennes and later sold them to the U. S. government.

[2] Who lived on the lower Susquehanna and were decimated by the Iroquois as well as by disease. *Jesuits*, I, 36.

[3] FP identifies the Conestogas as Andastes in *ibid.*, I, 36 n. A last remnant of the Conestogas was massacred by the Paxton Boys in 1763. See *Pontiac*, II, 130 ff.

[4] Jesuit missionaries except Nicholas Perrot (1644–1718), the famous *voyageur*, author of *Mémoire sur les Moeurs, Coustumes et Relligion des Sauvages de l'Amérique Septentrionale.* A Paris edition was published in 1864. See also *Frontenac*, 106 ff.

[5] Shea in his letter of June 19, cited above, mentioned having information on Champlain's wife, who became an Ursuline nun. See also *Pioneers*, II, 249.

[6] See note 1, FP to Abbé J.-B.-A. Ferland, September 10, 1856.

[7] Pierre Margry, FP's lifelong friend, a specialist in maritime and colonial French history, was born in Paris in 1818, and died in the city of his birth in 1894, one year after FP's death. When at the age of thirty he assisted Lewis Cass, then U. S. minister to France, in collecting documents, he acquired an interest in archival research. Later at Cass's recommendation he was employed by John R. Brodhead in a similar task. Probably at the time Margry was associated with Brodhead, he obtained work at the Archives de la Marine et des Colonies, where he eventually came to be the officer in charge.

Stimulated by his work with Cass and Brodhead, Margry embarked on his own project of collecting transcripts of documents on French colonial history. He soon amassed a vast accumulation from the Archives of the Marine and Colonies and from other repositories. One authority who has recently examined the large Margry collection preserved in the Bibliothèque Nationale concludes that Margry tired of the laborious task of copying and filched originals from the archives under his care. Be this as it may, Margry's manuscript volumes are protected for posterity while some of the collections he used have been exposed to hazards of fire and neglect.

The story of FP's relations with Margry is told in FP's letters. The $10,000 Congressional appropriation for the publication of Margry's fat six-volume series, *Découvertes et établissements des Français dans l'ouest et dans le sud de l'Amérique Septentrionale (1614–1754), Mémoires et Documents Originaux* (Paris,

1876–88), was passed, largely as a result of FP's efforts. Margry's volumes represented only a small part of his collection, but the La Salle materials were of tremendous interest to FP, enabling him to bring out his final revision of 1879. FP's personal copies of the Margry volumes in the Harvard College Library are filled with marginalia. Some of the documents, as FP's marginal comments reveal, were duplicated in O'Callaghan's *New York Colonial Documents*. John G. Shea gave Margry a thorough drubbing for this duplication in a hostile twenty-four-page review, *The Bursting of Pierre Margry's La Salle Bubble* (New York, 1879), a pamphlet reprint from the *New York Freeman's Journal*.

A sketch of Margry and a list of his publications is found in *Larousse du XXe Siècle*, edited by Paul Augé, IV (Paris, 1931), 679. Much additional material regarding Margry's life is found in the Margry letters to FP, PP, MHS, and in FP's letters to Margry.

[8] Or Abnaki, a name applied to the Algonquian tribes of New England living in Maine along the course of the Kennebec and other rivers.

[9] Father Joseph Bressani, Italian seventeenth-century Jesuit, a Canadian missionary. Félix Martin translated his journal from Italian to French, and John G. Shea translated the work from French to English.

To George Bancroft[1]

My dear Sir, Boston, Aug. 6, 1856

Your very kind reply to my note reached me yesterday. I am, as you suppose, familiar with the Brodhead MSS., in regard to which my excellent friend Dr. O'Callaghan has given me every facility. I have tried vainly to get something at Rome, but the Jesuits are very reserved, & Creuxius,[2] the Relations, & a few miscellaneous MSS are all that I have access to in regard to them. I hope, however, to get more at Paris. You speak of your vols. given you by Mr. Biddle on the Coligny enterprise in Florida.[3] This is to me a matter of peculiar interest. If agreeable to you, I would regard it as a great privilege to be permitted to examine them, a favor which I need not say I should find pleasure in acknowledging.

The work I have undertaken is one of great labor, but I am more & more satisfied that it will repay all pain necessary to accomplish it thoroughly. I shall spare no effort to do so, either as respects copiousness of material, or exactness of statement.

I have the honor to be
Very truly yours
Francis Parkman

ms: Bancroft Papers, Massachusetts Historical Society.

[1] George Bancroft (1800–91), Harvard class of 1817, Ph.D., Gottingen, 1820, was from 1867 to 1874 U. S. minister to Berlin. Bancroft's *History* (see

Introduction) was extremely important in FP's growth as a historian, and a long correspondence took place between the two men.

[2] Or Du Creux, *Historia Canadensis* (Paris, 1664), a summary of the yearly Relations of the Canadian Jesuits.

[3] Gaspar de Coligny's sixteenth-century Huguenot colony in Florida. See *Pioneers*, I, 22 ff.

To Edmund B. O'Callaghan

Boston,
My Dear Sir, Monday Aug 11, 1856

Many thanks for yr. kind note, & for the valuable gift which accompanies it. I shall prize it for its own sake & the giver's.

I feared that all application for the Lenox papers[1] would fail; and must content myself with borrowing. As for the other books, it is rather the spirit than the bodily possession that I crave, & should my kind friend, Bishop Fitzpatrick, fail in finding them, I shall be quite consoled if I can succeed in borrowing them.

With sincerest regard yr. much obliged friend

FRANCIS PARKMAN

MS: Papers of Edmund B. O'Callaghan, Library of Congress.

[1] James Lenox (1800–80), New York bibliophile and philanthropist whose great collection is now owned by the New York Public Library, reprinted a number of the Jesuit Relations. Although FP uses the term "Lenox papers," he may have referred to the "Lenox prints." See FP to G. W. Curtis, Oct. 12, 1875. FP, in *Jesuits*, II, 270 n., cites one of these, the *Relation* of 1676. Sabin, *Dictionary of Books*, XVI, 541, indicates Lenox printed only sixty copies of selected *Relations*.

To Abbé Jean-Baptiste-Antoine Ferland[1]

Reverend Sir, Boston Sept. 10, 1856

It gives me great pleasure to find myself in communication with a gentleman so well versed in a subject which I have, I may say from boyhood, regarded with the utmost interest. The early history of Canada is so full of dramatic incident, and noble examples of devoted heroism, that it is a matter of wonder that American writers have, until lately, so little regarded it. For my own part, I shall spare no effort to place it in its just light.

I am glad that the Canadian government have procured copies of documents in the French archives. Can you inform me whether these are understood to comprise *all* relating to Canada in the offices of Paris? If so, I shall be spared a visit to France. I mean to spend a part of the winter in Canada in search of material, and hope, among other things, to find a copy of your *Notes sur les Régistres*, and of your critique on Brasseur, of which I have hitherto failed to gain possession.

I need not say that I shall hold myself greatly your debtor if you can give me any suggestions which may aid me in my inquiries after material. There is no more important period in Canadian history than that of the civil and ecclesiastical organization, after the colony passed out of the hands of the "Hundred Associates." Any papers bearing upon this period would be particularly valuable.

Your *Notes*, I trust, will be continued. I have seen only the first number, & this is of so much value that a suspension of the publication would be very much to be regretted.

I have the honor to be

Very respectfully yours,
FRANCIS PARKMAN

MS: Gagnon Collection, Bibliothèque de la ville de Montréal.

[1] Abbé Jean-Baptiste-Antoine Ferland (1805–65), Canadian priest and historian, the first professor of Canadian history in a Canadian university, joined the faculty of Laval as professor in 1855, and in 1864 became a dean of the university. As indicated in FP's letter, Ferland published *Observations sur un ouvrage intitulé "Histoire du Canada," par M. L'Abbé Brasseur de Bourbourg* (Quebec, 1853), and *Notes sur les régistres de Notre Dame de Québec* (Quebec, 1854); but his best-known work is *Cours d'histoire du Canada* (2 vols., Quebec, 1864–65).

To Jacques Viger[1]

Sunday Ev'n'g—Beaver Hall
[October 13, 1856][2]

Dear Sir,

I return the first volume of the *Petit Régistre*, & the memoir of Father Martin, with many thanks. Enclosed with them is a copy of the work of which I spoke, and which I beg you to accept.

I shall set out for Ottawa tomorrow morning, and on my return, in a few days, I shall have the honor of calling on you, when I hope to be permitted a farther examination of the valuable manuscripts in your collection.

Very respectfully
Your obliged Servant
FRANCIS PARKMAN

ADDRESSED: Monsieur le Commandeur J. Viger 24 Notre Dame St.
MS: Panet Collection, Seminary Archives, Laval University.

[1] See note 5, FP to J. G. Shea, June 19, 1856.

[2] Date on MS has been placed in brackets. FP's *Journals*, II, 517 ff., indicate that he did visit Canada in 1856.

To George H. Moore[1]

8 Walnut St. Boston
Nov. 28 [1856][2]

My dear Sir,

I return to you the subscription list which Mr. Williams sent me. I am beating up here for more names, and this morning have got 23 copies subscribed for.—Mr. Sparks, 4, Mr. Prescott, 4, C. F. Adams, 3, etc. etc. Can't you get a few more? The thing ought to go on. It would be scandalous if it failed for want of encouragement. I hope to get 50 copies engaged in Boston. New York is able to do a great deal better if she will.

Very sincerely Yrs.
F. PARKMAN

MS: Miscellaneous Manuscript Collection, New-York Historical Society.

[1] George Henry Moore (1823–92), librarian, historian, bibliographer, in 1849 was elected librarian of the New-York Historical Society, a position he held until 1879, when he became librarian of the Lenox Library. A record of Moore's activities is found in R. W. G. Vail, *Knickerbocker Birthday* (New York, 1954). FP was well known at the New-York Historical Society, for he had been elected a corresponding member as early as 1847. FP to John Jay, Feb. 1, 1847, Miscellaneous MSS, Parkman folder, New-York Historical Society.

[2] This letter is dated by Buckingham Smith's *Collección de Varios Documentos para la Historia de la Florida* of 1857. A prospectus of the volume with names of subscribers is in the Miscellaneous Manuscript Collection, New-York Historical Society. FP, as indicated in the letter, obtained twenty-three subscriptions, including four for Jared Sparks, four for William H. Prescott, and three for Charles Francis Adams. Smith, who was born in Florida in 1810 and died in New York in 1871, obtained a portrait of Menéndez for FP as well as copies of MSS from Spanish archives while secretary of the U. S. legation in Spain, 1854–58. (*Pioneers*, I, 6). See also FP to C. E. A. Gayarré, June 27, 1857. There is reason to believe that FP would have portrayed the Spaniards in a more favorable light in *The Pioneers* if he had had access to more documentary material from Spanish archives. See Richard Sonderegger, *Francis Parkman* (Mexico, D. F., 1951), 27.

To Louis-Joseph Papineau[1]

8 Walnut St. Boston
Dec. 23, 1856

My Dear Sir,

On returning, a day or two since, from New York, I found a manuscript & letter which you have had the kindness to send me. Pray accept my cordial thanks for the favor, and for the no less valued expressions of good will with which it is accompanied. I have read the paper with interest, & find in it much that will be of service to me. If you will permit me to keep it during the winter, I will return it to your hands early in the spring.

Of many most agreeable recollections of Canada, I have none to which I revert with greater pleasure than to the day under your roof at Monte Bello. Believe me, dear Sir, I prize as no common privilege the opportunity which enabled me to become acquainted with yourself and your family, an acquaintance which I trust may be hereafter continued. I hope, most sincerely, that your southern journey may be a means of restoring Mademoiselle Papineau to health. Shall you not visit Boston on your return? If so, I beg you will not forget to inform me of your being here.

With my compliments and best regards to Madame, I have the honor to be

With the highest esteem
Your friend & Servant
FRANCIS PARKMAN

MS: Papineau and Bourassa Papers, Archives of the Province of Quebec.

[1] Louis-Joseph Papineau (1786–1870), French Canadian leader in the *Patriote* uprising of 1837 and for many years speaker of the legislative assembly, had one of the best libraries in Canada (including copies of items from Paris archives) at his seigneury *La Petite Nation*, at Montebello, where FP saw him in 1856.

To George Bancroft

Dear Sir,

Boston, Dec. 26, 1856

I return, with thanks, the documents which you were so kind as to lend me. The first, Ribault, is a transcript from the rare Hakluyt of

1582,[1] which the Hakluyt Society have recently printed among their collections. Like the journal of Cartier's 3d voyage, it owes its preservation to an English editor and translator. Gaillard's interesting notice is the source whence the writer of the sketch of De Gourgues in the Biby. Universelle[2] drew his information. I had sought for it in vain till I saw this copy. The manuscript of the Vicomte de Gourgue[s] is referred to by Charlevoix. Both he and Basanier make it the basis of their narrative. With a few trivial points of difference, it is the same with the two duplicate manuscripts preserved in the Bibliothèque Impériale. The latter, though substantially the same, differ[s] in title. One of them called "La Reprise de la Floride, par Rob. Prevost" is printed in Ternaux's collection, though, in all but spelling, nearly identical with Mr. Biddle's MS. I hold it an advantage to be able to refer to the latter, as to a fountain head of authority.[3]

In connection with your very obliging offer to mediate for me with Archbishop Hughes,[4] I beg to say that any documents bearing on the French in North America, prior to 1763 will be very welcome to me. I have reason to think that there are at Rome papers relating to the Jesuit and Franciscan missions in Canada and Louisiana. The period of the erection of Canada into a bishoprick and the nearly contemporary change in the civil administration—A.D. 1663—is one of great moment in the history of the country, and papers illustrating it may perhaps be found at Rome. My object being a general and not an ecclesiastical history, matters relating merely to the *internal affairs* of the Church do not fall within my province. I may add that my inquiries have been most kindly and freshly assisted by Bishop Fitzpatrick of Boston, Father Martin, S.J. the Grand Vicar Cazeau, of Quebec, and other eminent ecclesiastics. I shall regard it as a signal favor, if, through your kind word, I may be put in the way of adding to my store of information from the Roman archives.

With compliments to Mrs. Bancroft, I remain

Very respectfully,
Your obliged F. PARKMAN

MS: Bancroft Papers, Massachusetts Historical Society.

[1] *Divers voyages touching the discovery of America, and the islands adjacent*, edited by John W. Jones and printed for the Hakluyt Society (London, 1850). Jean Ribaut's journal is included in this reprint. See also *Pioneers*, I, 37–38 n.

[2] FP probably refers to a manuscript in the Bibliothèque Nationale describing the

expedition of Dominique de Gourgues against the Spaniards. See *Pioneers*, I, 5, 158 ff.

[3] FP's notes in *Pioneers*, I, 158–62 give further information on the points raised in this paragraph. FP's main source for his dramatic narrative of the De Gourgues expedition was a MS, presumably written by the soldier himself. Here, in his letter of December 26, 1856, FP discusses variations in copies of the MS.

[4] John Hughes (1797–1864), first archbishop of New York and a powerful Roman Catholic leader, is credited in the *Catholic Encyclopedia* with founding the Catholic school system. During the Civil War the government sent him to France to persuade Napoleon III not to recognize the Confederacy. In his role as a diplomat Archbishop Hughes probably came to know Bancroft. The Archbishop was pleased, he said, to aid Bancroft's friend, but reported that there was no particular friendship between the Holy See and France during Canada's colonial period, and communications from Canadian church representatives were sent to Paris, not Rome. The only exception would be Jesuit records. The Archbishop's letter of Feb. 18, 1857 was sent to FP by Bancroft (PP, MHS), and FP replied to Bancroft: "Many thanks for your obliging intercession in my behalf. In spite of what the Archbishop says, there are no doubt papers at Rome, could one but get at them. Whether the attempt succeeds or not, I am not the less a debtor to your kindness." FP to George Bancroft, Feb. 20, 1857, BP, MHS.

To Charles E. A. Gayarré[1]

Dear Sir, Boston, Feb. 4, 1857

I have the honor to enclose to you a note from Mr. Benj. F. French,[2] which I should have sent before, had not the severe illness of several of my family put all my correspondence in arrears. I am engaged in a general history of the French Empire in America, a subject which I think worthy of the most elaborate research. Just at present, I am at work upon La Salle & his discoveries. I have not yet reached the Colonization of Louisiana, a subject upon which I shall be under very great obligation to your works. It will be some time, however, before I take up this part of the history, and before finishing it, I mean to explore the archives of Paris. As to Mr. French's very friendly suggestions, they are of a kind which I should never have ventured to make for myself, and are entirely a result of his own goodwill. You will see from what I said above that though an easy access to the documents in the State Department of Louisiana would hereafter be of the utmost advantage to me, yet, for the present, I am busied in another quarter. Perhaps, however, you can put me on the track of some papers relating to La Salle besides those published in your History. The Jesuits, the Iroquois wars, & other kindred matters still remain to be written up. I have a great mass of papers on them.

M. Pierre Margry writes me that he made a catalogue of all papers on Louisiana in the Archives de la Marine, and that it was purchased by some one in America. Pray have you ever heard of such a catalogue? Is there not such a thing in one of your public offices?

I have the honor to be,

Yours truly
F. PARKMAN

MS: Charles E. A. Gayarré Papers, Department of Archives, Louisiana State University.

[1] Charles Étienne Arthur Gayarré (1805–95), the New Orleans historian, wrote *Histoire de la Louisiane* (2 vols., 1846–47), published in French in order to preserve the exact form of the original documents. Although it is little more than a series of extracts linked by a thread of narrative, FP found this work valuable. Gayarré's *Romance of Louisiana* (1848) was a mixture of history and fiction; but his later works united historical accuracy with vivid narrative: *Louisiana: Its History as a French Colony* (1852), and another, more formidable work on the same subject in 1854 together with additional histories of Louisiana under Spanish and American rule. Gayarré reported to FP in a letter of June 16, 1857, PP, MHS, that he had examined the State Archives at Baton Rouge and found nothing "beyond what was already known to me, relative to the subject of your investigations." At the close of his letter Gayarré expressed much interest in FP's theme of a history of the French empire in America, which should, he said, be translated into French. See also FP's reply to Gayarré of June 27, 1857.

[2] Benjamin Franklin French (b. 1799), a wealthy southern bibliophile who gave his library to the Fiske Free Library of New Orleans and later moved to New York, and was editor of a series of memoirs and narratives relating to Louisiana, published between 1846 and 1875. One of French's volumes, *Historical Collections of Louisiana* (5 vols., New York, 1852), IV, includes narratives of missionaries who accompanied La Salle. In the HCL copy which belonged to FP, we find his marginalia opposite French's explanatory footnotes, including such comments as "nonsense," "not so." In French's letter of introduction which FP mentions, French proposed that Gayarré persuade the Louisiana legislature to pass a resolution authorizing the sending of Louisiana MSS to FP through the Massachusetts State Department. Gayarré, a member of the legislature at this time, was unsuccessful in this project because of "politics," or hostility toward Massachusetts abolitionists. B. F. French to C. E. A. Gayarré, Jan. 1, 1857, Gayarré Papers, Dept. of Archives, Louisiana State University; B. F. French to FP, March 4, 1857, PP, MHS.

To Pierre Margry[1]

8 Walnut St. Boston,
Feb. 11, 1857

Dear Sir,

My long delay in answering your obliging communication has been the result of severe illness in my family, by which my correspondence has been thrown into arrears. This will be my excuse for so long delaying to send to you the enclosed note from Mr. Hunt, which reached me some time after Mr. Fairbanks left Boston.

I perfectly understand the difficulties under which you labor in respect to the documents under your charge, and the necessity of strict care & method. The works on which you are engaged will be of the greatest service to my researches. I shall be very glad to hear more particularly of their scope & character, & especially if there is a prospect that any portion of them will be published within this year or the next. I have caused copies to be made of the first volumes of the two collections made by you at the instance of M. Faribault. These, together with the Brodhead Collection, & that made by Mr. Poore, are all at my command, besides various papers supplied by my friend M. Papineau & other gentlemen *in Canada. These papers relate chiefly to the missions.* [*if however*] *I intend to publish at first, two volumes, extending to the year 1690.*[2] These, I hope, will be ready in about three years. If necessary, I shall visit Paris before the volumes are finished. On this point, no one is so well able to inform me as a gentleman, like yourself, so intimately acquainted with the contents of the archives of your own & other departments. Will you therefore have the kindness to tell me whether, in your opinion, I should find at Paris much additional material to elucidate the History of Canada from its discovery to 1690? From what I have said, you may form a tolerable idea of the papers already in my hands.

I shall expect your proposed works with the greatest interest, for I regard them as absolutely indispensable; & I trust that no unfortunate accidents will retard their publication.

I am, sir, with high esteem

Your Obedient Servant
FRANCIS PARKMAN

MS: Vignaud Papers, William L. Clements Library.

[1] See note 7, FP to John G. Shea, July 17, 1856.

[2] Three lines have been heavily underlined in the MS, probably by Margry. The two words in brackets are deletions by FP. See Key to Editorial Apparatus.

To Louis-Joseph Papineau

Dear Sir, Boston, Feb. 15, 1857

I return with many thanks the manuscript which you were so kind as to lend me. I find facts in it that are new and interesting. I have sent to Paris for copies of several of the documents mentioned in

Ida Agassiz, daughter of Louis Agassiz, Harvard's famous naturalist, the girl Parkman once hoped to marry.

Courtesy of the Massachusetts Historical Society

Parkman's writing guide or "gridiron," his colored spectacles, and his ink stand. At upper right is one of Parkman's notebooks; at lower right, one of his account books, in which he recorded his daily expenditures.

Courtesy of the late Elizabeth Cordner

your list. The quarto vol. is undoubtedly written by Perrot. I have known of its existence, but hitherto have been unable to get a copy.

I hope, very sincerely, that the health of Mademoiselle has been improved by your southern tour. We have just been so unhappy as to lose a little child, a boy of two years old, by scarlet fever.[1]

Hoping for the renewal of an acquaintance which I shall always regard as a privilege, I remain, dear Sir,—with compliments to Madame—

Very respectfully Yours
FRANCIS PARKMAN

MS: Papineau and Bourassa Papers, Archives of the Province of Quebec.

[1] Francis Parkman III (1854–57).

To George H. Moore

My Dear Sir, Boston March 5, 1857

Yr. two letters came yesterday. Thank you for your kind intentions respecting the vols. of yr. collections. Appleton says he will send you the full list.

I shall take pleasure in laying yr. request for the Duke of York document before the Soc. which meets a week from today. I am sorry that such a step is necessary, as it involves delay; but our regulations require it. I cannot doubt that all will be as you wish. You may rely on all I can do.

It would give me much pleasure to read a paper before the N. Y. Hist. Soc. & I should regard it as an honor, but for the present at least, I must decline it; if for no other reason than the conclusive one that I could not read a word by artificial light.

The diploma is all right. If anything has been omitted on my side, I will supply it when I next come to N. Y.

As I was writing the above, the "Articles of the Church of Leyden" were brought to me, for which pray accept my thanks. They will certainly excite interest here.

I will write again after the meeting. Meanwhile [I] am

Very truly yours,
F. PARKMAN

P.S. If necessary, I shall apply for the copy in my own name.

MS: Miscellaneous Manuscript Collection, New-York Historical Society.

To Lyman C. Draper

My Dear Sir, Boston, June 2, 1857

Pray accept my thanks for the two vols. of Mr. Smith's[1] history which were kindly sent me on behalf of the Hist. Soc. I have examined them with interest. The documentary parts are especially valuable. I hope soon to send to your very active & vigorous young society some documents bearing on the early history of your region. I shall remember you in my researches, & if anything comes to hand that may especially interest you, you shall know it.

I was glad to see by yr. circular that your league with Mr. Lossing[2] still continues & will soon issue in the publication of some of yr. treasures—but don't make the book merely *popular*.

I have never seen Martin's Historical Discourse. Can you spare me a copy?

I have just been writing La Salle's history, on wh. I have a great mass of new material;—it is to be incorporated in my general work.

Very sincerely Yrs.
F. PARKMAN

P.S. You ask if I have received the publications of yr. Soc. You sent me a pamphlet—the first Annual Report of Executive Committee 1855. This is all I have seen.

MS: Draper Correspondence, State Historical Society of Wisconsin.

[1] Probably William R. Smith's *History of Wisconsin* (Madison, 1854).

[2] Benson J. Lossing, a successful New York popularizer of American history, was Draper's literary partner for proposed volumes on Daniel Boone and other frontiersmen. The partnership lasted some sixteen years without tangible results. Hesseltine, *Pioneer's Mission: The Story of Lyman C. Draper*, 128 ff.

To John G. Shea

My Dear Mr. Shea, Boston, June 14 '57

M. Ferland has just sent me *Perrot* wh. I shall examine with interest. I have another shorter MS. of Perrot, wh. shall be at yr.

service. It is on the movements of the various tribes after the dispersion of the Hurons. I am going to Quebec for a few days. Can I serve you there?

Truly yr. friend
F. PARKMAN

MS: Redpath Library, McGill University.

To Charles E. A. Gayarré

Dear Sir, Boston, June 27, 1857

I beg leave to acknowledge yrs. of June 14,[1] & to thank you for the information contained in it. I have consulted with much advantage your documentary volumes published in 1846, as well as your "Louisiana," 1851, & "History of La. under the French Domination," 1854. I hope you have not abandoned this sort of research. There is now at Madrid a gentleman, Mr. Buckingham Smith,[2] of St. Augustine, engaged in investigation of the Spanish archives from which he has unearthed a mass of most interesting material, which he is beginning to print in the original. If these matters still interest you, you will find him a most useful correspondent. He is attached to the American legation, & has, I am told gained the confidence of the government to a degree which gives him free way to the archives. I trust he will be retained in his place, where he is doing a work for which he is every way admirably fitted.

Sincerely & Respectfully
Yours
FRANCIS PARKMAN

ADDRESSED: Hon. Charles Gayarré New Orleans.
MS: Charles E. A. Gayarré Papers, Department of Archives, Louisiana State University.

[1] FP's slip of the pen. Gayarré's reply is dated June 16, 1857. See note 1, FP to C. E. A. Gayarré, Feb. 4, 1857.

[2] See note 2, FP to George H. Moore, Nov. 28 [1856].

To John G. Shea

My Dear Mr. Shea, Boston, Sept. 25 1857

I have not seen the Oswego verses, & shall be glad of a copy.—I was glad to see that the Canadian Parliament have voted to take 50 copies of F. Martin's researches in the Huron country—so I hope we can see it in print. Gravier[1] seems to me excellently brought out, & I hope we shall get more. By the way, the Jogues papers will facilitate my operation in a matter, which though, episodical, is of such dramatic interest—this is the view of a heretic—that I am tempted to give it more space than is consistent with just historic proportion.

Truly Yr. friend
F. PARKMAN

MS: Parkman Letters, Library of Congress.

[1] Shea sent FP a copy of Jacques Gravier's *Relation*, probably that of 1693–94. Shea to FP, Sept. 14, 1857, PP, MHS. For an account of the early printings of the Jesuit *Relations*, see Winsor, *History*, IV, 295–316.

To George William Curtis[1]

My Dear Mr. Curtis Boston, Oct. 12 1857

Thanks for your kind recollection of my hobby in the matter of the Lenox prints.[2] They ought to be more accessible, as they are of a very decided value. Mr. L. was good enough to send them to me about three weeks ago—a great piece of good luck for me, as I had been at a loss how to get them, & Mr. L. seldom lets them out of his strong box.

All is topsy turvy here; the oldest respectabilities go down,—those who stood best & were "best" in all the senses of that abused word. There is a shade over us all.[3] Those who were rich yesterday & deserved to be so have nothing to stand on today but their own worth. Those who go down have at least the consolation of going in good company.

Yrs. truly
F. PARKMAN

MS: In the possession of the editor.

[1] George William Curtis (1824–92), American man of letters, orator, and friend of Charles Eliot Norton, James Russell Lowell, and Ralph W. Emerson, wrote "The Easy Chair" for *Harper's Magazine* and after 1863 was editor of *Harper's Weekly*. He had been in the Brook Farm community (1842–43) and was one of the first to fight for the enfranchisement of women, a movement that

FP opposed. However Curtis and FP agreed on civil service reform, and when Curtis in 1856 married Anna Shaw of Staten Island, FP's cousin, a friendship developed between the two men.

[2] Reprints of the Jesuit *Relations* by James Lenox. See Winsor, *History*, IV, 295 ff.; note 1, FP to E. B. O'Callaghan, August 11, 1856. Lenox probably kept the reprints in his "strong box" because he printed a limited number of copies.

[3] As a result of the Panic of 1857, a depression following the boom of the decade after the Mexican War. The failure of the Ohio Life Insurance Company of Cincinnati in August, 1857, marked the beginning of the panic in the urban centers of the Middle West and East.

To Lyman C. Draper

My Dear Sir, Boston March 14, 1858

I have received a very valuable vol. of the Wisconsin Historical Series, for which pray accept my thanks. Your society is showing an admirable degree of vitality, & in the energy of its action is beyond praise.

I sent, some months since a copy of Watson's facsimiles of autographs—2 vols. fol.—and of the facsimile of Washington's account books—1 vol.—to the Society, placing them in the hands of Mr. S. G. Drake,[1] who said he would forward them. I hope they came safely. Please let me know. I have some historical volumes which I wish to send, & will thank you to indicate in what manner it had better be done.

Very truly Yours
FRANCIS PARKMAN

MS: Draper Correspondence, State Historical Society of Wisconsin.

[1] Samuel Gardner Drake (1798–1875). See note 3, FP to L. C. Draper, July 28, 1851.

To Edmund B. O'Callaghan

My dear Sir, Boston, Mar. 17, 1858

Let me thank you once more for the publication, invaluable to me, of the Paris Documents, of which I have just received the last vol. & to which your notes and illustrations add so much that is useful. The debt I owe to the liberality of the State of New York & to the devoted labors of the editor, is such that I could not too emphatically express my obligation. I can only trust that your services will be as warmly appreciated elsewhere as with me.

My historical labors have met with very serious interruption, but, still advance, though slowly. I am in search of the vol. of maps published in connection with the *Documentary Hist. of N. Y.* but have not found one here for sale. Can you tell me of anyone who has one?

Very truly
Your friend & Servt.
FRANCIS PARKMAN

MS: Miscellaneous Manuscripts Collection, Boston Public Library.

To John G. Shea

My Dear Mr. Shea, Monday, July 26 1858

On Saturday I received the Cavelier, & the Faillon MSS.—which you need not have sent back at all. I have sent our friend the abbé two copies of Cavelier. I have made him understand—which by his note he seems to have mis-conceived—that the former volumes were wholly your gift. I fear the ancient roughness between the Brethren of Jesus & St. Sulpice still lingers on his mind.[1]

Yrs. faithfully
F. PARKMAN

MS: Redpath Library, McGill University.

[1] Abbé E.-M. Faillon was a Sulpician and Shea had been a Jesuit novice. See note 2, FP to J. G. Shea, June 19, 1856.

To Lyman C. Draper

My dear Mr. Draper, Jamaica Plain, July 30 1858

I shall be heartily glad to renew a personal acquaintance of which I have a very pleasant recollection. My house is four miles from town, on Jamaica Pond (Prince St. Jamaica Plain.) & here I shall look forward to seeing you, unless your visit should happen during the time when I am absent on a (historical) journey into Canada, which I attempted in the spring, but was thwarted by a severe attack of neuralgia in the head, which has not yet taken leave.

Mr. Sparks is still in Europe. I send you, per mail, a little book of some historical interest—a printed copy of a MS in my possession.

Hoping not to be disappointed of seeing you, I am

Yrs. cordially
F. PARKMAN

P.S. You will learn my whereabouts at *No. 8 Walnut St. Boston.* My letter address is always *Boston.*

MS: Draper Correspondence, State Historical Society of Wisconsin.

To Mary B. Parkman[1]

My Dear Molly, Paris Dec. 22 '58

I got yr. letter yesterday with Grace's remarkable designs. I was very glad to hear from home. I wrote from Halifax, & from here, a week ago. I am well lodged—Hotel de France, 239 Rue St. Honoré, have felt much better, since arriving, & find abundant occupations for the winter. I often see Anna Green, & have been at Howland's & Mrs. Wharton's. For the rest, I shun Americans like the pest, & have not even given my address to my Bankers—Hottinguer & Co.—to whom please direct. I tell them to send my letters to Wm. Green.[2] I passed the Empress day before yesterday, in the Bois de Boulogne, & received a gracious bow in return of my salute. On the previous day, the heir of the Empire, about 3 years old, was walking with his gouvernante & servants in the garden of the Tuilleries, while a line of S[Z]ouave sentinels kept the crowd at a safe distance. Paris is greatly changed since I was here, 14 years ago. The Emperor has made great improvements in many parts & added vastly to the beauty of the city. Tell Jack I cannot advise him to come, as the cigars are very bad. Give my love to Grace, Mother, & Lizzie & all.

Yrs. affectely,
F.

Enclosed is a line for Mary [Dwight] Parkman—
Grace can take it, if still at school.

MS: Parkman Papers, Massachusetts Historical Society.

[1] FP's sister, Mary Brooks Parkman (1830–66), was unmarried and lived with FP, his mother, and his youngest sister, Lizzie. As a young woman she took great joy in attending the Boston assemblies, and the Reverend Dr. Francis Parkman, her father, made every effort to obtain tickets for her. The Parkman Papers contain many of her early letters showing her enthusiasm for social affairs and her deep devotion to her family. A mention of the illness which apparently caused her death is made by FP in his letter to Mary Dwight Parkman of Dec. 6, 1863, in which he wrote that she was "unchanged."

[2] William Batchelder Greene (d. 1878) a graduate of West Point who also held a divinity degree from Harvard (1845), was a colonel in the First Massachusetts Heavy Artillery during the Civil War. Greene, a tall, handsome, soldier-clergyman, was a man to suit FP's tastes, "a capital fellow, and nothing of a parson." FP to Eliza Parkman, Jan. 19, 1859. See also Quinquennial folder on W. B. Greene, HA.

To Mary B. Parkman

Address (Hottinguer & Co. Bankers)
Paris, Hotel de France et de Bath.
239 Rue St. Honoré
Jan. 13, 1859

My dear Moll,

I got yr. letter yesterday, & Lizzy's some time ago. By this time, all mine will have come. I wrote Dr. B.[1] that I was floored with lameness. It still continues, but seems mending, so that I get about—drive all day (chiefly on omnibuses!!), dine at 6, & commonly spend the [*day*] evening at the cafes. I have seen Dr. Brown-Séquard,[2] who fixed Sumner's[3] head. He says he can soon cure the lameness, but that the head is quite another matter. He says, however, that it will not kill me, & at some remote period may possibly become better. He has 2 other cases of this kind, but says they are very rare. I am still unable to walk more than 5 minutes at a time.

This hotel is very comfortable, the servants very attentive, etc. G. Russell[4] has been very ill, but is better. The only Americans of whom I see much are Anna & Wm. Green. I am greatly obliged to Uncle C. for his remembrance, & hope the youngster will do honor to the name. He should be brought up to some respectable calling, & not allowed to become a minister.

Remember me to the Bigelows, Uncle C. & Aunt Mary.[5] Love to Jack. Ditto to Grace to whom I would send a little doll, if it would go into the letter. With love to mother & Lizzy,

Yrs. Affty
F.

ADDRESSED: Mary B. Parkman 8 Walnut Street, Boston, Mass. *U.S.A.* By Cunard Steamer, Postmarked Boston Jan. 30.
MS: Parkman Papers, Massachusetts Historical Society.

[1] Dr. Jacob Bigelow, FP's father-in-law.

[2] Dr. Charles-Édouard Brown-Séquard (1817–94), born at Port Louis, Mauritius, of an American father and a French mother whose names he joined, studied medicine in Paris and became an eminent authority on the pathology and physiology of the nervous system. Brown-Séquard taught medicine in the United States (at Harvard in 1863) and in France, where he made his permanent home. *Dictionnaire de Biographie Française*, sous la direction de M. Prevost et Roman D'Amat (7 vols., Paris, 1929–56), VII, 459.

[3] Brown-Séquard, according to FP, treated Charles Sumner after he was beaten over the head by Preston S. Brooks on the floor of the U. S. Senate on May 22, 1856. Senator Sumner three days before had delivered his famous speech, "The Crime Against Kansas," and had ridiculed Senator Andrew P. Butler of South Carolina. Butler's nephew, Brooks, a congressman from South Carolina, avenged his kinsman by the attack on Sumner, an incident which heightened the sectional controversy in the period immediately preceding the Civil War.

[4] Possibly FP refers to George Peabody Russell (1826–1909), Harvard class of 1856, Harvard Law School of 1858, who practiced law in Boston and later made his residence in England. "Class of 1856," Secretary's report of 1899, HA.

[5] According to Hall, *The Halls of New England*, 308, FP's mother's sister, Mary Brooks Hall (1796–1869), died unmarried.

To Eliza Parkman[1]

(Hottinguer & Co.)
Paris, Jan. 19, 1859
Hotel de France & de Bath
239 Rue St. Honoré

My Dear Liz,

My knees are somewhat better, & I am about all day. Sleep well, etc. So much for my corporeal state. I mean to stay here some time, as I am better off than elsewhere. G. Russel is much better. I see Anna Green almost daily. Green is a capital fellow, and nothing of a parson. Annie R[obbins?][2] wrote me a long letter, in wh. she advises me to leave Paris as the contrast between outward gaity & inward sin must grate dreadfully on my feelings! I used to think her a woman of sense & understanding. She also thinks that I keep up a sentimental correspondence with Mrs. Bigelow![3] What the devil are your sex made of? Also suggests that I should leave my hotel & live at a boarding house kept by a female friend of hers, where I should be surrounded by such kind people! I shall stop off that sort of thing. Love to mother, Molly,

& P. P. Remembrance to Mary & Mrs. B. also the Dr. Love to Grace, for whom I have tried to find something that would go into a letter, but can't.

Yrs. affcty F.

P.S. Will you see Mary [Dwight] Parkman, & give my kind regards. Love to Aunt Mary

ADDRESSED: Miss E. W. S. Parkman 8 Walnut St. Boston Mass. U.S.A. (per Cunard Steamer *Liverpool*)
MS: Parkman Papers, Massachusetts Historical Society.

[1] FP's youngest sister, Eliza W. S. Parkman (1832–1905), his companion in later life after the death of his mother in 1871. See Introduction.

[2] Conjectural reading of the name is Robbins. An Annie S. Robbins' letters are in the Shattuck Papers, MHS, in the 1870's and 1880's, but no mention of FP is made.

[3] FP's mother-in-law.

To Mrs. Edward Twisleton[1]

Hottinguer & Co. Bankers
Hotel de France & de Bath
239 Rue St. Honoré Paris
Feb. 5 1859

Dear Mrs. Twisleton,

From an oversight of my bankers, to whom it was intrusted, your note of Dec. 19 did not reach me till yesterday. Thank you most cordially for your kind expression of sympathy. You knew Kate,[2] & can judge the unutterable extent of my loss. She was one of those friends in America who have always preserved a warm remembrance of you & never ceased to regret your absence. When I called at your home, I brought her daguerreotype with me, thinking you might like to see it. I shall hope for an opportunity hereafter. Your kind and affectionate estimate of her character is perfectly truthful. Knowing her so well in her early life, I wish you could have known her too in her last years, for you would then feel, even more strongly than now, her inestimable value to all near her.

I am glad the books reached you safely. They had to pass through the hands of the custom house officials, & this will account for the broken seal of a note in one of the parcels, the carriage of sealed letters, as you know, being illegal. The note itself of course remained unopened.

When you write to your sister Mary[3] pray give her my kindest regards. She has been to me the truest and most valued of friends.

It is scarcely necessary to assure you how sincerely and heartily I remain

Your friend and servant
FRANCIS PARKMAN

MS: Parkman Papers, Massachusetts Historical Society.

[1] Ellen, Mary Dwight Parkman's attractive sister, married an Englishman, Edward Twisleton, in 1852. There is evidence that FP unsuccessfully courted Ellen in 1848. See note 1, FP to Mary Dwight Parkman [1852].

[2] Catherine Bigelow Parkman, FP's wife, died on September 4, 1858, following the birth of her daughter Katharine on August 28, 1858. "Parkman Genealogy," by Mary Bigelow Coffin.

[3] Mary Dwight Parkman.

To Mary B. Parkman

My Dear Molly, Paris, Feb. 30 1859

I got yr. letter of Feb. 8 about a week ago. I am a little less lame, & get on well enough. The omnibuses of Paris—of which there are about 700—are made with railings etc. in such a way that with a little science, I can swing myself to the top with the arms alone, & here I usually spend the better part of the day smoking cigarettes & surveying the crowds below. I have formed an extensive acquaintance among omnibus cads & the like, whom I find to be first-rate fellows in their way—also have learned pretty thoroughly the streets of Paris, where much may be seen from the top of an omnibus. When hungry or thirsty, I descend to any restaurant, café, or "buffet" that happens to be near, whether of low or high degree, if only clean. In fair weather, an hour or two may always be spent pleasantly enough between 3 & 5 o'clock in the open air under the porches of the cafes on the Boulevards, where all Paris passes by.

In one respect I have gained greatly from Brown-Séquard's treatment. The muscles which ever since my first lameness, have been very much reduced & weakened, are restored wholly to their natural size & strength, so that when the neuralgic pain subsides, I shall be in a much better condition than before.

I enclose a story for Grace, which *she is not to be allowed to carry* about *with her* at least out of the house.

Yrs. affty
F.

MS: Parkman Papers, Massachusetts Historical Society.

To Eliza Parkman

My dear Lizzy, Paris Ap. 14, 59

The inflammation in my eyes is better, so that I get about again. Head also better, for some days past. John[1] was here—also Mayer.[2] I hope Grace has her doll. Will you ask Molly to see that John Morris sets out the small "cuttings" in the hotbed at Brookline. He knows where to plant them. Tell Dr. B. that it is slow work, & requires time. If my eyes continue to mend, I shall hang on here for the present. Knees are better.

Yrs. affecty
F.

MS: Parkman Papers, Massachusetts Historical Society.

[1] Possibly the Reverend John Cordner, FP's brother-in-law.

[2] Brantz Mayer, FP's Baltimore friend.

To Ephraim George Squier

8 Walnut St.
Dear Squier, Boston, Aug. 15 1859.

Yr. note has reached me, but minus the prospectus wh. it seems, has miscarried, but wh. may yet turn up. I can proffer no farther aid than the slight one of requesting a place for my name on the subscription list. I have lately come from Europe, whither I hope soon to return. My wife's recent death, with other causes, has of necessity changed my scheme of life for a time. I heard of your marriage[1] some time ago.

With all good wishes for your plans, believe me,

Yrs. sincerely,
F. Parkman

MS: Huntington Manuscripts, Henry E. Huntington Library.

[1] In 1858 Squier was married to Miriam Florence Folline, who divorced him in 1873 and later married Frank Leslie, for whom Squier had been an editor.

To John G. Shea[1]

8 Walnut St. Boston
July 21, 1860

My Dear Mr. Shea,

Coming a few days since to Boston, I found a parcel, forwarded from the public library, containing the new issues of your series—the *Relations* of Montigny St. Cosme, etc. and the *Bataille du Malangueulé*[2]—a most generous supply of each. The portrait of Beaujeu, & the notice of his life, especially interested me. I had no idea of the existence of the former, till I learned it from you, and much that you say of him is altogether new to me. The French orthography of Monongahela puzzled me at first. I remember a remark of an English prisoner —Smith, I think—among the Indians of that region that they had difficulty in managing the letters *m n* and *l*, often pronouncing them indiscriminately, so that Monongahela might easily enough be sounded *Malangueulé*.

Very truly
Yr. obliged friend
F. PARKMAN

P.S. I scarcely need say that any MS. in my hands is quite at your service, for publication in whole or part.

MS: Parkman Letters, Library of Congress.

[1] This letter is written in an almost unreadable scrawl, but in the next few months FP's handwriting improves, perhaps an indication of a gradual improvement in his health.

[2] An advance copy of Shea's printing of De Montigny de St. Cosme and Thaumur de la Source's *Relation de la Mission du Mississippi du Séminaire de Québec en 1700* (New York, 1861) and an edition of *Relations Diverses sur La Bataille de Malangueulé* (New York, 1860), including a portrait of Daniel H. M. L. Sieur de Beaujeu, the commander at Fort Duquesne who led the successful attack on Braddock on July 9, 1755. See *Montcalm and Wolfe*, I, 216 ff.; Jacobs, *Diplomacy and Indian Gifts*, 144, 144 n.

To Joel Tyler Headley[1]

Sir, Feb 22 [1861]

I [*find*] see in the March number of [*the March*] *Harpers' Monthly*, a paper mentioned in the index as "by J. T. Headley," describing the siege of Detroit by the Indians under Pontiac. The whole is however taken substantially from the "History of the Conspiracy of Pontiac etc" written by me. In great part, indeed, it is a paraphrase of [*Chapters*] portions of that work. Sometimes the words, are preserved; and [*very*] [*throughout*], the structure of the narrative [*are preserved*] is closely followed throughout. Nothing is added, except a few embellishments without historical foundation. All remarks & illustrations being borrowed from my work. You will at once see the impropriety of permitting the matter to stand [*farther*] without a recognition of the source whence the account was substantially, and all but verbally derived. I cannot doubt, therefore, that you will comply with my request that you make, in the next number of the *Monthly*, a satisfactory acknowledgement, of a nature so explicit, as to save me the unpleasant necessity of placing the affair in the hands of a literary friend to publish a statement of the facts, with such comments as the case would then require. Have the goodness to [*send*] return an early answer.

Yr. obt. Servt.
F. P.

MS: Draft, Parkman Papers, Massachusetts Historical Society.

[1] Joel Tyler Headley (1813–97), New York journalist and author of some thirty biographies, was one of the noted popularizers of American history in his day. His *Napoleon and his Marshals* (2 vols., New York, 1846) sold thousands of copies, and the *Nation* said his *Washington and His Generals* (2 vols., New York, 1847) was one of the five secular volumes on every American bookshelf. In the March, 1861 issue of *Harper's New Monthly Magazine*, Vol. XXII, 437–55, Headley published a dramatic article on Pontiac, complete with engravings of Indians and soldiers in action. As FP says in his letter to Headley, the article was almost completely taken from *Pontiac*, an example of the plagiarism that caused Edgar Allen Poe to give Headley the name of "the autocrat of all quacks." *DAB*.

Headley's reply of March 2 [1861], PP, MHS, stated that a note crediting FP had been accidentally left out of the article. "I am vexed beyond measure at the occurrence," Headley said, "for nothing so annoys me as to be put in a position by others when it is necessary to explain my conduct." Despite Headley's resentment, he did make a public apology through newspapers. (Headley to FP, May 16, 1861, PP, MHS.) The date of FP's draft is established by this letter.

Wm. H. Russell[1] and Our Duty

[August 28, 1861]

To the Editors of the *Boston Daily Advertiser:*

I see with regret, in some quarters, vehement tirades against the correspondent of the London Times, for his account of the rout of Bull Run. Whether his statements are candid or not, to assail this author with vituperation is a miserable error. There may be question as to this factor or that, but there is none that our arms have been disgraced and our courage impugned. These wordy effervescences can provoke nothing but contempt. None but a coward requites an insult with a volley of impotent abuse. Our safety and our honor demand a different answer. We are entered upon a course where it is ruin to turn back, ruin to turn aside, ruin to hesitate. For God's sake, let us tread it like men, and discharge our strength against the ranks of armed treason, not vapor it off in harmless scolding. The not very flattering narrative of Mr. Russell and the insolent comments of the London Times demand for their only answer, the shout of onset and the cheers of conquering battalions.

F. P.

PRINTED: *Boston Daily Advertiser,* August 28, 1861.

[1] William Howard Russell (1820–1907), British correspondent for the London *Times* watched from a convenient vantage point the First Battle of Bull Run of July 21, 1861. What Russell, in the company of congressmen and their wives and with the help of opera glasses, saw formed the basis for his account of the battle, "The Defeat at Manassas," an eight and one-half-column article in the August 6, 1861 issue of the *Times.* The article revealed the great contempt of a veteran correspondent for the conduct of green Union troops. Using such phrases as "the disgraceful conduct of the troops," and "cowardly route," he aroused the anger of the American press, became known as "Bull-Run Russell," and eventually resigned from the staff of the *Times* because of the unpopularity of his article. *The History of the Times: The Tradition Established, 1841–1884* (London, 1939), 367 ff., gives an account of the incident.

The Nation's Ordeal

[September 4, 1861]

To the Editors of the *Boston Daily Advertiser:*

Every day the gravity of the nation's position seems more and more impressed on the minds of the people. Enthusiasm is giving place

—at least it is to be hoped so—to a deeper and intenser purpose. All is at stake; the die is cast; we must do or perish. The peril, the solemnity of the hour cannot be too earnestly pondered. It is well to survey our stormy horizon, not in despondency and trembling, but in the firmer spirit of one who observes his ground, takes account of his dangers, and forearms himself against the worst. Our house is divided against itself. Our own blood has risen in arms against us, and we grapple for life or death with a fraternal foe, the most restless and war-like of mankind; ambitious, aggressive, and now maddened with an insane hate. With such an adversary there is no safety but in conquest. He or we must be humbled. If we but act the part of men, the conflict is one of no doubtful issue; but it is one which may tax our strength and constancy more than the less momentous struggle of the Revolution taxed those of our fathers. Nor is Southern treason our only danger; for if those among ourselves who have neither conscience to feel the course of right, nor manhood to feel the course of honor, nor wit to feel the course of safety,—if the counsels of such should prevail, then indeed would all be lost. The nation might hide her dishonored head and wait in ignominy the sure steps of her dissolution.

This might seem enough, but this is not all. Other storms are threatening in the outer darkness. There are contingencies, not probable, perhaps, but only possible, which it behoves us to consider and confront. The commercial interest, with its profits cut off, and the aristocratic interest eager for the ruin of republicanism, might, in case of a new reverse to our arms, or a protracted war, bring foreign interference into the contest. If we listen to the dictates of a foreign power, or of all foreign powers combined, and suffer ourselves to be turned from our great enterprise, there is but one result,—disintegration, decay, contempt, ruin. But if we stand to our work, doing that which truth and human liberty demand of us, then the whirlwind and the storm will be our portion. Yet let us not hesitate, nor shrink for an instant from the stern alternative. Marathon would grow dim before the splendor and the majesty of such a conflict, and the heroic tale would ring through unborn centuries, how, to vindicate the right, a nation of freemen stood against the world in arms.

Our position is a solemn and critical, but not a melancholy one. Perhaps, even, it is one not to be lamented. There is close analogy between the life of nations and of individuals. Conflict and endurance are necessary to both, and without them both become emasculate. Rome grew colossal through centuries of war. Out of the agony of civil strife came constitutional liberty to England, and vigor and unity to France. The individual is rare and the nation never yet was seen which the continuous smiles of fortune could not weaken or pervert. Our own unmatched prosperity has wrought its inevitable work. We are a *parvenu* nation with the faults and follies of a *parvenu*. Rising with astounding suddenness to wealth and greatness, we have not always been noted for the modesty or the dignity with which we have filled our new position. A too exclusive pursuit of material success has notoriously cramped and vitiated our growth. In the absence of a high interest or ruling idea, a superficial though widespread culture has found expression and aliment in a popular literature commonly frivolous and often corrupt. In the absence of any exigency to urge or any great reward to tempt it, the best character and culture of the nation has remained for the most part in privacy, while a scum of reckless politicians has choked all the avenues of power. Already, like a keen fresh breeze, the war has stirred our clogged and humid atmosphere. The time may be at hand when, upheaved from its depths, fermenting and purging itself, the nation will stand at length clarified and pure in a renewed and strengthened life. It behoves us, then, less in fear than in hope, to bide the tempest; for among its blackest clouds shines a star of promise.

It was said of Washington, that in the Revolution, he was slow to draw the sword, but, having drawn it, he threw away the scabbard. The North has been slow to draw the sword, but the steel is bare at last, and now let her, too, throw away the scabbard.

F. P.

PRINTED: *Boston Daily Advertiser,* September 4, 1861.

To Henry W. Longfellow[1]

Boston November 20, 1861.

Dear Sir. Will you permit your pupils of the class of 1844 to offer you a simple expression of grateful remembrance and profound sympathy?[2] You may have forgotten that while reading the plays of Molière you allowed us to meet you in your new library, and received us as friends. The eighteen years that have passed since then, with all the changes they have brought, have served only to make more permanent the recollection of those hours as among the most agreeable of our college course; and if it is true, as we believe it is, that next to the offices of religion the thoughts which are most soothing to an inconsolable grief are those of the happiness which in times past we have bestowed on others, you will not deem it an act of intrusion on our part that we now recall to your remembrance our uncancelled debt of gratitude and respect.

And subscribe ourselves,
Yours with great regard.
EDMUND DWIGHT[3]
GEO. S. HALE
CHAS W. DABNEY
FRANCIS PARKMAN
H. B. SNOW[4]

MS: Longfellow Papers, Harvard College Library.

[1] Henry Wadsworth Longfellow (1807–82) was "Smith Professor of the French and Spanish Languages and Literature, and Professor of Belles-Lettres" *(Harvard Catalogue,* 1840–41) at Harvard from 1835 to 1854. FP's class records in the Harvard Archives do not identify the courses he took from Longfellow, although he studied French and Spanish (as well as Latin, Italian, and Greek). In 1854, Longfellow retired and devoted himself to writing at his large house on Brattle Street, where many pleasant evenings were spent in his study with friends, discussing revisions of his translation of Dante's *Divine Comedy.*

[2] In July, 1861, Longfellow's wife, Frances Appleton, whom he had married in 1843, was burned to death when her dress caught fire from either a lighted match or burning wax as she sat near an open window. Although the details of her death vary greatly, Longfellow's recent biographer says that the poet tried to wrap a rug around her to smother the flames, but that he was burned so badly he could not attend her funeral when she was buried at Mount Auburn on her eighteenth wedding anniversary. Longfellow, it is said, was semidelirious at the time of her death, and as long as two years later he would burst into tears at the memory of his wife's tragic fate. Edward Wagenknecht, *Longfellow: A Full-Length Portrait* (New York, 1955), 252.

[3] The letter is in Edmund Dwight's hand, but with individual signatures.

[4] Charles Henry Boylston Snow. See note 7, FP to George B. Cary, Dec. 15, 1844.

Where Are Our Leaders?

[January 8, 1862]

To the Editors of the *Boston Daily Advertiser:*

Our ship is among breakers, and we look about us for a pilot.

An endangered nation seeks a leader worthy of itself—the ascendant spirit which shall render its redundant energies into effective action. In a struggle less momentous it found such leaders; men who were types of the national heart and mind, and whose pre-eminence our enemies were forced in bitterness to confess. Out of three millions, America found a Washington, an Adams, a Franklin, a Jefferson, a Hamilton; out of twenty millions, she now finds none whose stature can compare with these. She is strong in multitudes, swarming with brave men, instinct with eager patriotism. But she fails in that which multitudes cannot supply, those master minds, the lack of which the vastest aggregate of mediocrity can never fill. As well an army without generals as an imperilled nation without its counsellors and guides. Where are they? Why is mediocrity in our high places, and the race of our statesmen so dwindled? Schools, lyceums and newspapers have not engendered them. A half-culture, shallow, if not unsound, has spread far and wide; but the high traits of a high and finished manhood have grown rarer and rarer yet. The people have ceased to call for them and they have well nigh ceased to appear; for here, as in things less vital, demand and supply act and react with inevitable and deadly reciprocity. The people have demanded equality, not superiority, and they have had it;—men of the people, that is to say, men in no way raised above the ordinary level of humanity. In degrading its high offices, the nation has weakened and degraded itself. When log-cabins, raccoons, and rail-splitting became rallying cries of potent influence on the course of elections, the fact was mournfully significant. When the President declared that every volunteer regiment raised at his summons could furnish men fit to conduct the government, in that strange assertion he spoke the popular mind;—great men were a necessity only in the days that are past and gone; we have outgrown them; we, the people, are sufficient to ourselves—to us all things are possible. The people are and ought to be the masters, but a wise master will choose skilled and faithful servants, and prize them at their worth. They have chosen to be served, not by patriot statesmen, but by dextrous politicians, fluent demagogues, or, at best, by men who, whatever their merit, could never by any attribute of a conspicuous superiority disturb a perverted self-love or confute the maddest theory of universal equality. A high culture has not been in request. It is scarcely too much to say that it has of late been banished from the arena of public life; and thus, shut out from this great field of exercise and stimulus, our best culture has become, in great part, nerveless and emasculate.

If the people will learn that no expansion of territory, no accumulation of wealth, no growth of population, can compensate for the decline of individual greatness; if they can learn to recognize the reality of superior minds, and to feel that they have need of them; to feel, too, that in rejecting and ignoring them they prepare the sure though gradual ruin of popular government,—that beneficent lesson would be cheaply bought by years of calamity and war. In the thickening storm we may discern already the rainbow of a brighter future. The nation in its jeopardy will welcome all who can give it help. Those who have shrunk—often with an overstrained fastidiousness—from the mean contacts and repugnant compliances which public life has exacted, may now listen to the call of patriotism without compromising self-respect. Then, wherever such there are, let them stand forth, for the country has need of all its manhood.

F. P.

PRINTED: *Boston Daily Advertiser,* January 8, 1862.

To Mary Dwight Parkman

My Dear Mary, Jamaica Plain, Ap. 4, 1862.

I have heard the news of you & Mrs. Twisleton from Mrs. Cabot,[1] and though perforce a bad correspondent, have had you daily in mind. My horse does not understand your absence, and tries to turn down Boylston St. whenever he passes it. I am daily here—in Jamaica Plain —and am at last really busy, having formed a partnership with Spooner,[2] wh. will absorb all the working faculties I have left. So you find me a man of business. I am content with the move, & resolved to give the thing a fair trial and, by one end of the horn or the other, work a way out of a condition of helplessness. At all events, this is my best chance, & I will give it a trial. Spooner wants me to go to England & France in the Fall, to look up new plants. The thing has difficulties & risks, not a few under my circumstances; but is attractive, & doubly so as it gives me a prospect of meeting you. So I cherish it, as probably an illusion, but still a very pleasing one. Turning tradesman has agreed with me so far. Several bushels of historical MSS. and fragments of abortive chapters have been packed under lock & key, to bide their time.—Will you not send me a line? You know how welcome it would be.

Miss B.[3] has returned, & a note *from her sister* advised me of the fact, and expressed a hope that I would come & see her, as she was "Sure it would give her pleasure"! I admired, reflected, and after waiting a few days, went. A simple friendly interview was the result, both ladies being present through the greater part of it, as I took pains to inquire for Miss M. Here the matter rests.

With cordial regards to Mrs. Twisleton & remembrances to Nelly & Harry[4]

Affecty Yrs
F. P.

ADDRESSED: Mrs. S. Parkman.
MS: Parkman Papers, Massachusetts Historical Society.

[1] Sisters of Mary Dwight Parkman, Ellen and Elizabeth, or Mrs. Twisleton and Mrs. J. Elliot Cabot.

[2] William H. Spooner, a nurseryman who specialized in roses, was a prominent leader in the Massachusetts Horticultural Society, and as late as 1892 advertised his plants in the *Boston Directory*, p. 1918.

[3] Miss "B.," or "Miss P." or "B" has been impossible to identify. Since she is not referred to as "P," the inference is that "B" was her given name's initial, and "P" the initial of her surname. Howard Doughty in his able article, "Parkman's Dark Years," *Harvard Library Bulletin*, Vol. IV (Winter, 1950), 53–85, has thoroughly explored the possibilities of linking the mysterious "Miss P" with Pamela Prentiss of Keene (see note 2, FP to his father, July 29, 1841); but she had married Judge Henry F. French on September 29, 1859 and had become the stepmother of Daniel Chester French, the sculptor, son of the judge by an earlier marriage. Margaret French Cresson, *Life of Daniel Chester French: Journey Into Fame* (Cambridge, Mass., 1947), 11. FP's *Journals*, I, 286, refer in 1844 to a "Miss P." whom FP called on at the home of Dr. B[igelow], presumably the Dr. Jacob Bigelow who became his father-in law in 1850.

[4] Mary Dwight Parkman's children, Ellen and Henry (1850–1924). "Harry" was a frequent visitor in the home of FP. Henry's letters to his mother in the Parkman Family Papers, HCL, often mention his "jolly" Uncle Frank and his Aunt Lizzie with affection. Lizzie was particularly fond of Henry and Ellen as well as their mother, whom she addressed as "My dearly Beloved" in letters. *Ibid.*

To Mary Dwight Parkman

My Dear Mary, Boston Ap. 27 '62

Do not take the length of my notes as the measure of my regard. I do not get used to your absence, and miss you, if possible, more & more. I am busy, nevertheless, and with a good deal on my hands;

quite as much, I often find, as my head will endure; but I shall give it a trial, & if it breaks down, it is no doing of mine. Spooner is animated at the look of our affairs and augurs success in spite of the war. I spend the day out of town, looking after matters at several separate places, which keeps my horse in lively motion. Having had a friend to whom one has been accustomed to speak himself freely, it is not easy to reconcile oneself to the loss—so, as I leave the stable every morning, I look across the Public Garden at your window with a fresh feeling of regret. I am as well as usual and mean to be better or worse before the year is out. Mother & sisters all well. The George Parkmans have given a family party!!![1] B. is busy with theatricals for the benefit of the sanitary. I have not seen her since I wrote last, but shall go soon. I think that at the close of the last interview there were distinct evidences of pique.

With cordial esteem to Mrs. Twisleton,
Affectionately
F. P.

P.S. I should be very glad of a few post stamps of the higher priced sorts to pay the amount—say [$5.00] £ 1.00 or so wh. I will pay to Mrs. Cabot—but don't give yourself any trouble about this.

F. P.

ADDRESSED: Mrs. S. Parkman Baring Bothers & Co. London
MS: Parkman Family Papers, Harvard College Library.

[1] George Parkman, FP's cousin and classmate, had been a recluse since the murder of his father by Dr. John W. Webster. See note 4, FP to E. G. Squier, April 2, 1850.

To Mary Dwight Parkman

Private Jamaica Plain
My Dear Mary, June 22, 1862

I am half reluctant to trouble you with my own affairs at this time, & to tax your thoughts when they are so heavily burdened. And yet I think you would not wish me to do otherwise. I have told you my relations with Miss P. &, as you know, omitted nothing essential bearing on the case. Since writing to you, I have once seen her—a half hour's friendly conversation ended, as usual, by an urgent request to come again. In short, I stand on precisely the same ground I have always taken, & which, I scarcely need say, I have been of late more than ever guarded in keeping & defining. As I was going away, however, she made some allusion to Mrs. Jeffries Wyman,[1] in a way designed to engage my attention. She then, with apparent hesitation said that Mrs. W. had spoken ill of her & of me. I desired her to say what had been spoken. Little appeared, however, but a general expression of unfriendly feeling towards me on Mrs. W's part, with a few items of trivial gossip. At length B. touched the true point, remarking that Mrs. W. had said that I was in the habit of visiting at the Agassiz's. I replied that I had long been in the habit of doing so. [*Miss*] She then alluded to Miss. Ida Agassiz,[2] & by various remarks and indirect questions, endeavored to learn my feelings towards her. I expressed the cordial esteem and friendship I feel towards her. While this was going on, B's face was by turns ashy pale & deeply flushed. To account for her emotion she professed great anger against Mrs. W. who, she said, had insulted her by telling her that I had deserted her and was "moving heaven & earth to marry Miss Agassiz" and that she "thought it her duty" to tell Miss Agassiz, to which B. said that she had replied that she would not have me abused as I was the truest friend she had. All this part of the reported dialogue, I have reason to think a fiction. She then repeated various unfriendly remarks of Mrs. W. who is well known for a very unguarded & dangerous tongue, and who, to judge from these questionable quotations had a very comprehensive but very perverted idea of my relations with every young lady with whom I have spoken for the last two years. She herself ascribed her avowed hostility to me chiefly to my having "put her down"—her own alleged expression—when she made an ill-natured remark touching a young lady of Cambridge. I remembered the incident, the place being my mother's tea-table, & the young lady Miss. Martha Parsons. Mrs. W. as perhaps you know, is a familiar friend of my sister Lizzy.

As it seemed clear that my name was in the way of being used in a way not only detrimental to me but unpleasant to others, I told Lizzy of Mrs. W's assertions & surmises, explaining that I had never stood to Miss P. in any other relation than that of a friend, & that from the first I had made it clear to her by every possible means that this must always be the case. Lizzy much distressed, repaired to Mrs. W. who confessed to using in reference to me the expression, "I hate him & he hates me," confessing also that she had no particular justification for either part of the statement. For the rest, it seemed that she was somewhat less in fault than at first appeared. B., knowing her intimacy in my mother's family had long used her as a medium of information concerning me, & as Mrs. W. affirmed, her gossip was not gratuitously uttered, but called forth by questions. B. had struck up an intimacy, betrayed with little reserve her own feeling, & left Mrs. W. to infer that it was, in some measure at least, reciprocal. An unfriendly and exceedingly gossipping disposition did the rest. The risks from this state of things are evident, B's jealousy centres on Miss Agassiz, and her superlative powers of intrigue will, above all others, be directed to injure me here. Her diplomacy is as hardy as it is subtle & she never shrinks from risks. I should be deeply grieved if a shadow should be cast over the friendship with which Miss Agassiz honors me. I have no reason to think that this is yet the case, yet against this and other mischief which may spring out of the affair, I would gladly make some provision. My position towards B. is completely known to you, & I believe you think that though a difficult and delicate it has not been an unworthy one. I have considered her interests far more [*attentively*] anxiously than she herself has done. Will you have the kindness to write a letter to me—or better perhaps to Lizzy—simply indicating your knowledge of the affair and that you think my course in it has not been one which ought to discredit me—such a letter as may be shown if the occasion should demand it, and which, coming from you, will refute the most ingeniously devised slander. It need not & ought not to involve any vital reflection on B.—merely vindicating me with as little injury to her as may be. I believe I have been considerate of her to a fault, but I heartily rejoice that no overstrained scruple prevented me from making you acquainted with the position.

I trust, Dear Mary, that you are beginning to recover your strength, and that what is around you can avail in some degree to distract & engage your thoughts. I don't know whether or not I am disinterested enough to wish you to stay abroad.

Affecty.
F.

MS: Parkman Family Papers, Harvard College Library.

[1] Wife of Dr. Jeffries Wyman (1814–74), Harvard class of 1833, M.D. Massachusetts Medical College, 1837. In 1847, he was appointed Hermsey Professor of Anatomy at Harvard.

[2] Ida Agassiz (1837–1935), second of

Louis Agassiz's three children by his first wife (Cécile Braun), came to America with her sister Pauline after her father married Elizabeth Cary Cabot of Boston in 1850. *DAB* under Louis Agassiz. Alexander, her brother, had already joined his father. In 1854, the Agassiz family moved from Oxford Street to Quincy Street and a delightful home "with no luxury but every comfort." Ida assisted her stepmother in teaching French and German in the "Agassiz School" for young men and women, which Mrs. Agassiz (later president of Radcliffe) established to augment her husband's income as a professor. Ida and Pauline, it is said, were "young handsome creatures . . . full of life and gaiety," and favorites with the young people of Cambridge. See *Memories of Fifty Years* by Emma Forbes Cary (privately printed, Boston, 1947), 118 ff.; Edward Waldo Forbes, "The Agassiz School," Cambridge Historical Society *Publications* (Cambridge, 1955), XXXV, 35–55.

To the Lingerers

[August 12, 1862]

To the Editors of the *Boston Daily Advertiser:*

Several of the newspapers have published replies to certain expressions, used by a late speaker, supposed to impugn the patriotism or manhood of certain classes of our citizens. Every one who knows anything of the matter, knows that such attacks—if intended as such—were utterly baseless; for, East or West, on every memorable field, cultivated New England has stood in the front rank of battle, from where Peabody,[1] shattered with unhealed wounds, rode to his death at Shiloh, to where Putnam[2] and Lowell[3] died on the banks of the Potomac and the James. And the records of the war have shown that a prompt courage in the face of death, a cheerful and unflinching hardihood under toil, privation, and exposure, has been nowhere more conspicuous than in that gallant youth, trained in ease and perhaps in luxury, which New England has sent from colleges, from "learned professions," or from homes of abundance.

But this is nothing to the purpose. We write, not to those who have gone, but to those who stay behind,—those who, rich or otherwise, of "Beacon Street" or any other street, sound in wind and limb, with time to spare, and no strong ties to constrain them, can yet linger at home. With the country ringing to the note of war, hosts mustering to the fray from far and near, the nation's life and honor trembling on the ordeal of battle, these worthless young imbeciles still follow, as far as they may, their wonted round of amusement and ease; watering-places, races, streets, theatres, drawing-rooms. Their dull blood will not stir at the blast of the trumpet. Neither the impulses of patriotism, nor the love of adventure, nor the thirst for honor, nor the fear of shame can rouse them from this miserable lethargy. Those who no less now than of old are the inspiration and the reward of youthful valor, will well know how to punish cowardice and sloth. The scorn of men, and of women, should pursue all who, without cogent reason, stand idle lookers-on in this time of peril.

Wear a shoulder-strap, if you can get it; but in these days, the rough coat of a private soldier is more honorable than a citizen's broadcloth. Enlist and fight your way to a commission, those of you who have a lurking spark of manhood, and, for the rest, let them stay at home and bask out their torpid lives in ignominy.

F. P.

MS: Printed, *Boston Daily Advertiser*, August 12, 1862.

[1] Colonel Everett Peabody, Harvard class of 1849, was killed at Shiloh on April 6, 1862. Francis H. Brown, *Harvard University in the War of 1861–1865* (Boston, 1886), 43.

[2] William Lowell Putnam, Harvard class of 1861, second lieutenant, Twentieth Massachusetts Volunteers, was killed at Ball's Bluff, Virginia, on Oct. 21, 1861. *Ibid.*, 348–49.

[3] James Jackson Lowell, Harvard class of 1858, first lieutenant, Twentieth Massachusetts Volunteers, died at Nelson's (or Fraser's) farm, Virginia, on July 4, 1862. *Ibid.*, 114–15.

To Mary Dwight Parkman

Jamaica Plain
Sep. 27, 1862

My Dear Mary,

If I wrote as often as I think of you, you would have a letter daily, to say no more. We are in the midst of war, & begin to feel it. Wilder Dwight[1] was buried yesterday, and everybody is bidding good-bye to some friend or other. I spent a day & night at the camp at Readville—Frank Lee's[2] regiment—Edward Cabot[3] lieut. col. & Charly Dabney[4] major. They know their work & will do it. No regiment better led has left this state. Lee is in his element. All, I think, had hard work to get away and go with a very mixed feeling, but all three will do their part nobly. The men are worthy of the officers. It is a picked corps. When I left them, I was sick of life—but I will not utter what lies at my heart, even to you.

Many thanks, dear, for your kind note about B. I have it by me, but don't think there will be any need to show it—indeed I am sure there will not. I have not seen B. & probably shall not. Q. A. S.[5] knows the case, & if any insinuations are cast out against me, his word will suffice. On consideration, I thought it best to tell him. He was interested but not surprised, having had a pretty clear perception of B's possibilities.

The starved and desperate vagabonds of the rebel army have been handled with an admirable address by your acquaintance Lee. No doubt, now, of their fighting qualities, but they have been badly beaten, and left some 20,000 men as the price of their excursion into Maryland.

Sept. 29—Above is a fine piece of gloom and azure melancholy. I should do best to tear it up. Set it all to the account of a visit to Readville—the banners I was not to follow,—the men I was not to lead, the fine fellows of whom I could not be one. I thought I had known what deprivation is, but I had not. It was the lamentation of the moth, in despair, because, being burned already, he cannot fly into the candle. At present, he is resigned, if not consoled. Q. A. S. is restive, but restrained by thinking of Pauline,[6] who is in a tremor at the thought of his going. I am a bad patriot, & tell him to stay at home. Among all the doubts, one thing seems sure—slavery has its death blow, and the North, through Abe Lincoln, her feeble and ungainly mouthpiece, has vindicated herself at last.—You have heard the release of Harry Russell.[7] He got off very easily, considering what was threatened & expected. Savage[8] is among friends of Prof. Rogers,[9] in Virginia, but so badly wounded, that there is little hope for him. Nobody knows, I believe, what is Quincy's[10] condition. So I close this cheerful epistle. Don't believe, though, that we are so gloomy after all, for this community still contrives to be jolly, though under evident difficulties.

Very Affect[y].

F. P.

ADDRESSED: Mrs S. Parkman

MS: Parkman Family Papers, Harvard College Library.

[1] Wilder Dwight, Harvard class of 1853, lieutenant colonel, Second Massachusetts Volunteers, had been a Southern prisoner, but was exchanged and died from wounds at Boonesborough, Maryland, on September 16, 1862. Brown, *Harvard University in the War*, 65.

[2] Francis L. Lee (1823–86), Harvard class of 1843, FP's college friend (see note 3, FP to Henry O. White, April [1843]), colonel of the Forty-fourth Massachusetts Infantry, a regiment that included about forty alumni of Harvard. The regiment participated in several battles, including the siege at Washington, N. C. It was mustered out in June, 1863,

but called out to assist in suppressing draft riots in July of the same year. Brown, *Harvard University in the War*, 20.

[3] Edward Clark Cabot (1818–1901) served less than a year as lieutenant colonel in Lee's regiment. A noted architect, professor of architecture at the Massachusetts Institute of Technology, he designed the Boston Athenaeum in 1845, the Boston Theatre (1852–53), and the hospital of The Johns Hopkins University, which opened in 1899.

[4] Charles William Dabney, FP's classmate. See FP to Dabney, Feb. 10, 1845.

[5] Quincy A. Shaw, FP's cousin and companion on the Oregon Trail.

[6] Pauline Agassiz Shaw, his wife. See note 2, FP to his mother, June 12, 1846.

[7] Henry Sturgis Russell (1838–1905), Harvard class of 1860, first lieutenant, Second Massachusetts Infantry, was taken prisoner at Cedar Mountain, Virginia. After rejoining the Union forces, he rose rapidly in rank and in June, 1865, was promoted to brigadier general. Brown, *Harvard University in the War*, 148.

[8] James Savage (1832–62), Harvard class of 1854, lieutenant colonel, Second Massachusetts Infantry, died at Charlottesville, Virginia, on October 22, 1862, from wounds received at the battle of Cedar Mountain. *Ibid.*, 75.

[9] William Barton Rogers (1804–82), geologist and educator, occupied the chair of natural philosophy at the University of Virginia from 1835 to 1853. In 1862, he became the first president of the Massachusetts Institute of Technology, a post he held until 1870 and again from 1878 to 1881. In 1849, he married Emma Savage of Boston, James Savage's sister.

[10] Samuel Miller Quincy (c. 1832–87), Harvard class of 1852, colonel, Second Massachusetts Infantry, was taken prisoner at Cedar Mountain, confined at Libby Prison, exchanged in 1863, and commanded his regiment at Chancellorsville. *Ibid.*, 59; Quinquennial folder on S. M. Quincy, HA.

Why Our Army Is Not the Best in the World

[October 14, 1862]

To the Editors of the *Boston Daily Advertiser:*

Never was an army on foot with rank and file like ours. The most valuable classes of our people are represented in it, and, in large measure, compose it—agricultural, commercial, mechanical, literary, scholastic, clerical, in short, all we have that is worth having will find its type shouldering a musket and wheeling at the word of command. And as for our commanders, if we have not yet given to the world that perilous production, "a Napoleon," we have at least some six or eight generals of whom no nation need be ashamed. But when we come to officers of subordinate rank—lieutenants, captains, majors, colonels—and ask how well they are fitted for the duties of command, the lamentable reply must be that the greater number are not fitted at all. He is a worthless officer who can only command the obedience of his men because military rules give him power to enforce it. The fallacies of ultra democracy cannot safely be applied to the organization of armies. The leader ought at least to be as good a man as he who follows, and yet many an officer in federal pay might, with great propriety, change places with half the privates who obey his mandates. Village demagogues, city "b'hoys" and the like, are the last men to be entrusted with the honor of the nation and the lives of her soldiers. Whether fraternizing with their men in the old familiarity of the bar-room or the town hall, or, in the spirit of Jack in office, establishing a brutal despotism of buck and gag, the effects are about equally bad.

It is much to have a leader who is afraid to run away, who knows what the point of honor means, and on whom the brand of cowardice would bring results more terrible than death. It is much to have a leader in whom his soldiers can recognize one who by nurture, by associations, by acquirements, by character, has an inherent claim to their respect. Such there are, and not a few, and we may congratulate ourselves that nowhere has the proportion of such been greater than in the regiments of Massachusetts. Yet here, as elsewhere, there is woeful abundance of a different element, and hence has come neglect, inefficiency, disorder, drunkenness, defeat, shame. Were all the federal regiments officered as well as they are manned, treason would this day lie groveling in the dust. Of those who have gone into battle, some have borne themselves admirably, some indifferently, and a few shamefully, and the assertion is a safe one, that out of the merit or demerit of their officers, nearly all the difference has sprung. Instances have not been wanting where one gallant man, and he not of the highest rank, has breathed his own spirit through an entire corps and rescued it from the disorder and demoralization into which his associates in command were suffering it to fall. A good officer makes good soldiers; a bad officer makes bad soldiers, be the original metal of what temper it may.

It is not in managing to pass an examination in the drill-book, but in the intrinsic character and spirit of the man that the most essential requisites must be sought. Our social influences have not been favorable to the development of such requisites, but they are to be found among us, nevertheless; and to use them and develope them to the utmost is a paramount necessity if the nation is to have a real military strength,—if every war is not to drain her of men and money to an extent wholly disproportioned to results achieved. Such men are to be found in all the intelligent classes of our society. Education: using the term in the comprehensive sense which includes the influences which spring from favorable associations and surroundings—can never fail to produce them. New England nurture has been of anything but a martial stamp, and yet she has drawn a most efficient, faithful, and brave body of officers from the ranks of her educated young men. We look with hope to see a military element infused into all our schools and colleges. It is not for us to enlarge on these topics. Democracy has learned the weak points of her armor. At least she has ample means to learn them. In peace, as in war, she cannot dispense with competent and right minded leaders. If she demands them, they will come in time. If not, her future is black with disaster.

F. P.

PRINTED: The *Boston Daily Advertiser,* October 14, 1862.

Conservatism

[October 17, 1862]

To the Editors of the *Boston Daily Advertiser:*

Well is it said that extremes meet. The Conservatism that anchors on rottenness and grapples to forms without life,—that struggles with infatuated dullness to dam back the flowing current instead of guiding it to safe and beneficent issues, is destruction in disguise. Conservatists and destroyers, timid respectability on one hand, and Woods,[1] Vallandighams,[2] and copperheads[3] on the other, circle on their convergent paths till they seem on the point of joining hands. At least, the latter, with their customary astuteness have contrived to make those in whose nostrils they are an offence, colaborers and tools in their devil's work.

Eighteen months of war have wrought ruin enough; and there is more in store; but, like thunderstorms in a thick and fever burdened air, the war has been a fearful minister of good. The weeks that preceded the final outrage at Fort Sumter, are never to be forgotten: menace upon menace, insult upon insult; demands outrageous alike to God and man, urged with an unheard of insolence and passively received, till it seemed that all manhood, all honor, all conscience had fled the nation, and that she would drain the cup of her abasement to the uttermost dregs. It was the climax towards which many years had tended. More and more, the mean and bad elements of the nation had risen in influence. Material interests and base political rivalries ruled us. There was no limit to their exactions, and seemingly no limit to concession and sacrifice in their behalf. The national mind and heart were fast subsiding into one vast platitude, over whose level monotony great thoughts and noble purposes did not rise, and would scarcely have been tolerated if they had risen. More and more, worth and character had withdrawn from public life. Rarely did a man above the stamp of mediocrity appear among those who made or administered the laws. All that was best and ablest dwindled in obscurity, and an ill-instructed zeal, often assumed to cover mean designs, was left to battle after its own fashion with unscrupulous self-interest and the passions of demagogues and adventurers. Yet there was peace, such as it was; or rather the stagnation which precedes the ebullitions of inward corruption. Treason grew audacious with long-continued triumphs, never dreaming that, though buried deep in ashes, the old fire was not dead. From threats and intrigue, it passed to open violence. The rebel cannon at Fort Sumter were the resurrection of our manhood. With that infatuated blast, the forked flame leaped up, and to its utmost bounds the renovated nation burned with heroic fire.

Who can ever forget the day when from spires and domes, windows and housetops, the stars and stripes were flung to the wind, in token that the land was roused at last from deathly torpor. They were the symbols of a new life; portentous of storm and battle, yet radiant with hope. Our flag was never so glorious. On that day, it became the emblem of truth and right and justice. Through it, a mighty people proclaimed a new faith,—that peace, wealth, ease, material progress, were not the sum and substance of all good. Loyalty to it became loyalty to humanity and to God. The shackles of generations were thrown off. We were a people disenthralled, rising from abasement abject and insupportable. An electric life thrilled to the heart of the nation, and they who had stood aloof, in despondency and scorn, from the foul arena of party strife, now with an eager and buoyant alacrity, offered their breasts to the cannon. Women, with sympathies bounded till now by the circles of private life, threw into the conflict lives more valued than their own. Shall these sacrifices be vain? Shall that bright hope be the herald of the opening day, or was it but the sinister gaping of the clouds that portends a thicker night? Must we again be the vassals of outrage and wrong, entangled in the same wretched meshwork of compromises and compliances? Shall all that is noble in our national life again be borne down and smothered, and the bats and owls of society again flock from their hiding-places, triumphant and clamorous? To buy a transient and hollow peace, a brief interval of material prosperity, shall faith, honor, conscience, loyalty, all that makes the soul of a nation, be choked and starved into annihilation, and shall this ruin be wrought in the name of Conservatism? It would be a wholesale crime, as unavailing as monstrous. It would be a suicidal folly. To the eye, the mockery of a cure.

> "While rank corruption, mining all within,
> Infects unseen."

It would make a desert, and call it peace. The safety of the nation lies in being true to herself. A true peace must be hewn out with the sword. We fight against incarnate wrong, and, come what may, we must crush it.

F. P.

PRINTED: *Boston Daily Advertiser,* October 17, 1862.

[1] Leonard Woods (1807–78), clergyman and president of Bowdoin College for twenty-seven years. His popularity suffered in the closing years of his administration because of his extreme pacifist views, for he bitterly opposed the use of force against the South. In 1865, however, he presided with dignity when his college conferred a degree of doctor of laws on U. S. Grant.

[2] Clement Laird Vallandigham (1820–71), Ohio politician and leader of the Peace Democrats ("Copperheads" or "Butternuts"), who advocated a union restored by peaceful negotiation instead of by war. In 1863, Vallandigham was banished to the Confederacy, but he returned to the North to oppose Lincoln's policies.

[3] See note 2, above.

To John G. Shea

8 Walnut St.
Boston
3rd May 1863

My Dear Mr. Shea,

Returning from a short absence I find on my table your beautiful impression of the *"Novum Belgium,"*[1] which I shall prize as a most interesting addition to my collection of French-American books.

Doctors are false prophets. I have been assured that I had very little chance of meddling in literary matters with impunity for the rest of my natural life, but I never believed so, & I think I shall convince the Faculty that I had the right to it. So the Novum Belgium,

I hope, will come into play before long, and serve me in other ways than as a passive ornament to the shelves of a bookcase.

Very truly Yrs.
F. PARKMAN

MS: Parkman Letters, Library of Congress.

[1] After Father Isaac Jogues' captivity among the Mohawks and his rescue by the Dutch (*Jesuits*, II, 47 ff.), he wrote the narrative of *Novum Belgium, Description de Nieuw Netherland* . . . , which remained in manuscript form until John G. Shea printed it with notes in his Cramoisy Press series (New York, 1862).

The Weak Side of Our Armies

[June 30, 1863]

To the Editors of the *Boston Daily Advertiser:*

One lamentable fact is established by a host of concurrent witnesses,—a deficiency in character and qualification in a vast proportion of our officers. Often, the officers have been first to run. The superb material which fills the ranks of our armies has lost three-fourths of its efficiency from incompetent, negligent, or cowardly leadership, with its inevitable results of indifferent discipline and indifferent morale. Is it that the North does not produce men fit to command, or that, producing them, she does not use them?

The principle of military honor underlies all other qualifications to command, the principle that induces, nay, compels a man to face wounds and death rather than incur the insupportable stigma of cowardice. In the South, a community essentially military, this spirit is rife. So in a less degree, in the Northwest, where a civilization of imperfect and disproportioned development has not smothered the instincts natural to man, and always strongest in the strongest and richest nature. For, since the world began, no nation has ever risen to a commanding eminence in the arts of peace, which has not at some period of its history, been redoubtable in war. And, in every well-balanced development of nations as of individuals, the warlike instinct and the military point of honor are not repressed and extinguished, but only refined and civilized. It belongs to the pedagogue, not to the philosopher, to declaim against them as relics of barbarism. Luxury and commerce have sometimes emasculated a people naturally warlike. The former has injured us only partially, but the spirit of trade, in the excess of its predominance, has done us a wide-spread and deadly mischief. The morality of commerce has become confounded with universal morality, and the word honor, to the minds of half of those who use it, means little but commercial honor. The pride of a good bargain has overborne the pride of manhood, and much that is vital to worth and nobleness is treated as illusory. So, from highest to lowest, this influence pervades this vigorous and practical race, courageous, indeed, as all roused and energetic peoples are, but not spurred to acts of courage by the same exacting and unanswerable demand which urges, on the one hand, ruder nations, and, on the other, nations of a more balanced and normal civilization. The ambition to be a good business man is nowise akin to the ambition to be a good soldier. No wonder that, from among the masses of our people, trusty officers are rare. Not that they are not to be found, for, happily, there are many, in all classes, whose native manhood is too vigorous to be repressed or perverted from its true instincts. Those, too, who by education and associations have gained a more liberal and balanced development than falls to the general share, have, as a class, proved excellent officers, and displayed the mettle and endurance which might be expected from those on whom the brand of fear would entail an intolerable punishment.

But, for the most fruitful and deplorable source of our military short-comings, we must look elsewhere than to the character of the population. Full as it is of vitality and courage, no candid man can doubt that, with every drawback, a force might in a little time be created out of it that might defy the world in arms, and march to assured and speedy conquest of the valiant traitors who have faced us so fiercely and so long. The fitness to command, hitherto kept latent by our social and political influences, might readily be called forth in this time of necessity. A military pride, such as the times demand, and will long continue to demand, might readily be fostered and the morale of the army raised to the highest pitch of efficiency. Officers appointed with a single eye to their fitness, merit sought out and promoted, demerit degraded,—such a system in short as has been followed by every successful commander, who ever turned citizens into soldiers,—would make us a people more formidable in war than any the world has seen. But, if a political and not a military principle is to control our organizations, if Bowery boys are made brigadiers, and if regimental officers are to be appointed, not because they are fit for the work, but because they are able and willing to serve the ends of some unworthy politician, if political subserviency is to be the criterion of military merit, and an honest reputation won in the brave and faithful discharge of duty is a bugbear in the eyes of those who pull the wires, then we must resign ourselves to an inglorious war and a ruinous peace. Politicians, great and small, have had a problem to solve,—how to win a victory without permitting the rise of a reputation which shall eclipse them. The latter requisition has been reasonably well fulfilled, but woefully to the sacrifice of the former. The armed slaveholder, backed by the passion, ignorance, and blindness, which he has drilled to do his work of treason, is a perilous enemy, but less insidious and less dangerous than the selfish politician.

F. P.

PRINTED: *Boston Daily Advertiser,* June 30, 1863.

The Chiefs of the Nation

[July 4, 1863]

To the Editors of the *Boston Daily Advertiser:*

We are a people wonderfully endowed, mightier in transformations than the Wizard of the North. Give us the raw material, and that, too, of the rawest,—weak, perhaps, and rotten withal,—it is all we ask. Quick as thought, by the magic of our institutions, behold generals, statesmen and foreign ministers. And why not? For no reason whatever, provided that this mode of production proves safe, economical and expedient; provided that it gives us the results we need, and with which in the present posture of our affairs, we cannot well dispense.

Our former copartner, now our foe, has long adopted a different system, the results of which we have groaned under for a generation and more. This is no time for clinging to mere theories of government, right or wrong. We must look to practical issues. Democracy has played her low cards long enough. She must play trumps now or lose the game. She wants men to represent her, men to lead her, not swarms of interwrithing worms to batten on her entrails. It is perilous to deal in figures of speech, and we would fain do honor to the ability, the fidelity, the patriotism which some of those in offices of trust have put forth in this dire exigency. There is good coinage in the public treasury, but not enough of it, nor of the highest alloy, while the base and the counterfeit is heaped there by the cartload.

Never, since history recorded the life of nations, was such a people so led, or rather so entangled in such a political meshwork. We have no allusion to this party or that. Men and parties will change, but the same bad system rules rampant over all. Still the same withering machinery of caucuses and conventions, the same combinations, wheel within wheel, of adroit and selfish managers, the same organized scramble of mean men for petty spoils, clogging the avenues and outlets of public opinion, jealously vigilant of the rostrum and the press, and limiting the votes of an acquiescent people to such candidates as may suit, not the national interests, but their own. As freemen and sovereigns we go to the polls and cast our votes, not after our own judgment, but at the dictation of self-constituted knots and combinations of men whom we can neither esteem nor trust. If we did otherwise, our vote would be thrown away. A many-headed despotism, exercised in the name of the largest liberty. If to degrade public morals, sink the national reputation, weaken the national counsels, root out the race of statesmen, and place a pliant incompetency in control of our destinies,—if these are the ends of government, then is our political management a masterpiece of human wit. They know better at the South. Through all the illusions and falsehoods with which that fierce and selfish aristocracy has encompassed itself, runs a vein of sound political truth. We may take a lesson of our enemy. If we do not, he may master us. Perhaps we have misunderstood the nature of a true democracy. It is a thriftless household that chooses for itself servants untaught and untrusted; yet, far more than any household, a great and mighty nation has the necessity and the right of being well and truly served. The wisest and the ablest are not too good for her, and her freedom consists in holding them under a sharp accountability, not in degrading them till they are unfit to do her work. "Let the best rule," is the maxim of aristocracy. "Let the best serve," is the maxim of the only healthful and permanent democracy.

Who are the best? They are gone; their race is died out. Surely as effect follows cause, for a half century, they have withered and dwindled away. The race, we mean, of legislators and statesmen, minds trained to apply great principles to practice, to grapple with great affairs, to guide the nation with a wise and temperate vigor along the giddy heights of that grand destiny which awaited her, and perhaps awaited her in vain. When will such men return? When a deep and abiding sense of our deep need of them has seized and possessed the national heart, when the fallacies that have deluded us so long shall be thrown from us as debasing and perilous illusions, and the national mind rises to a true conception of republican freedom.

F. P.

PRINTED: *Boston Daily Advertiser,* July 4, 1863.

Aristocrats and Democrats

[July 14, 1863]

To the Editors of the *Boston Daily Advertiser:*

It was a strange union that linked us to the South, and one that can never be renewed until we have thrust regeneration, total and absolute, into the innermost being of our adversary. Meanwhile, to consider for a moment, how well and boldly he has fronted us—how, with means scarcely the tithe of ours, he has stood at bay for two long years, and despite the zeal, the devotion, the courage of a mighty people, has led his warlike hordes to plunder at our thresholds. There is much to be learned from him, and, if we are as sagacious as we have been wont to think ourselves, we may draw profit from our adversity.

A head full of fire, a body ill-jointed, starved, attenuated, is matched against a muscular colossus, a Titan in energy and force—full of blood, full of courage, prompt for fight, and confident of victory. Strong head and weak body against strong body and weak head; oligarchy against democracy.

A few men—the leaven of the whole fermenting mass might almost be counted on the fingers—may be said to form the South, for they control and animate it. A truer aristocracy never existed, or a worse one when considered in its origin and foundation. But that which it most imports us to feel is the fearful efficiency of its education. We of New England are a bookish people. With us, the idea of education is inseparable from school-houses, school-masters, lyceums, public libraries, colleges, and diplomas. Yet these are but secondary agencies; pallid, nerveless, and emasculate, beside those mighty educational powers which spring out of the currents of life itself, the hopes, the fears, the responsibilities, the exigencies; the action or the idleness, the enjoyment or the suffering; the associations, the friendships, enmities, rivalries, and conflicts, which make the sum of each man's vital history. Not that the Southern aristocracy is ignorant of books. Of its number, are men high in scholarly accomplishment, valuable to those who know how to use it; futile in the mere votaries of the lamp. The culture of the South has long been the heart and focus of its political life, while that of the North has been rather an excrescence upon the vital system than a part of it. But this alone is not the education which has held back the mighty surges of democracy and dammed the Nile with bulrushes.

From his cradle the slave oligarch is taught that he holds a place of power and peril, isolated, pelted with opprobrium, beset with swarming foes,—a post to be held only by every effort of will and brain. A small class of men are linked together by a common interest and a common spirit; the pride, more than feudal, which belongs to their unbridled power over those who are less than vassals, is chafed to redoubled intensity by attacks from these whom they despise no less than they hate. With them, politics are a battleground where the issues are victory or ruin, and where passion, self-interest, self-preservation, urge to intensest action every power of their nature. Hence the vigor of their development, which can find no match either in our own best instructed classes, so weak in political influence and political training, or in that swarm of professed politicians, who, like flies in August, suck each his petty nutriment from the body of the long-suffering nation.

The Southern leaders knew the North chiefly through three classes of its population. They knew the merchants, whom they scorned as the feudal noble scorned the rich burgher, and the politicians in whom they found no concession too abject, no abasement too deep. Here lay their hope. In the subserviency of self-interest and low ambition, seeking to abase the nation to their level, the slaveholder saw his triumph. But there was another class, whom, despising not less, he hated with a bitter hate, the abolition agitators, whose clamors wakened the earthquake under his feet. That he should recognize the sound and earnest basis of this agitation was not in human nature. He saw it only in its extravagance, fanaticism and obstreperous weakness; classed it indiscriminately with that morbid brood of moral and social crudities which, to his thinking, was the natural progeny of pestilent New England, and the spawn of sickly minds besotted with the little learning said to be so dangerous.

These classes the Southern leaders knew, or thought they knew, and, knowing them, vainly thought they knew the Northern people. They knew, at least, that the Northern people were politically without a head. The eagle soared on our banners; the crow, the buzzard, and the owl, clamored in our council-halls. But they never dreamed how, under a surface of froth and scum, the great national heart still beat with the pulsations of patriotic manhood. The error has been their ruin.

They confront us in an antagonism as fierce and inevitable as that of steel white hot to the flood that quenches it. Oligarchy and Democracy, the strong head and the strong body, cannot live side by side. In war we can in time master them. In peace, every advantage will be with the concentrated will, the trained and subtle intellect. Our safety is in the destruction of their system and the purging of our own; in the development and use of the statesmanship latent among us, and long kept latent by the perverted action of our political machinery. An incalculable waste of wealth, time, life and honor, would have been spared to us, had the servants of the people been worthy of their trust.

F. P.

PRINTED: *Boston Daily Advertiser*, July 14, 1863.

Our Best Class and the National Politics

[July 21, 1863]

To the Editors of the *Boston Daily Advertiser:*

We mean our cultivated class, rich or not rich. We do not mean the untaught or half-taught offspring of the rich, a class than which none among us is more insignificant. Those we mean are few in number and very weak in political influence.

In other free countries the culture of the nation is a strong and vital member of the body politic, giving and receiving life from the national veins; in despotisms it is the most dreaded foe of the despot, the centre of the national aspirations, the corps of the national heart. With us the case is reversed. Our cultivated class, from the fact of its culture, is in a great measure thrown aside from the broad and turbid current of our political life. It has been blamed for this, charged with inertness, squeamishness, and the like, but only with a very partial justice. Volition governs individuals, but the character of classes is simply a question of cause and effect.

In the main, this political nullity,—for it is little better,—comes of a vigorous and good stock; partly from that "Brahmin caste" which, as one of its members tells us, has yielded a progeny of gentlemen and scholars from the days of the Puritans; partly from the practical energy which has raised itself to place and fortune. It gives us admirable lawyers, excellent physicians and divines, good literary men, good men of science, here and there a finished scholar, here and there an artist, with accomplished dilettanti, intelligent travelers and well bred gentlemen. And, though it has long ceased to play any very active part in the dusty arena of political turmoil, its patriotism was not dead, but only dormant. Witness Ball's bluff, Shiloh, Cedar Mountain, and Antietam, Fredericksburg, Gettysburg, and the Peninsula, and the memory of those who at the blast of war rejoiced that at last they could serve their country without shame. Witness the necrology of Harvard University. Of her graduates, dead the past year, at and under the age of forty, thirty-five out of forty-three died on the battlefield, or from the wounds and diseases of war. Numbers more will bear its marks to their graves; and had all borne themselves as they, treason ere this would have groveled in the dust.

The well-instructed class has been jostled from political life far less by its own shortcomings than by the action of our political machine. Small rewards, in infinite number, the spoils of office, have called up an infinite swarm of small men, hungry, eager, clamorous, banded together in vast combinations, playing into each other's hands, and looking askance at those who will not utter their shibboleth. What can a handful do against a host in a country where the bought vote of the unlettered boor can neutralize the vote of the wisest and the best? Fall into the ranks or leave the service: here is the virtual demand of all those vast aggregations in which, under the covering mantle of a professed principle, self-interest and petty ambition hunt their game. The necessities, the exactions are too repugnant, the prize too small. Deplorable enough that the places of trust of a great nation should carry so little honor, confer so little social consideration; but, by a swift and steady progress, we have come at last to that ominous pass where "the post of honor is a private station." Not that the political-swarm think so. The prize in their eyes is a glittering lure, and the solid spoils a bait to be scrambled for in every posture of moral and mental gymnastics. Human nature has not much changed since the birth of Adam. It is in vain to expect any body of men to display much alacrity to reach an object which must be pursued through weariness, disgust and nausea, and which when obtained is not worth keeping. We mean that most of the ablest and best instructed minds of the nation, entering upon political life, would do so, not only without pecuniary gain, but at a pecuniary sacrifice, and would reap in return little but the satisfaction of doing a much needed service to the country. Honor to those, for such there are, with whom this consideration has had a prevailing weight. There are a few of the best culture who have entered, and for a time, remained in public life from little other consideration than simple patriotism. Their influence is a drop to the ocean, a cheaper quality than theirs will pass current in the political exchange. They are matched with as good talkers, as good declaimers; better managers, more practiced, adroit, and pliant. In short, they have found themselves in an element foreign and disagreeable to them, and have generally withdrawn after a time, consoling themselves that they have done their part.

This cultivated class is sometimes charged as relatively weak and unpractical. To a partial degree the charge is just. No class in the country has more natural elements of force, but these are not and cannot be fully developed. It lacks a career. All below it are impelled by stimulants and tempted by opportunities such as no other country can supply. Fortune, position, reputation, are within the possibilities of the humblest, and thousands upon thousands are straining nerve and muscle to ascend those heights to whose summits—though none of the loftiest —distance and the unknown still lend their mighty enchantment. The farmer's son dreams of the palatial mansion and the merchant prince, and the Demosthenes of the village debating club beholds in a vision the glories of the Senate Chamber and the White House. Here is the inspiration of a life-time. Each stoutly fights his way to the surface of the vast and shallow expanse, but here he must stop. Neither he nor his children after him can go farther. They must remain where they are, or sink again towards the bottom.

But the man with whom the fancied splendors, so potent at a distance, are robbed of every rag of their illusion, shares none of this invigorating and fertilizing stimulus. Special careers, and good ones, are open to him. He may give himself to the professions;—as, for example to the law, though without the prospect of the vast political and social elevation which in some other countries rewards the successful jurist. In the so called learned professions, however, this class has found its chief field of activity and acquitted itself well and honorably. In science and letters it has played a creditable part. For the pursuits which have for their object, directly and simply, the accumulation of money, it has shown little inclination. The full development of manhood, however, is not to be found in any one of these special pursuits; neither in the law when separated from the practical application of its broad principles to great affairs; nor in literature; much less in science. Despotisms fear literature; they encourage science as a harmless escape for a dangerous mental activity. Literature draws her strongest vitality from the pulsations of the great national heart; and let us most earnestly hope that those who best represent her may always be found, as they have been found since the outbreak of this great war of principles, in an intense and vital sympathy with those pulsations.

And here one is tempted to launch upon a boundless sea of disquisition. But we have touched our limit, and transcended it.

F. P.

PRINTED: The *Boston Daily Advertiser,* July 21, 1863.

To Mary Dwight Parkman

My Dear Mary, Boston Dec. 6th 1863

I began, some two months since a letter to you which was never sent & never finished. The same impulse, though acting somewhat differently, urges me to write now. Ida Agassiz was married yesterday. Unless I greatly mistake, you knew that her engagement could not be a matter of indifference to me. A kind note from her, telling me of it, took me wholly by surprise. She & I had been on terms of cordial friendship. She is certainly a most exceptional person, for though Mrs. Agassiz & at least one other person had suggested to her that there was more than friendship in my regards for her, she seems not to have believed it, but rather to have believed that the attitude which I had studiously assumed towards her expressed all that I felt. The truth is, that, for a year or two, my dearest wish has been to make her my wife; but during all that time I have carefully avoided the expression of anything beyond a simple though a very cordial friendship. And, to my astonishment, she seems to have been completely deceived. I took this course because I thought, & still think, that under the circumstances, it was the best. My health is too doubtful, and everything like exertion of mind, especially under stimulus, is too dangerous, not to say ruinous, for me to place myself, and ask another to be a sharer with me, in a position, in which exertion might be called for by necessity. A life time of disability has so far affected my position that I am not—or rather should not be if married—in the position of ease which the conditions of my health imperatively require. I waited therefore till either my health or my pecuniary condition should become more favorable. Both were improving, & on the very morning in which I received her note, I was pleasing myself with the thought that a time perhaps had come when without hazard to myself or unfairness to her, I might frankly state my feelings & the circumstances which had induced me to hide them, & without asking for any present response, ask leave to continue the same relations of intercourse as hitherto. She being at Nahant, I had not then seen her for several months, when her note came telling me of her engagement, and with characteristic unconsciousness, asking me to share with Henry Higginson[1] the friendship I felt for her. You may judge if the surprise was a pleasant one—for I had known nothing of this very old affair. It was more than a month before I had a night of tolerable sleep. As was inevitable the effect on my head was very bad, though not so serious as at one time I thought it would prove. I accepted her desire—as well as I could—wrote a note to Henry & went to see him—as hard work as I remember ever to have done. The rebels who sabred & shot him were the best friends he ever had. Last winter, she refused him decidedly, he went to the war, reckless, possibly, of his life, came back wounded, moved her compassion, & gained his wish. I like him, for a manly good fellow who, I hope, will make her happy. I have avoided seeing her, but, accidentally, met her twice, the first time, contrary to expectation, [*when*] at the side of his couch when I went to see him. You may judge if I slept the better for it. She feels towards me a cordial goodwill. Mrs. Agassiz knows what I have told you & is the kindest of friends. She—Ida—also knows at last, as I had never doubted that she had long known, or suspected.

The marriage which I had dreaded more than death is over, and thanks to the long preparation, without the expected torture. The lightning-like suddenness of the first stroke made it one of the most painful of my life. I do not regret my acquaintance with her—on the contrary, I value it. What remains is a friendship, cordial, I am sure, on both sides &, on both, founded on a solid base.

I have just met Mr. Hurd,[2] who desires to be remembered. Pray give my best regards to Mrs. Cleveland,[3] & remembrance to Nelly & Harry.[4] I look forward earnestly for your return. It will be more pleasure than I can tell you to see you again. Mrs. Cabot is well—I saw her yesterday. My sister Mary[5] is unchanged.

Affectionately
F. P.

ADDRESSED: Mrs. S. Parkman 4 Via Sistina Rome, Italy.
Postmarked Boston Dec. 9; Paris Dec. 22.
MS: Parkman Family Papers, Harvard College Library.

[1] Henry Lee Higginson (1834–1919), banker, Union soldier, founder of the Boston Symphony Orchestra, entered Harvard in 1851, the class of Alexander Agassiz, Ida's brother. He studied music after leaving college in his freshman year and about 1854, according to Ida, attended a "delightful German class," of which she was the teacher, much adored by her students. (Forbes, "The Agassiz School," Cambridge Historical Society *Publications*, XXXV, 39.) He enlisted as a second lieutenant in the Second Massachusetts Infantry and rose to major in another unit, the First Massachusetts Cavalry, fought at Antietam, and was severely wounded in a skirmish with the Confederates at Aldie, Maryland. During his long convalescence, he returned to Boston to marry Ida Agassiz. After the war he became one of Boston's most successful bankers. FP mentions Higginson in later letters without any antagonism as a rival for Ida's hand. Higginson was chairman of the committee which obtained subscriptions for FP's memorial on the edge of Jamaica Pond. Quinquennial folder on FP, HA. The fund was oversubscribed, and extra funds were used to set up the Parkman memorial fund to purchase books for the Harvard College Library Canadian Collection.

[2] Perhaps FP refers to Francis Parkman Hurd (1820–84), M.D. Harvard, 1839. Quinquennial folder on F.P. Hurd, HA. An Augustine Heard (1827–1905), Harvard class of 1847, who engaged in the China trade and became an American minister to Korea in 1890, was a correspondent of Mary Dwight Parkman.

[3] Sarah Perkins Cleveland, a correspondent of Mary Dwight Parkman.

[4] Mary D. Parkman's children. See note 4, FP to Mary D. Parkman, April 4, 1862.

[5] Mary Brooks Parkman. See note 1, FP to Mary B. Parkman, Dec. 22, 1858.

Southern Treatment of Federal Prisoners

Jamaica Plain, Sept. 29, 1864.

To the Editors of the *Boston Daily Advertiser:*

Gentleman:—My brother, John Eliot Parkman,[1] late captain's clerk, U. S. ship Aries, has recently arrived from an eight months' imprisonment in the South. The following statements were made by him in the family circle, without thought of their publication. At my request he consents that they should be made public.

On the seventh day of January last, his boat was overset in a gale, after boarding the rebel blockade-runner Dare, stranded near Georgetown, S.C. Another boat was also overset, and those who reached shore, four officers and twenty-four men, were captured by a body of Georgia cavalry. They were confined that night in a negro house, and after remaining wholly without food from the morning of the seventh to the evening of the eighth, were marched to Charleston, where they arrived on the twelfth. Those who dropped from exhaustion were placed on carts. Major White, the commanding officer, treated them with harshness, but two or three of the cavalry secretly declared themselves Union men, and gave the prisoners tobacco.

At Charleston they were placed in the State prison, in a room where all the glass was broken from the windows, and, as they had no blankets, the cold at night was very severe. The place was full of vermin of various kinds. Neither here nor elsewhere, except in a single instance, was straw or any substitute for it allowed them to sleep on. They slept on the bare floor, or the bare earth, wet or dry. In the prison of Charleston their food was a dish of mush, made of very coarse corn meal, often sour. In the middle was placed a lump of fat pork or other meat. Sometimes rice was substituted for the meal. The dish, which was rarely or never washed, was thrust in once a day, and the four prisoners shared it as they could, without plate, cup, spoon, knife or fork. At the end of three weeks, a female relative of the jailer, learning their condition, brought them plates and spoons of her own, and washed them daily.

At first, they were allowed to walk in the jail yard during an hour, once a fortnight. This liberty was afterwards extended, and at length they were allowed to take the air for a short time nearly every day. One end of the yard was assigned to them; the remainder was occupied by a crowd of confederate convicts and deserters, the sentinels walking between.

They were one hundred and twenty-five days in the Charleston prison. Thence, they were sent to Macon, where they arrived on the eighteenth of May. Six hundred prisoners from Richmond had arrived the day before, and other arrivals soon increased the number to about sixteen hundred, all officers. They were confined in a space of two and a half acres, enclosed by a high fence of boards with a platform near the top for the sentinels. Within this fence, and distant from it ten or fifteen feet, was a rope, or, in some parts, a wooden railing. This was called the "dead rope," and the sentinels were ordered to shoot any prisoner who should touch it. On one occasion a federal officer was shot through the back and killed in my brother's presence, though, when he received the shot, he was two or three paces distant from the rope. No redress could be had; the sentinel escaped unpunished.

There were two buildings within the enclosure, one a kind of barrack, assigned to the higher officers; the other a shed open on all sides. These sheltered but few of the prisoners. The rest had no shelter except tents made of their own blankets by those who had them. The heat of the sun was intense. There were occasional heavy rains, flooding the enclosure, compelling most of the prisoners to sleep, if they slept at all, in mud and water. After a delay of several weeks, other sheds were erected, and nearly all had eventually a kind of shelter. The condition of the federal soldiers at Andersonville was incomparably worse; more than thirty thousand men being packed in an enclosure scarcely large enough to permit motion, and exposed, without shelter, to the intensity of the southern sun. Death, insanity, and idiocy were fearfully rife among them. Men often seized the dead rope with both hands, and called on the sentinels to shoot. They were taken at their word.

At Macon, the prisoner's ration was one pint of coarse Indian meal, one-third of a pound of bacon, rancid, and sometimes full of worms, a handful of "cow peas" and rice, and a little salt. The prisoners were divided into messes of ten. To each was given a mess-kettle and frying pan. With the rest they supplied themselves if they could. Those who had money could buy a tin cup for five dollars. Escapes of prisoners were not infrequent, but all were found, by means of trained dogs kept for the purpose, and soon brought back.

The Fourth of July was a memorable day at Macon. Some secret unionist had contrived to convey a miniature American flag within the enclosure. This was carefully kept till the morning of Independence Day, when it was raised on a stick. All the prisoners who could stand gathered around it. Repeated cheers were given, and the Star Spangled Banner was sung by the whole assemblage. Other national airs followed. The enthusiasm became intense, and my brother saw rough East Tennesseeans and sturdy officers from the northwest with eyes streaming with tears. The confederates, though greatly exasperated, dare not attempt any other interference than remonstrances.

About the end of August, the prisoners were removed to Charleston. Six hundred of them, with half that number of guards, formed the first party. They were placed in cattle-cars, where, as there was no room for all to lie down, many were compelled to keep a half-sitting, half-kneeling position for a day and two nights, causing extreme pain, and in some cases permanent injury. Near Charleston eighty men escaped. All were brought in within ten days, having been hunted in the swamps with hounds. Their appearance was frightful. Their clothes were torn to shreds, their flesh lacerated with briars, their skin blistered with the heat, and their features swollen with the stings of mosquitoes. The confederates asserted that two of the fugitives had been severely bitten by the dogs, and were then in hospital.

At Charleston the six hundred prisoners were confined in the yard of the jail, without shelter for the greater part. The crowd was suffocating and the heat intense. They were exposed without respite to the sun when the thermometer was at 100 deg. The suffering was far greater than at Macon. In about a week, however, they were removed to a workhouse, used for negroes. It was filthy, yet comparatively endurable. Thence they were soon removed to the Roper hospital. Those who would give their parole were allowed to remain; the rest were sent to jail. At the hospital the accommodation and shelter were good, and here my brother remained until his exchange, early in September.

All the prisoners suffered from some form of illness, and the health of many is completely broken.

The above are the more essential statements made by my brother. Many significant particulars are omitted for the sake of brevity.

FRANCIS PARKMAN

PRINTED: *Boston Daily Advertiser,* September 30, 1864.

[1] John Eliot Parkman (1833–71), FP's younger brother (another brother, George, died in infancy). As a young man "Jack," as he was known, several times made the circuit of the world while engaged in "mercantile occupations." His *Boston Evening Transcript* obituary of December 23, 1871, states that he had "considerable natural ability as a writer," and this assertion is verified by the entertaining letters Jack sent his family from the Far East in the 1850's. In writing to his mother from Calcutta on June 11, 1854, he described his experience when his ship, the *Marcellus,* capsized while approaching the city: ". . . I was in the upper cabin at the time the accident occurred—the water rushed in with tremendous force filling the cabin and smashing down everything in its way, taking me with it of

course, but just as I was going overboard I caught hold of the cabin window and held on with all my might entirely under water for I should think fifteen seconds (it seemed many minutes) when the ship righted enough to get my head out of water so that the men on the dry side of the ship could see me and toss me a rope . . . the second mate and three men were drowned. . . ." (PP, MHS).

In May, 1861, he enlisted as a captain's clerk and served on three U. S. vessels in addition to the *Aries*, or *Ares*. In January, 1871, he was appointed secretary of Commodore Roger N. Stembel, U.S.N., commanding the North Squadron of the Pacific Fleet. He served on the U.S.S. *Pensacola* and died as a result of an accident on December 20 of that year. The log of the *Pensacola* shows that on this date her colors were lowered to half-mast "on account of the death of John Eliot Parkman, Commodore's Secretary." I am indebted to Admiral Samuel E. Morison for this information, which he found in Navy Department records.

When FP's Chestnut Street study was recently dismantled, a number of John Eliot's pen-and-ink and wash drawings of scenes and people of the Far East were found. These have been placed in FP's reconstructed study in the Colonial Society of Massachusetts headquarters at 87 Mount Vernon Street in Boston.

For the circumstances of John Eliot's death, see note 2, FP to Lt. Leonard E. Chenery, Jan. 10, 1872.

To Charles Eliot Norton

50 Ches[t]nut St.
Wed. 9 Nov. [1864][1]

My Dear C.

I have a paper on Indian social & political organization, & the traits which produced it or were produced by it. It [*embodies*] is the result of a very careful study of every thing—I speak literally—of the least value which has been written on or near the subject in early or recent times. Though written for another purpose, the paper with a slight alteration will answer for a review.[2] There are 60 pages of 200 words.

If you think it may suit your purpose for the N. A. I will send it for examination.

Truly Yrs.
F. Parkman

P.S. The tribes especially referred to are the "sedentary" agricultural races—not our wandering New England Indians. Much will be wholly new to most people.

MS: Norton Papers, Harvard College Library.

[1] Endorsed by Norton, "Nov. 9, 1864."

[2] This paper was published in the *North American Review*, Vol. CI (July, 1865), 28–64, under the title of "Manners and Customs of Primitive Indian Tribes." It was based almost entirely on Jesuit Rela-

tions, which FP stated were "by far the most full and trustworthy authority." *Ibid.*, 28. Most of the material in the article later appeared in the introduction to *Jesuits*, I, 3–87.

To George E. Ellis

50 Chestnut St., 28 Nov. [1864][1]

My dear Friend,—Running my eye over this paper, I am more than ever struck with its egoism, which makes it totally unfit for any eye but that of one in close personal relations with me.

It resulted from a desire—natural, perhaps, but which may just as well be suppressed—to make known the extreme difficulties which have reduced to very small proportions what might otherwise have been a good measure of achievement. Having once begun it, I went on with it, though convinced that it was wholly unsuited to see the light.

Physiologically considered, the case is rather curious. My plan of life from the first was such as would have secured great bodily vigor in nineteen cases out of twenty, and was only defeated in its aim by an inborn irritability of constitution which required gentler treatment than I gave it. If I had my life to live over again, I would follow exactly the same course again, only with less vehemence. Very cordially,

F. PARKMAN.

PRINTED: Farnham, *Life of Francis Parkman*, 315.

[1] Farnham's *Life of Francis Parkman* dates this letter as Nov. 28, 1868. The accompanying autobiographical letter was apparently written sometime in 1864, however. It is possible that FP kept the autobiographical letter in his possession for four years before turning it over to Ellis. The original MS of the cover letter is not in the Parkman or Ellis Papers at the Massachusetts Historical Society.

To George E. Ellis

AN AUTOBIOGRAPHICAL LETTER[1]

[1864][2]

[The first seven pages of the manuscript are missing.]

Allusion was made at the outset to obstacles which have checked the progress of the work, if the name of obstacles can be applied to obstructions at times impassable and of such a nature that even to contend against them would have been little [*less*] else than an act of self-destruction. The case in question is certainly an exceptional one; but as it has analogies with various other cases, not rare under the stimulus of our social and material influences, a knowledge of it may prove of use. For this as for other reasons, the writer judges it expedient to state it in full, though in doing so much personal detail must needs be involved.

His childhood was neither healthful nor buoyant.[3] His boyhood though for a time active, was not robust, and, at the age of eleven or twelve, he conceived a vehement liking for pursuits, a devotion to which at that time of life far oftener indicates a bodily defect than a mental superiority. Chemical experiment was his favorite hobby, and he pursued it with a tenacious eagerness which, well guided, would have led to some acquaintance with the rudiments of the science, but which in fact served little other purpose than injuring him by confinement, poisoning him with noxious gases, and occasionally scorching him with some ill-starred explosion.

The age of fifteen or sixteen produced a revolution. At that momentous period of life retorts and crucibles were forever [*laid aside*] discarded, and an activity somewhat excessive took the place of voluntary confinement. A new passion seized him, which, but half gratified, still holds its force. He became enamoured of the woods, a fancy which soon gained full control over the course of the literary pursuits to which he was also addicted. After the usual boyish phases of ambitious self-ignorance, he resolved to confine his homage to the Muse of History, as being less apt than her wayward sisters to requite his devotion with a mortifying rebuff. At the age of eighteen, the plan which he is still attempting to execute was, in its most essential features, formed.[4] His idea was clear before him, yet attended with unpleasant doubts as to his ability to realize it to his own satisfaction. To solve these doubts he entered upon a training tolerably well fitted to serve his purpose, slighted all college studies which could not promote it, and pursued with avidity such as had a bearing upon it, however indirect.

The task, as he then reckoned, would require about twenty years. The time allowed was ample, but here he fell into a fatal error, entering on this long pilgrimage with all the vehemence of one starting on a mile heat. His reliance, however, was less on books than on such personal experience as should, in some sense, identify him with his theme. His natural inclinations urged him in the same direction, for his thoughts were always in the forests, whose features, not unmixed with softer images, possessed his waking and sleeping dreams, filling him with vague cravings impossible to satisfy. As fond of hardships as he was vain of enduring them, cherishing a sovereign scorn for every physical weakness or defect, deceived, moreover, by a rapid development of frame and sinews, which flattered him with the belief that discipline sufficiently unsparing would harden him into an athlete, he slighted the precautions of a more reasonable woodcraft, tired old foresters with long marches, stopped neither for heat nor rain, and slept on the earth without a blanket. Another cause added not a little to the growing evil. It was impossible that conditions of the nervous system, abnormal as his had been from infancy, should be without their effects on the mind, and some of these were of a nature highly to exasperate him. Unconscious of their character and origin, and ignorant that with time and confirmed health they would have disappeared, he had no other thought than that of crushing them by force, and accordingly applied himself to the work. Hence resulted a state of mental tension, habitual for several years, and abundantly mischievous in its effects. With a mind over-strained and a body over-taxed, he was burning his candle at both ends.[5]

But if a systematic and steady course of physical activity can show no better results, have not the advantages of such a course been overrated? In behalf of manhood and common sense, he would protest against such a conclusion; and if any pale student, glued to his desk, here, seek an apology for a way of life whose natural fruit is that pallid and emasculate scholarship of which New England has had too many examples, it will be far better that this sketch had not been written. For the student there is, in its season, no better place than the saddle, and no better companion than the rifle or the oar. A highly irritable organism spurred the writer to excess in a course, which, with one of different temperament, would have produced a free and hardy development of such faculties and forces as he possessed. Nor, even in the case in question, was the evil unmixed, since from the same source whence it issued came also the habits of mind and muscular vigor which saved him from a ruin absolute and irremediable.

In his own behalf, he is tempted to add to this digression another. Though the seat of derangement may be the nervous system, it does not of necessity follow that the subject is that which, in the common sense of the word is called 'nervous.' The writer was [*once*] now and then felicitated on 'having no nerves' by those who thought themselves maltreated by that mysterious portion of [*the*] human organism.

This subterranean character of the mischief, rarely declaring itself at the surface, doubtless increased its intensity, while it saved it from being a nuisance [*from*] to those around.

Of the time when, leaving college, he entered nominally on the study of law—though in fact with the determination that neither this nor any other pursuit should stand in the path of his projects—his recollection is of mingled pain and pleasure. His faculties were stimulated to their best efficiency. Never, before or since, has he known so great a facility of acquisition and comprehension.[6] Soon, however, he became conscious that the impelling force was growing beyond his control. Labor became a passion, and rest intolerable, yet with a keen appetite for social enjoyments in which he found not only a pleasure, but in some sense, a repose. The stimulus rapidly increased. Despite of judgment and of will, his mind turned constantly towards remote objects of pursuit and strained vehemently to attain them. The condition was that of a rider whose horse runs headlong, the bit between his teeth, or of a locomotive, built of indifferent material, under a head of steam too great for its strength, hissing at a score of crevices, yet rushing on with accelerating speed to the inevitable smash.

A specific sign of the mischief soon appeared in a weakness of sight, increasing with an ominous rapidity. Doubtless to study with the eyes of another is practicable, yet the expedient is not an eligible one, and the writer bethought him of an alternative. It was essential to his plans to gain an inside view of Indian life. This then was the time at once to accomplish the object and rest his failing vision. Accordingly he went to the Rocky Mountains, but he had reckoned without his host. A complication of severe disorders here seized him, and at one time narrowly missed bringing both him and his schemes to an abrupt termination, but, yielding to a system of starvation, at length assumed an intermittent and much less threatening form. A concurrence of circumstances left him but one means of accomplishing his purpose. This was to follow a large band of Ogillallah Indians, known to have crossed the Black Hill range a short time before. Reeling in the saddle with weakness and pain, he set forth, attended by a Canadian hunter. With much difficulty the trail was found, the Black Hills crossed, the reluctance of his follower overcome, and the Indians discovered [*the*] on the fifth day encamped near the Medicine Bow range of the Rocky

Mountains. On a journey of a hundred miles, over a country in parts of the roughest, he had gained rather than lost strength, while his horse was knocked up and his companion disconsolate with a painful cough. Joining the Indians, he followed their wanderings for several weeks. To have worn the airs of an invalid would certainly have been an indiscretion, since in that case a horse, a rifle, a pair of pistols, and a red shirt might have offered temptations too strong for aboriginal virtue. Yet to hunt buffalo on horseback, over a broken country, when, without the tonic of the chase, he could scarcely sit upright in the saddle, was not strictly necessary for maintaining the requisite prestige. The sport, however, was good, and the faith undoubting that, to tame the devil, it is best to take him by the horns.

As to the advantages of this method of dealing with that subtle personage, some question may have arisen in his mind, when, returning after a few months to the settlements, he found himself in a condition but ill [*suited*] adapted to support his theory. To the maladies of the prairie, succeeded a suite of exhausting disorders, so reducing him that circulation at the extremities ceased, the light of the sun became insupportable, and a wild whirl possessed his brain, joined to a universal turmoil of the nervous system which put his philosophy to the sharpest test it had hitherto known. All collapsed, in short, but the tenacious strength of muscles hardened by long activity. This condition was progressive, and did not reach its height, or, to speak more fitly, its depth, until some eighteen months after his return. The prospect before him was by no means attractive, contrasting somewhat pointedly with his boyish fancy of a life of action and a death in battle. Indeed, the change from intense activity to flat stagnation, attended with an utter demolition of air-castles, may claim a place, not of the meanest, in that legion of mental tortures which make the torments of the Inferno seem endurable. The desire was intense to return to the prairie and try a hair of the dog that bit him, but this kill-or-cure expedient was debarred by the certainty that a few days' exposure to the open sunlight would have destroyed his sight.

In the spring of 1848, the condition indicated being then at its worst, the writer resolved to attempt the composition of the "History of the Conspiracy of Pontiac," of which the material had been for some time collected and the ground prepared. The difficulty was so near to the impossible that the line of distinction often disappeared, while medical prescience condemned the plan as a short road to dire calamities.

His motive, however, was, in part, a sanitary one, growing out of a conviction that nothing could be more deadly to his bodily and mental health than the entire absence of a purpose and an object. The difficulties were threefold; an extreme weakness of sight, disabling him even from writing his name except with eyes closed; a condition of the brain prohibiting fixed attention except at occasional and brief intervals, and an exhaustion and total derangement of the nervous system, producing of necessity a mood of mind most unfavorable to effort. To be made with impunity, the attempt must be made with the most watchful caution.

He caused a wooden frame to be constructed of the size and shape of a sheet of letter-paper. Stout wires were fixed horizontally across it, half an inch apart, and a movable back of thick pasteboard fitted behind them.[7] The paper for writing was placed between the pasteboard and the wires, guided by which, and using a black lead crayon, he could write not illegibly with closed eyes. He was at the time absent from home, on Staten Island, where, and in the neighboring city of New York, he had friends who willingly offered their aid. It is needless to say to which half of humanity nearly all these kind assistants belonged. He chose for a beginning that part of the work which offered fewest difficulties and with the subject of which he was most familiar, namely the Siege of Detroit. The books and documents, already partially arranged, were procured from Boston, and read to him at such times as he could listen to them, the length of each reading never, without injury, much exceeding half an hour, and periods of several days frequently occurring during which he could not listen at all. Notes were made by him with closed eyes, and afterwards deciphered and read to him till he had mastered them. For the first half year, the rate of composition averaged about six lines a day. The portion of the book thus composed was afterwards partially rewritten.

His health improved under the process, and the remainder of the volume,—in other words, nearly the whole of it—was composed in Boston, while pacing in the twilight of a large garret, the only exercise which the sensitive condition of his sight permitted him in an unclouded day while the sun was above the horizon. It was afterwards written down from dictation by relatives under the same roof, to whom he was also indebted for the preparatory readings. His progress was much less tedious than at the outset, and the history was complete in about two years and a half.

He then entered upon the subject of "France in the New World," —a work, or series of works, involving minute and extended investigation. The difficulties which met him at the outset were incalculable. Wholly unable to use his eyes, he had before him the task, irksome at best where there is no natural inclination for it, of tracing out, collecting, indexing, arranging, and digesting a great mass of incongruous material scattered on both sides of the Atlantic. Those pursuing historical studies under the disadvantages of impaired sight have not hitherto attempted in person this kind of work during the period of their disability, but have deputed it to skilled and trusty assistants, a most wise course in cases where it is practicable. The writer, however, partly from the nature of his subject and his plan, though in special instances receiving very valuable aid, was forced in the main to rely on his own research. The language was chiefly French, and the reader was a girl from the public schools, ignorant of any tongue but her own. The effect, though highly amusing to bystanders, was far from being so to the person endeavoring to follow the meaning of this singular jargon. Catalogues, indexes, tables of contents in abundance were, however, read, and correspondence opened with those who could lend aid or information. Good progress had been made in the preliminary surveys, and many books examined and digested on a systematic plan for future reference, when a disaster befell the writer which set his calculations at naught.

This was an effusion of water on the left knee, in the autumn of 1851. A partial recovery was followed by a relapse, involving a close confinement of two years and a weakened and sensitive condition of the joint from which it has never recovered. The effects of the confinement were as curious as unenviable. All the irritability of the system centered in the head. The most definite of the effects produced was one closely resembling the tension of an iron band, secured round the head and contracting with an extreme force, with the attempt to concentrate the thoughts, listen to reading, or at times to engage in conversation. This was, however, endurable in comparison with other forms of attack which cannot be intelligibly described from the want of analogous sensations by which to convey the requisite impressions. The brain was stimulated to a restless activity impelling through it a headlong current of thought which, however, must be arrested and the irritated organ held in quiescence on a penalty to avert which no degree of exertion was too costly. The whirl, the confusion, and strange undefined torture attending this condition are only to be conceived by one who has felt them. Possibly they may have analogies in the savage punishment once in use in some of our [*state*] prisons, where drops of water were made to fall from a height on the shaved head of the offender, soon producing an effect which brought to reason the most contumacious. Sleep, of course, was banished during the periods of attack, and in its place was demanded, for the exclusion of thought, an effort more severe than the writer has ever put forth in any other cause. In a few hours, however, a condition of exhaustion would ensue, and both patient and disease being spent, the latter fell into a dull lethargic state far more supportable. Excitement or alarm would probably have proved wholly ruinous.

These were the extreme conditions of the disorder which has reached two crises, one at the end of 1853; the other in 1858. In the latter case it was about four years before the power of mental application was in the smallest degree restored, nor, since the first year of the confinement has there been any waking hour when he has not been in some degree conscious of the presence of the malady. Influences tending to depress the mind have at all times proved far less injurious than those tending to excite or even pleasurably exhilarate, and a lively conversation has often been a cause of serious mischief. A cautious vigilance has been necessary from the first, and this cerebral devil has perhaps had his uses as a teacher of philosophy.

Meanwhile the Faculty of Medicine were not idle, displaying that exuberance of resource for which that remarkable profession is justly famed. The wisest, indeed, did nothing, commending his patient to time and faith; but the activity of his brethren made full amends for this masterly inaction. One was for tonics, another for a diet of milk; one counselled galvanism, another hydropathy; one scarred him behind the neck with nitric acid, another drew red-hot irons along his spine with a view of enlivening that organ. Opinion was divergent as practice. One assured him of recovery in six years, another thought that he would never recover. Another, with grave circumlocution, lest the patient should take fright, informed him that he was the victim of an organic disease of the brain, which must needs despatch him to another world within a twelvemonth, and he stood amazed at the smile of an auditor who neither cared for the announcement nor believed it. Another, an eminent physiologist of Paris, after an acquaintance of three months, one day told him that, from the nature of the disorder, he had at first [*disorder*] supposed that it must in accordance with precedent be attended with insanity, and had ever since been studying him to discover under what form the supposed aberration declared itself, adding, with a somewhat humorous look, that his researches had not been rewarded with the smallest success.

In the severer periods of the disorder, books were discarded for horticulture, which benign pursuit has proved most salutary in its influences. One year, four years, and numerous short intervals lasting from a day to a month, represent these literary interruptions since the work in hand was begun. Under the most favorable conditions, it was a slow and doubtful navigation, beset with reefs and breakers, demanding a constant lookout and a constant throwing of the lead. Of late years, however, the condition of the sight has so far improved as to permit reading, not exceeding, on the average, five minutes at one time. This modicum of power, though apparently trifling, proves of the greatest service, since, by a cautious management, its application may be extended. By reading for one minute, and then resting for an equal time, this alternate process may generally be continued for about half an hour. Then, after a sufficient interval, it may be repeated, often three or four times in the course of the day. By this means nearly the whole of the volume now offered has been composed. When the conditions were such as to render systematic application possible, a reader has been employed, usually a pupil of the public schools. On one occasion, however, the services of a young man, highly intelligent, and an excellent linguist, were obtained for a short time. With such assistance every difficulty vanished, but it could not long be continued.

At present the work, or rather the series of separate works, stands as follows. Most of the material is collected or within reach. Another volume, on the Jesuits in North America, is one third written. Another, on the French Explorers of the Great West, is half written, while a third, devoted to the chequered career of Louis de Buade, Comte de Frontenac, is partially arranged for composition. Each work is designed to be a unit in itself, independently of the rest, but the whole, taken as a series, will form a connected history of France in the New World.

How far, by a process combining the slowness of the tortoise, with the uncertainty of the hare, an undertaking of close and extended research can be advanced, is a question to solve which there is no aid from precedent, since it does not appear that [*the*] an attempt under similar circumstances has hitherto been made. The writer looks, however, for a fair degree of success.

Irksome as may be the requirements of conditions so anomalous, they are far less oppressive than the necessity they involve of being busied with the past when the present has claims so urgent, and holding the pen with a hand that should have grasped the sword.

MS: Dictated, Parkman Papers, Massachusetts Historical Society.

[1] A second, similar autobiographical letter was written to Martin Brimmer sometime in 1886 with instructions that it be given the Massachusetts Historical Society after FP's death. It is a dictated MS in the Parkman Papers and has been printed in the appendix of Henry Dwight Sedgwick's *Francis Parkman* (Boston, 1904). Since this second letter is in large part repetitious and is available in printed form, only significant excerpts are quoted in the footnotes below. Brimmer (1829–96), Harvard class of 1849, whose father was mayor of Boston, was active in Massachusetts politics, a member of the St. Botolph Club, which FP helped to found, and a prominent member of the Massachusetts Historical Society. Quinquennial folder on Martin Brimmer, HA.

[2] Near the end of this letter, FP describes his plans for writing and publication. It is apparent that the letter was written late in 1864, or possibly in the early part of 1865.

[3] In his 1886 letter to Brimmer, FP gave additional information about his childhood: "As a child I was sensitive and restless, rarely ill, but never robust. At eight years I was sent to a farm belonging to my maternal grandfather on the outskirts of the extensive tract of wild and rough woodland now called Middlesex Fells. I walked twice a day to a school of high but undeserved reputation about a mile distant, in the town of Medford. Here I learned very little, and spent the intervals of schooling more profitably in collecting eggs, insects, and reptiles, trapping squirrels and woodchucks, and making persistent though rarely fortunate attempts to kill birds with arrows. After four years of this rustication I was brought back to Boston, when I was unhappily seized with a mania for experiments in chemistry."

[4] In his 1886 letter to Brimmer, FP enlarges on his early writing plans: "Before the end of the sophomore year my various schemes had crystallized into a plan of writing the story of what was thus known as the 'Old French War' . . . for here, as it seemed to me, the forest stage drama was more stirring and the forest stage more thronged with appropriate actors than in any other passage of our history. It was not till some years later that I enlarged the plan to include the whole course of the American conflict between France and England; or, in other words, the history of the American forest; for this was the light in which I regarded it. My theme fascinated me, and I was haunted with wilderness images day and night.

"From this time forward, two ideas possessed me. One was to paint the forest and its tenants in true and vivid colors; the other was to realize a certain ideal of manhood, a little mediaeval, but nevertheless good."

[5] In the second letter he writes: "The first hint that my method of life was not to prove a success occurred in my junior year, in the shape of a serious disturbance in the action of the heart, of which the immediate cause was too violent exercise in the gymnasium. I was thereupon ordered to Europe."

[6] Concerning his law school period he writes in the second letter: "Here, while following the prescribed courses at a quiet pace, I entered in earnest on two other courses, one of general history, the other of Indian history and ethnology, and at the same time studied diligently the models of English style."

[7] FP had two frames, one of wood, and another of metal. Both are preserved in his reconstructed study at the Colonial Society of Massachusetts in Boston. W. H. Prescott's "noctograph" was quite similar, a frame covered with red leather with sixteen horizontal brass wires. The noctograph has a back and front cover to protect the frame, and, when the covers are closed, it resembles a leather-bound notebook. It was often on exhibit in the museum of the Massachusetts Historical Society.

To Charles Francis Adams[1]

Dear Sir, Boston 15 March 1865

I take the liberty of sending you the proofs of an historical book[2] of mine which Messrs Little, Brown, & Co. are to publish here. I wish to make an attempt towards its publication in England, & though not at all sanguine of success—as the subject is American—I am sure that the chance of succeeding would be better if the publisher should receive it through you. I shall feel much indebted to you if you will send it to Messrs Sampson Low [*&*] Son & Co, 14 Ludgate Hill, with the enclosed letter, which, as you will see, contains my proposals to them. I address Messrs Low because I think them more likely than others to take up an American book, though I should be glad to have it brought out by any [*other*] respectable publisher.

Let me take this opportunity of expressing my sense of the debt owed by all loyal Americans to the judgment & ability which have rendered services of such value to the national safety & honor.

Pray give my compliments & cordial remembrance to Mrs. Adams.

I have the honor to be, Dear Sir,

with the highest consideration

Truly Yours

FRANCIS PARKMAN

P.S. Mr. Hillard has just left the enclosed note to you, which I send with the others.

MS: Adams Papers, Massachusetts Historical Society.

[1] Charles Francis Adams (1807–86), son of John Quincy Adams and father of Henry Adams, the historian, was the American minister to Britain in the years 1861–68, a turbulent period in American diplomacy described in Henry Adams' *Education.* In his reply to FP of April 13, 1865, C. F. Adams indicated that he had forwarded the proofs to Sampson and Low and added: "I am greatly obliged to you for the friendly terms in which you refer to my labors here. If in the midst of the perils of the country, I shall have been able to contribute any mite to diminish them, the reflection will be a superabundant compensation to me for the remainder of my days."

[2] *The Pioneers.*

To John G. Shea

Jamaica Plain
Near Boston
18 May 1865

My Dear Mr. Shea,

I received your note yesterday & send you today a proof of the head of Menendez[1] wh. I have had engraved. It is a facsimile—size of original—of the head alone, as the book will not be large enough for the entire picture.

The engraving sent me by Mr. Smith[2] is of course at your service, should you want it, & I, and I think my publishers, will be happy to hear any suggestion you may wish to make with regard to the steel plate.

I take this opportunity of sending you the title pages, Introduction, & Contents of the volume for wh. the plate was engraved. I intended to send them soon in any case. They will tell their own story, & I should feel much obliged by a mention of the plan and the intended publication [*within a short time*] in the Magazine. The [*book*] plates are all cast & the book will probably appear in Sept. having been withheld this spring in consequence of the excitement of the times (1 vol. 420 pp, 2 maps)

Believe me ever
Very truly Yrs
F. P.

MS: Parkman Letters, Library of Congress.

[1] This portrait of Menendez de Avilés, the villain of FP's saga of the Huguenots in Florida, is reproduced in *Pioneers* I, 96.

[2] Buckingham Smith. See note 2, FP to George H. Moore, Nov. 28 [1856].

To Charles Eliot Norton

Jamaica Plain
29 May 1865

My Dear C.

I have on hand a completion of the paper[1] of wh. I have just returned proofs. It is on the religious ideas of primitive Indians, a subject which, though a great deal has been talked & written about it, has not been critically or closely examined. I have been led to conclusions different from those currently accepted. The paper, with the notes and illustrations, will be a good deal shorter than the first. If you want it, it will be at your service, I retaining right of future use.

I send you with this the title pages, Introduction, Contents, etc of a forthcoming book, & should like to have you run your eye over them. I don't know if it is in the way of the North American to make any announcement in advance of literary births, but if this is the case, a mention would oblige.

F. P.

[P.S.] If convenient, I should be glad to have 12 copies of "Manners & Customs of Indians" struck off for me at my expense.

MS: Norton Papers, Harvard College Library.

[1] Published in the *North American Review*, Vol. CIII (July, 1866), 1–18, under the title of "Indian Superstitions." A large portion of the article is based on Nicolas Perrot's *Mémoire sur les Moeurs, Coustumes et Relligion des Sauvages de l'Amérique Septentrionale* (Leipzig and Paris, 1864).

To George E. Ellis

My Dear Mr. Ellis, Boston 3 June 1865

I leave you the sheets of my book, as I am going to Washington[1] for a week or two, and shall have no time to come & see you. I hope to do so when I come back—about the middle of the month.—Shall be glad if you will look over the sheets at your leisure.

Very truly yours,
F. Parkman

ADDRESSED: Rev. Dr. Ellis Charlestown Kindness of Mr. John H. Ellis.
MS: H. H. Edes Papers, Massachusetts Historical Society.

[1] As a member of the library committee of the Boston Athenaeum, FP was largely responsible for the superb collection of Confederate imprints in the Athenaeum described in Walter Muir Whitehill and Marjorie Lyle Crandall, *Confederate Imprints: A Check List Based Principally on the Collection of the Boston Athenaeum* (Boston, 1955). As a historian FP knew the value of assembling materials printed in the South during the period of the Confederacy. In June, 1865, FP, traveling with his friend Dr. Algernon Coolidge, purchased a number of Confederate newspapers, government documents, books, and tracts, for the most part Richmond publications. FP's expense account, amounting to $418, is reproduced in *ibid.*, 5.

To Grace Parkman[1]

Washington
7 June 1865

My Dear Gracy,

I was sorry not to see you & Katy before I went away, but I had no time to come. I reached Washington yesterday morning and went over to the camps where there are still about a hundred thousand soldiers, though a great many are going off every day. I am just about to go again, but wish first to write a line to you. Dr. Coolidge[2] is here too. I hope when I come home that you & Katy will be able to come to Brookline. There were no plants in pots left, and it was too late to move any others, so I could not do anything for your garden. With love to Katy.

Affecty. Yrs.
PAPA

Dr. Coolidge wishes you to tell Aunt Mora that the ladies have come safely to Washington.

I do not mean to stay here many days, so should not get a letter if you wrote it.

MS: Parkman Papers, Massachusetts Historical Society.

[1] Grace Parkman (1851–1928), FP's eldest daughter, with her sister "Katy," lived with "Aunt Mora," or Mary Bigelow, FP's sister-in-law. See Introduction. In 1879, Grace married Charles P. Coffin, an attorney of Lynn, Massachusetts. Mary Bigelow Coffin, "Parkman Genealogy." FP made a crude drawing of a cat's head in the upper right-hand corner of the MS.

[2] Dr. Algernon Coolidge (1830–1912), M.D., Harvard, 1853, was a direct descendant of Thomas Jefferson through his mother, Eleanor Randolph Coolidge. He had served in the Sanitary Commission during the war, and his twin brother Major Sidney Coolidge had been killed at the battle of Chickamauga. Quinquennial folder on A. Coolidge, HA. Coolidge was a desirable companion for FP, for he wished to see his Virginia relatives in Richmond and Charlottesville.

To Katharine Parkman[1]

Tuesday A.M.
[1865?][2]

My Deer Katy,

Me and Creem are wel. We send u our luv. We do not fite now. We have milk every day. One day, when i was playing under the evergreens, Creem would not lap her milk till she had come and told me that it was reddy, and we both went and lapped it together. Papa holds me every night to [*make*] keep me tame. Give my luv to Grace and ant mora. Tell ant mora that Doctor Forkland is engaged to Abby Adams. They told me I must not tell of it yesterday, but today it is out. Tell Grace that Mrs. Dannil D [. . .] asked about her and says she is coming to see her when she comes home. It is dredful hot hear.

Yors till deth
FLORA
her M[paw mark]*ark*

(I struggled so my paw has not made a good mark)

P.S. Plese bring me a skulpin.
P.P.S. Papa says to thank Grace for her letter, and he is glad she is having such a good time.
N.B. This is a lok of my fer, with best luv of yors in haste [lock of soft gray fur attached].

PUSS.

MS: Parkman Papers, Massachusetts Historical Society.

[1] Katharine Parkman (1858–1900), FP's youngest daughter, in 1879 married John Templeman Coolidge. See Introduction.

[2] This letter is very difficult to date, but there are family letters in the Parkman Papers indicating that Mary Bigelow took FP's daughters to Nahant in the summer of this year. If this letter was written in the summer of 1865, Katy would have been almost eight years old, and the language FP uses makes it plausible that the letter was sent in this year.

To Charles Eliot Norton

Jamaica Plain
9 Aug. 1865

My Dear Charles,

I have lately sent—as you were absent—a copy of "Pioneers of France" to Mr. Lowell[1] (for the N. A. Rev.) I shall be glad to have it noticed in the "Nation," & write to you for instructions. Shall I direct a copy to you, & do you prefer a copy *now*, [*in sheets*] stitched, or a bound copy when one can be had—say early in Sept. about which time the book will probably be published? You will perfectly understand that in sending you a copy, I have no idea of engaging you to a *favorable* notice. I know that you understand the obligations of criticism too well to feel yourself so engaged; and, for my own part, I should prefer that my reviewer should stand aloof, for the time, from personal regards. I propose to send you the book, not because I wish a friend to praise me, but because [*I believe*] I am told that you are a critic of the "Nation."

I have the article on Ind. superstitions ready. It will make some 20 pages of the review, & is at your service whenever wanted.

I am glad to see a word of justice for Isaac Taylor in the "Nation"—of which, by the way, I have great hopes as an elevator of the general standard of literary taste.[2]

Returning from a journey southward and endeavoring to visit yourself & family, I found you gone

Faithfully
F. PARKMAN

MS: Norton Papers, Harvard College Library.

[1] James Russell Lowell (1819–91) Harvard class of 1838, poet, editor, critic, and reformer, one of the foremost men of letters of his time, joined Charles Eliot Norton in editing the *North American Review* in 1864.

[2] The *Nation*, established by FP's friend Edwin L. Godkin in 1865, became an influential critical weekly. For a number of years FP contributed anonymous reviews to it, including a remarkable critique of himself, "Mr. Parkman and His Canadian Critics," Vol. XXVII (August 1, 1878), 66–67, in which he defended his works against Abbé Casgrain's criticisms. In the issues of July 27, 1865, and August 10, 1865, the *Nation* carried obituary articles on Isaac Taylor (1787–1865), British inventor and author of *History of the Transmission of Ancient Books to Modern Times* (London, 1827) and *The World of the Mind* (London, 1857).

To Lewis H. Morgan

My dear Sir— Boston, Sept. 24th 1865

I have received your letter of Sept. 20th, and am very glad to hear from you.[1] I fully agree with you as to the possibility of deriving very important results from the analysis and comparison of Indian practices and institutions. My own examinations have been made with an historical, not an ethnological, object, though I have always felt much interest in the ethnological aspect of the subject. The article in the *North American*, together with that which is to follow it, will eventually form the introduction to a book on the Jesuit Missions among the Indians. This is the reason why the scope of the articles is confined chiefly to the Iroquois and Algonquin tribes, these being the tribes concerned in the Missions.

All that I have been able to discover strongly inclines me to the belief that the natives of Mexico and Peru are radically of one family with our Northern Indians, though I cannot say that I have reached as yet any clear conviction. The "Medicine Lodge"[2] is certainly a very curious subject, and I wish I could say that I had unravelled it. It has no analogy, at least in form, in either the Iroquois or Algonquins, but I incline to think that it belongs to the same class of superstitions with the "Medicine Dances" and "Medicine Feasts" of those tribes. You are probably aware that it is not wholly confined to the Mandans and Minnitarees.[3] I have seen a Sioux chief of one of the western bands severely scarred with the traces of it.

I am sorry to say that I have never had any extra sheets of the article in the *North American,* as the publishers of that review object to having them struck off.

With great respect
Yours truly
F. PARKMAN

A weakness of sight obliges me to write this by the hand of another person.

MS: Dictated, University of Rochester Library.

[1] Lewis Henry Morgan (1818–81), the anthropologist, published his celebrated *League of the Ho-Dé-No Sau-Nee or Iroquois* in 1851, the same year that FP's *Pontiac* appeared. Morgan's *League of the Iroquois* has been acclaimed as "the first scientific account of an Indian tribe ever given to the world." FP reviewed it in the May, 1851, issue of the *Christian Examiner* with the observation that ". . . here a new sun has arisen, revealing the scene before us in all its breadth and depth. Mr. Morgan's work," he wrote, "on the aboriginal tribes of New York is a production of singular merit." Morgan's *Systems of Consanguinity and Affinity* of 1870, a remarkable achievement in originality and independence of research, is overshadowed by his *Ancient Society* of 1887, a work that attracted the attention of European writers.

In his letter to FP of September 20, 1865, PP, MHS, Morgan says: "It is gratifying to find so many of my statements confirmed by the observations of other investigators." Referring to his *League* he wrote, "My book was based almost entirely upon original materials, and when I wrote it I had access to but a limited number of the early French writers."

[2] In his letter of September 20, Morgan brings up the subject of the "Medicine Lodge" as "an unexplained enigma." This subject has occupied the attention of many American anthropologists since Morgan's time, but perhaps the best study is Leslie Spier's "The Sun Dance of the Plains Indians, Its Development and Diffusion," *Anthropological Papers of the American Museum of Natural History,* (New York, 1921), XVI, Part VII, 451–527.

[3] Minitari or Hidatsa Indians of Siouan linguistic stock.

INDEX

(See also Index in Volume II)

INDEX

INDEX

INDEX

INDEX

INDEX

INDEX

Letters of Francis Parkman is set in various sizes of Caslon Old Face on the Linotype machine, and in the Caslon type 471 produced for American Type Founders, here exhibited on the title page. Caslon was created by William Caslon, the English type founder, in the eighteenth century. Its individual letters often reveal seeming irregularities which, when combined in words and sentences, give a pleasant, moving effect. For this and other reasons, it is considered one of the most legible types developed since the founding of printing in the fifteenth century.

University of Oklahoma Press